BRITISH PAMPHLETEERS
VOLUME ONE

Seaven off these foules or byrds were found and taken in tymolne ffeddro at Crowley, 1588. wtherof
fowre died in shoot span affter they were taken, w.
offer three lyved longer, as it is to see in the bodies
pindid of them.

Queen Elizabeth Allegorised

BRITISH
Pamphleteers

VOLUME ONE
FROM THE SIXTEENTH CENTURY
TO THE FRENCH REVOLUTION

EDITED BY
George Orwell & Reginald Reynolds

LONDON
Allan Wingate
MCMXLVIII

First published Mcmxlviii
by Allan Wingate (Publishers) Ltd
64 Great Cumberland Place London W1

Composed in Monotype Garamond & Caslon Old Face

Printed in Great Britain by
Spottiswoode Ballantyne & Co Ltd
London and Colchester

CONTENTS

CONTENTS

LIST OF ILLUSTRATIONS

INTRODUCTION

By George Orwell

*T*HE *present collection of pamphlets contains twenty-five specimens, reproduced either in whole or in part. They have been chosen for their representativeness as well as for their literary merit, and between them they cover the two centuries between the Reformation, with which English pamphleteering may be said to have started, and the War of American Independence. Later it is planned to issue a second series which will carry the history of the pamphlet down to our own times.*

Mr. Reginald Reynolds, who has compiled and arranged this book, had to make his selection from a vast amount of material, as can be seen from the fact that 22,000 pamphlets and tracts of various kinds circulated in London merely between 1640 and 1661. The difficulty in a job like this is not merely to pick out the best pieces, but also to decide what is and what is not a pamphlet. To ask 'What is a pamphlet?' is rather like asking 'What is a dog?' We all know a dog when we see one, or at least we think we do, but it is not easy to give a clear verbal definition, nor even to distinguish at sight between a dog and some kindred creature such as a wolf or a jackal. The pamphlet is habitually confused with other things that are quite different from it, such as leaflets, manifestoes, memorials, religious tracts, circular letters, instructional manuals and indeed almost any kind of booklet published cheaply in paper covers. The true pamphlet, however, is a special literary form which has persisted without radical change for hundreds of years, though it has had its good periods and its bad ones. It is worth·defining it carefully, even at the risk of seeming pedantic.

A pamphlet is a short piece of polemical writing, printed in the form of a booklet and aimed at a large public. One cannot lay down rigid rules about length, but evidently a leaflet containing nothing but the words DOWN WITH MUSSOLINI would not be a pamphlet, and neither would a book of the length of Candide *or* The Tale of a Tub. *Probably a true pamphlet will always be somewhere between five hundred and ten thousand words, and it will always be unbound and obtainable for a few pence. A pamphlet is never written primarily to give entertainment or to make money. It is written because there is something that one wants to say* now, *and because one believes there is no other way of getting a hearing. Pamphlets may turn on points of ethics or theology, but they*

7

always have a clear political implication. A pamphlet may be written either 'for' or 'against' somebody or something, but in essence it is always a protest. As Mr. Reynolds points out, pamphleteering can only flourish when it is fairly easy to get one's writings printed, legally or illegally. Probably a slight flavour of illegality is rather beneficial to the pamphlet. When there is genuine freedom of speech and all points of view are represented in the press, part of the reason for pamphleteering disappears, and on the other hand, if one is obliged to break the law in order to write at all, one is less afraid of uttering libels. Violence and scurrility are part of the pamphlet tradition, and up to a point press censorship favours them. It will be seen that a number of the pamphlets in this collection are anonymous, or were printed abroad and then smuggled into England. This was normal in the sixteenth and seventeenth centuries, when almost all governments were both oppressive and inefficient. No one, when in power, would allow his adversaries a fair hearing, but at the same time there was no police force worth bothering about, and illegal literature could circulate freely. In a modern totalitarian state, pamphleteering after the seventeenth-century manner would be impossible. Clandestine printing, if it can be practised at all, is so desperately dangerous that no one who undertakes it has much time for literary graces. The baroque English of the seventeenth-century pamphlets does not give the impression of coming from people who were frightened for their skins. Here are a couple of sentences from the anonymous Tyranipocrit. *Notice the profusion of adjectives:*

> *But tell me thou proposturous impious world, if thou canst, who hath taught thee to punish the transgressors of the second Table of God's Commandments more than the first? Who hath taught thee to hang poore artlesse theeves and to maintain tyrants, and rich artificiall, proud, hypocritical, partial theeves, in their impious practices?*

And here is the Digger Gerard Winstanley, who was bankrupted by the Civil War and meanly persecuted under the Commonwealth:

> *And you zealous preachers and professors of the City of London, and you great officers and soldiery of the army, where are all your victories over the Cavaliers, that you made such a blaze in your land, in giving God thanks for, and which you begged in your fasting days and morning exercises? Are they all sunk into the Norman power again and must the old prerogative laws stand? . . . Oh, thou City, thou hypocritical City! Thou blindfold, drowsy England, that sleeps and snorts in the bed of covetousness, awake, awake! The enemy is upon thy back, he is ready to scale the walls and enter possession, and wilt thou not look out?*

Who would bother to use language like that when political controversy has to be carried on by means of stickybacks and chalkings on pavements?

Good pamphlets are likely to be written by men who passionately want to say

8

something and who feel that the truth is being obscured but that the public would support them if only it knew the facts. If one had not a certain faith in demo-cracy, one would not write pamphlets, one would try to gain one's ends by in-triguing among influential people. This is another way of saying that pamph-leteering will flourish when there is some great struggle in which honest and gifted men are to be found on both sides. The pamphlets in this collection have been chosen to cover the period as completely as possible, but it will be noticed that only four of them belong to the years between 1714 and 1789: and of those only one (Paine's Common Sense) deals with English internal affairs. Mr. Reynolds remarks on this 'interval' in political controversy, and points out the reason. During that period—after the Protestant Succession had been secured and before the outbreak of revolution in France—there was no clash of ideologies. The political struggle had ended with the complete victory of one faction, the wars against France were not wars for survival, and the controversies over Negro slavery or the exploits of the East India Company only touched minorities. In the two preceding centuries it had been different. Issues were being fought out which affected every thinking person, and in which each side genuinely felt the other to be sinning against the light. In its broad outlines the intellectual situation was curiously similar to that of our own day.

All the pamphlets in Mr. Reynolds's collection, up to and including Swift's, are really volleys in a single great battle. It is the battle of Catholic against Protestant, Feudalism against Capitalism. At the beginning the struggle is between England and Spain, then between King and Parliament, then between Whig and Tory: and mixed up with this—growing out of it, one should perhaps say—is the struggle of the victorious Parliamentary party against its own left wing. Looking back at the main encounter, it is easy to see that the forces repre-sented by Cromwell deserved to win, since they at least offered a hope for the future, whereas their adversaries did not. But, as some observers realised at the time, their victory brought no actual benefit, but merely the promise of one. Its outcome was the rise of modern capitalism, which can only be regarded as a pro-gressive event in so much that it has made possible another change which has not yet happened. If one judges capitalism by what it has actually achieved—the horrors of the Industrial Revolution, the destruction of one culture after another, the piling-up of millions of human beings in hideous ant-heaps of cities, and, above all, the enslavement of the coloured races—it is difficult to feel that in itself it is superior to feudalism. At the time of the Civil War, the long-term effects of a Parliamentary victory could not be foreseen, but the war was hardly over before it became clear that the causes for which the rank and file had believed themselves to be fighting were largely lost. The old tyranny had been overthrown, but neither liberty of opinion nor social equality had been brought much nearer. To-day the whole process seems familiar, like one of the classic openings at* *chess. It is as though history, while not actually repeating itself, were in the habit of moving in spirals, so that events of hundreds of years ago can appear to be happening at one's elbow. Certain figures, arguments and habits of mind always recur. There is always the visionary, like Winstanley, who is equally persecuted by both parties. There is always the argument that one must go forward or go back, and the counter-argument that the first necessity is to consolidate the position that has been won. There is always the charge that the revolutionary extremist is really an agent of the reactionaries. And once the struggle is well over, there is always the conservative who is more progressive than the radicals who have triumphed. It is fitting that the last pamphlet in the series dealing with the Catholic-Protestant struggle should be* A Modest Proposal, *in which Swift—not a Catholic and not a Jacobite, but certainly an adherent of the losing side—puts in a word for the downtrodden Irish.*

The most encouraging fact about revolutionary activity is that, although it always fails, it always continues. The vision of a world of free and equal human beings, living together in a state of brotherhood—in one age it is called the Kingdom of Heaven, in another the classless society—never materialises, but the belief in it never seems to die out. The English Diggers and Levellers, represented by three pamphlets in this series, are links in a chain of thought which stretches from the slave revolts of antiquity, through various peasant risings and heretical sects of the Middle Ages, down to the Socialists of the nineteenth century and the Trotskyists and Anarchists of our own day. One thing that can be detected here and there in these pamphlets is a half-belief that the ideal society has existed at some time in the past, so that a true revolution would really be a return. In Winstanley's pamphlets the word 'Norman' recurs over and over again. Everything that is oppressive and unjust—the King, the laws, the Church, the aristocracy—is 'Norman': by which Winstanley implies that the common people of England were once free and that the bondage in which they live is a foreign thing which has been forced upon them comparatively recently. In less crude forms, this belief still survives in our own time. Living before the machine age, Winstanley and his associates necessarily thought in terms of primitive peasant communes, and did not foresee that man might be freed from brute labour as well as from inequality. Their programme, unless one thinks a low standard of living desirable in itself, is out of date. But their essential predicament is that of any intelligent democratic Socialist to-day.

One ought not to press the analogy between the seventeenth and the twentieth centuries too hard, because the factors now involved are more complicated and the mental atmosphere has been altered by the coming of the machine and the decay of religious belief. Still, the general similarity is striking, and therefore the question arises: why has our own age not been to the same extent an age of pamphleteering?

It should be noticed that this is *a pamphleteering age, so far as mere bulk of output goes. Pamphlets are published in such a haphazard way that it would be impossible to discover how many are appearing at any given moment, but during the fifteen years or so since Hitler came to power, the number has certainly been enormous. All through those years, however bad the paper situation might be, Conservatives, Socialists, Communists, Anarchists, Pacifists, Trotskyists, currency reformers, vegetarians, opponents of vivisection, trade unions, employers' associations, minor political parties or fractions within parties, religious bodies ranging from the Catholic Church to the British Israelites, miscellaneous research groups and, of course, official and semi-official organisations of all kinds were pouring forth pamphlets in an unending stream. The figure mentioned by Mr. Reynolds, of 22,000 pamphlets circulating in London between 1640 and 1661, is impressive, but the contemporary rate of outpout is probably faster. I know no way of checking this, but it seems likely that between 1935 and 1945 (the flood appears to have slackened in the past year or two) pamphlets were being issued in Britain at the rate of several thousands a year. And yet in all those acres of print there has been very little that was either worth reading for its own sake or had any noticeable effect. There have been short books, such as* Guilty Men, *which have had a wide circulation and have influenced public opinion, but these are hardly pamphlets, if one accepts the definition I have given above. As for pamphlets possessing any literary merit, they are no longer to be found. The pamphlet survives, it even flourishes if one judges merely by numbers, but something has happened to it, and it is worth enquiring the reason.*

One thing one must take notice of first of all is the decay of the English language. This is all the more important because pamphlets are intended as propaganda and are not normally produced by people who are writers first and foremost. In any age one can write fairly good prose if one takes the trouble, but a purely political kind of literature is likely to be better when the language which lies ready to hand is uncorrupted. As an illustration, here are a couple of extracts, one from Mr. Victor Gollancz's recent pamphlet, Leaving them to their Fate, *the other from John Aylmer's* Harborowe for Faithfull and Trewe Subjectes. *They are similar enough in subject-matter to allow of a comparison. Both writers are engaged (though not from the same motives) in pointing out that the people of England are better off than those of Germany.* Leaving them to their Fate *is more simply and vigorously written than the majority of modern pamphlets, so that the comparison is not an unfair one. Here is the twentieth century:*

> *So that is the situation at the moment of writing on March 30th. The people of Germany are eating seed potatoes, and policemen, I am*

informed, are falling at their posts. The ration is to be maintained at about 1000 calories for the month of April. This is being achieved partly by raiding the very last reserves, and partly by the diversion of small shipments on their way to Britain, against a guarantee of very early replacement from supplies that would otherwise go to Germany. What will happen in May is anybody's guess . . . During the whole period of which I have been writing the average daily calories of the British people, according to repeated official statements, have been 2850, as against the 2650 stipulated by UNRRA as necessary for full health and working efficiency. On March 11th, after the cut in fats and dried egg, the figure was actually given by Dr. Summerskill as 2900. And the stocks of food and feeding stuffs in this country owned and controlled by the Minister of Food, exclusive of stocks on farms or held by secondary wholesalers and certain manufacturers, were estimated to total on the last day of March this year no less than a round four million tons.

Here is the sixteenth century (I am modernising the spelling):

Now compare (the Germans) with thee: and thou shalt see how happy thou art. They eat herbs: and thou beef and mutton. They roots: and thou butter, cheese and eggs. They drink commonly water: and thou good ale and beer. They go from the market with a salad: and thou with good flesh fill thy wallet. They likely never see any sea fish: and thou hast thy belly full of it. They pay till their bones rattle in their skin: and thou layest up for thy son and heir. Thou art twice or thrice in thy lifetime called upon to help thy country, with a subsidy or contribution: and they pay daily and never cease. Thou livest like a Lord, and they like Dogs. God defend us from the feeling of their misery.

I am not claiming that the second extract is in all ways better than the first. The modern way of writing has its virtues, which are due partly to the spread of the scientific outlook. Evidently the sixteenth-century writer, even if he had heard of such things as calories, would never bother with the kind of precise statement that is attempted in the first extract. One thing that strikes one all through the earlier pamphlets in this collection is the lack of any reasoned argument: very seldom is there anything more than assertion backed up by doubtful authority. In the last century or two we have grown to have a better idea of what is meant by evidence and proof, and language itself has grown more precise and capable of a wider range of meaning. Still, who could read those two passages one after the other and not feel that an enormous deterioration has happened? What has fallen is the average level of prose, the phraseology that one uses when one is not picking one's words for aesthetic reasons. 'Thou hast thy belly full of it'—'pay till their bones rattle in their skin'—'God defend us from the feeling of their misery'— that is not the kind of language that would come naturally to the compilers of

12

White Papers or the publicists of the Fabian Society. So much the less chance that any purely political writing will be art as well as propaganda.

But the modern pamphlet suffers another serious disadvantage in the fact that the public is not, so to speak, pamphlet-conscious. Unlike a novel or a book of verse, a pamphlet has no assured channel by which it can reach the readers most likely to appreciate it. The pamphlets of Milton, Swift, Defoe, Junius and others were literary events, and they were also a recognised part of the political life of the period. Nowadays this would probably not be the case, even if pamphlets of comparable power were appearing. Indeed, because of the manner in which pamphlets are distributed, it would be possible for a first-rate piece of work to pass almost unnoticed, even if the author of it were already known as a writer of books or newspaper articles.

Pamphlets are not only produced in great numbers, but some of them sell tens or scores of thousands of copies. However, their circulation is as a rule largely spurious. The majority of them are produced by political parties or groups, which make use of them, along with posters, leaflets, processions, pavement-chalking and what-not, as part of their general propaganda drive. At public meetings they are forced on members of the audience, who buy them as a way of paying for their seats; or they are circulated to party branches and zealous individuals who give a standing order for all the literature of the party they support; or they are given away free or sent through the post to M.P.s and other public men. In all cases many or most of the copies disposed of simply lie about unread, or go straight into the waste-paper basket. Moreover, even if one is interested in getting hold of a particular pamphlet, it is often very difficult to do so. Pamphlets are issued by a multitude of different organisations, including many which disappear or change their names soon after they have come into being. No bookseller stocks or even attempts to stock all of them, they are nowhere listed in any comprehensive way, and only a small proportion of them are ever noticed in the press. Even the keenest collector of pamphlets could not hope to keep track of anywhere near the whole output. It can be seen that a pamphlet is always liable to miss its potential public, and, although appearing as a separate booklet, to have less effect and receive less attention than it would if it were published as an article in a monthly magazine.

Of course, most pamphlets do not deserve attention. Most of them are rubbish. This must have been true at all times, but there are reasons, apart from those I have mentioned already, that work against even the occasional appearance of good pamphlets in our own day. Pamphlet literature has come to be thought of not only as propaganda, but essentially as party propaganda. It expresses not the outlook of an individual but the 'line' of some organised movement, or group, or committee, and even the actual writing is not necessarily done in its entirety by any one person. Pamphleteering after the old style, when some independent writer with a grievance to air, or a plan to propose, or a rival to attack, would take his manuscript to the printer, perhaps a clandestine printer, and then hawk the product round the streets at a few pence a time, is almost unheard of. Few people would know how to set about doing it, and the very occasional pamphleteer who does publish at his own expense is usually some uninteresting kind of crank or outright lunatic. On the other hand commercial publishers seldom interest themselves in pamphlets, i.e., political pamphlets. If one wants to write in this particular form one is practically obliged to do it under the wing of some organised body, with all the sacrifices of spontaneity and even of honesty that that implies.

There are five anonymous pamphlets in Mr. Reynolds's collection. Of the other twenty, nineteen—and, in Mr. Reynolds's opinion, probably the twentieth as well—are the work of individual persons. And in a less definable way they all, when compared with modern political writing, give an impression of individuality, which comes out in their language and in a certain exuberance of argument. Until quite recently there was no accepted political jargon. Even a venal writer, hired like a lawyer to turn black into white, chose his diction for himself, and probably also chose the line that he would take in building up his case. Look for instance at the extract from Royal Religion, *in which Daniel Defoe has been commissioned to 'write up' William III as a model of piety. We may assume that Defoe's motives were not very lofty ones and that he did not undertake this pamphlet because he was burning with zeal to say just that particular thing. And yet how lively he manages to make it! It is like a volley of custard pies, every one of them bang on the target. A modern political hack, boosting some doubtful cause, would be very unlikely to show the same humour and ingenuity, because he could never allow his imagination to range so freely. Party orthodoxy would not only take all the colour out of his vocabulary, but would dictate the main lines of his argument in advance.*

In Some Cautions for Choice of Members of Parliament *the Marquis of Halifax attacks the party system, which was beginning to govern political life by the end of the seventeenth century. Since then, various of the evils he mentions have swollen vastly, and fresh ones have appeared. If one thinks out what is involved, it is difficult to see how the growth of the party system could have been avoided in England, but there can be no doubt about the deadening effect that it has had on political thought and writing. It must be so, because collective action demands a sort of gregarious thinking, while literature has to be produced by individuals. It follows that, except by some kind of accident, good pamphlets cannot appear when this class of literature is under the control of closely organised groups. The typical modern pamphlet is either a predigested version of some longer work on sociology or economics, or it is a handbook intended to provide speakers with talking-points and quotable figures, or it is simply an extended slogan. Good pamphlets will begin to appear again when the pamphlet is looked upon as a means of getting a hearing for individual opinions, and when it seems normal, if you have something that you urgently want to say, to print and distribute it yourself without much expectation of profit.*

Whether a literary form survives or perishes may be determined by mechanical factors which have nothing to do with its intrinsic merits. The three-volume novel, for instance, went out partly because the lending libraries decided against it, and it is probably for economic reasons that the 'long-short' story, called in French a nouvelle (*the story of from fifteen to thirty thousand words, say*)*, has not flourished in England. The pamphlet, I have suggested, has decayed partly because it has been captured by professional politicians, and hence has ceased to be taken seriously or to attract gifted writers. It is hard to imagine Swift or Milton, or even Defoe or Tom Paine, bothering to write pamphlets if they were alive now. The sort of public that they would aim at would have to be reached in some other way. The pity is that in a pamphlet one can do things that are possible in no other medium. The pamphlet is a one-man show. One has complete freedom of expression, including, if one chooses, the freedom to be scurrilous, abusive and seditious; or, on the other hand, to be more detailed, serious and 'highbrow' than is ever possible in a newspaper or in most kinds of periodical. At the same time, since the pamphlet is always short and unbound, it can be produced much more quickly than a book, and in principle, at any rate, can reach a bigger public. Above all, the pamphlet does not have to follow any prescribed pattern. It can be in prose or in verse, it can consist largely of maps or statistics or quotations, it can take the form of a story, a fable, a letter, an essay, a dialogue or a piece of 'reportage'. All that is required of it is that it shall be topical, polemical and short. How great a variation is possible can be seen even in the twenty-five specimens assembled here, ranging as they do from earnest argument through satire and rhetoric to sheer abuse.*

The great function of the pamphlet is to act as a sort of foot-note or marginal comment on official history. It not only keeps unpopular viewpoints alive, but supplies documentation on events that the authorities of the day have reason to falsify. A good example in this collection is the description of the trial of Penn the Quaker, The People's Ancient and Just Liberties Asserted, *which has the appearance of being truthful and gives an interesting picture of nascent totalitarianism. Outrages of this kind, and indeed all minor controversial events, such as plots, real or imaginary, riots, massacres and assassinations are likely to be documented in pamphlet form or not at all. It is a job that needs doing in all ages, and surely never more than in the present one.*

Introducing Anthony Benezet's Caution and Warning, *Mr. Reynolds remarks that in the middle years of the eighteenth century such issues as Negro slavery 'at least gave the pamphleteers something to write about'. In our century, dearth of subject-matter is not one of the things that a pamphleteer suffers from.*

Probably there never was an age that so cried out for his activities. Not only are the ideological hatreds bitterer than ever, but minorities are suppressed and truth perverted in a way never before dreamed of. Wherever one looks one sees fiercer struggles than the Crusades, worse tyrannies than the Inquisition, and bigger lies than the Popish Plot. It might be argued that in England, with its free and reasonably varied press, there is not much scope for the pamphleteer; but this will not be endorsed by anyone who has ever tried to get a hearing for a genuinely unpopular cause. Certainly the British press has juridical freedom, which is not a sham but a very real blessing, and in the modern world an increasingly rare one. But it is not true that the British press adequately represents all shades of opinion. Nearly always it is safe to put one's political opinions on paper, but to get them into print, and still more to get them to a big public, is not so easy. Because of the way in which newspapers are owned and operated, not only can minority opinions—and even majority opinions, when they are not backed by some influential group—go almost unheard, but events of the utmost importance can pass unnoticed or can reach the public only in some shrunken and distorted form. At any given moment there is a sort of all-prevailing orthodoxy, a general tacit agreement not to discuss some large and uncomfortable fact. Take one recent example out of the scores that could easily be assembled: the expulsion of some twelve million Germans from their homes in East Prussia, the Sudetenland, etc. How much mention has this deed, for which Britain must be held at least partly responsible, received in the British press? How strongly has the British public reacted to it? Indeed, if the necessary enquiries could be made, would it be surprising to find that a majority of adult British citizens have not even heard of it?

It is true, of course, that events of this kind do not go altogether undocumented in pamphlet form. As I have said, the actual number of modern pamphlets is very large. But they are poor things, not much read and seldom deserving to be read—mere fragments of party orthodoxy describing a short parabola from printing-press to waste-paper basket. In general they are not written by people who are primarily writers, because no one who feels deeply about literature, or even prefers good English to bad, can accept the discipline of a political party. It would be difficult to name a single eminent English writer who has produced a pamphlet during the last fifteen years. There is no Swift or Defoe living to-day, but even those who are nearest to them never bother to write pamphlets. In order that they should begin doing so, it is necessary that people should once again become aware of the possibilities of the pamphlet as a method of influencing opinion, and as a literary form: in other words, that the prestige of the pamphlet should be restored. It is hoped that this collection and the one that will follow it, quite apart from being worth reading for their own sakes, will contribute towards that end.

NOTE: In these pamphlets and extracts the original spelling, punctuation and use of capitals have been followed; but some adaptation of the orthography was found desirable. The old *ſ* has been replaced by *s*, *v* has been used in place of *u* and *w* in place of *uu* (where modern orthography would require it) and *j* for *i*. We have also given in full the words where sixteenth-century English employed abbreviations (e.g. *repugnant* for *repugnãt*) in order to facilitate the reading of these early texts, and we have not always followed the original pamphlets in the use of italics.

I would like to record my personal gratitude to all who have helped, including those who checked the proofs with me. But they are too numerous to be named, without the danger of omission through inadvertence.

R. R.

THE FIRST BLAST OF THE TRUMPET

*K*NOX'S First Blast (*in 1558*) *was not merely the first against the 'monstrous regiment' (i.e. rule) of women, but perhaps the first British political pamphlet. The conditions of political pamphleteering are (1) that there is a well-established printing trade, and (2) that there must be some means, legal or otherwise, to use printing as a means of spreading political ideas. The Tudor despots gave little legal scope for such a use of printing in England during the early years of the printing trade; so it is natural that the first head-on attack on one of the Tudors had to be the work of a Scot (originally anonymous) and printed abroad.*

The pamphlet from which two brief extracts follow here was the first of a long series of religio-political works with which this volume is largely concerned. It is important to realise that, for some 200 years after the Reformation in Britain, politics and religious controversy were inseparable. But Knox, in his able and fiery onslaught on Mary Tudor, went far beyond any attack on her Catholicism or on the restoration in England of Papal authority. This Presbyterian Trumpet sounded even more loudly against feminism in politics, and asserted the Rights of Man in opposition to the outrageous pretension of women to rule over him. The extracts which follow those from Knox in this book show how widely he flung his challenge; for the author of the reply to Knox was, as we shall see, concerned with vindicating Mary's Protestant successor as a victim of Knox's tirade against women rulers.

The political effect may easily be surmised. Elizabeth, who reversed Mary's policy in religion, was not attracted by the Scottish Presbyterian who had attacked all of her sex and declared them unfit to rule, with the best arguments he could produce to indicate that such 'regiment' was against God's will and Holy Writ. The attitude of the Protestant queen towards both Scots and Calvinists may have been not a little affected by this unforeseen effect of the Blast intended for her Papist predecessor.

Elizabethan pamphlets, during the years which followed, frequently attacked social evils (such as usury, which had always been a subject of denunciation from the pulpit, and was still officially disapproved). They even attacked the Church on occasion. But such illegally printed and secretly circulated works as those of 'Martin Marprelate' never attacked the Crown or the Government as such. The

Puritan scribbler of the Tudor period was, in fact, fanatically loyal to the monarchy—at least so long as it remained Protestant—but bitterly opposed to the State Church as it took its shape under the reign of Elizabeth. Knox's pamphlet, though accidentally so, is therefore the outstanding exception to this rule, for it reached out of the past to attempt what Knox himself might have hesitated (and no other Protestant writer dared) to do. Of the Catholics we shall speak later.

THE FIRST BLAST OF THE TRUMPET AGAINST THE MONSTROUS REGIMENT OF WOMEN

By John Knox

To promote a woman to beare rule, superioritie, dominion or empire above any realme, nation, or citie, is repugnant to nature, contumelie to God, a thing most contrarious to his reveled will and approved ordinance, and finallie it is the subversion of good order, of all equitie and justice.

In the probation of this proposition, I will not be so curious, as to gather what soever may amplifie, set furth, or decore the same, but I am purposed, even as I have spoken my conscience in most plaine and fewe wordes, so to stand content with a simple proofe of everie membre, bringing in for my witnesse Goddes ordinance in nature, his plaine will reveled in his worde, and the mindes of such as be moste auncient amongest godlie writers.

And first, where that I affirme the empire of a woman to be a thing repugnant to nature, I meane not onlie that God by the order of his creation hath spoiled woman of authoritie and dominion, but also that man hath seen, proved and pronounced just causes why that it so shuld be. Man, I say, in many other cases blind, doth in this behalfe see verie clearlie. For the causes be so manifest, that they can not be hid. For who can denie but it repugneth to nature, that the blind shal be appointed to leade and conduct such as do see? That the weake, the sicke, and impotent persones shall norishe and kepe the hole and strong, and finallie, that the foolishe, madde and phrenetike shal governe the discrete, and

Causes why women shuld not have preeminence over men.

21

give counsel to such as be sober of mind? And such be al women, compared unto man in bearing of authoritie. For their sight in civile regiment, is but blindnes: their strength, weaknes: their counsel, foolishenes: and judgement, phrenesie, if it be rightlie considered.

Private examples do not breake the generall ordinance.

I except such as God by singular priviledge, and for certein causes knowen onlie to him selfe, hath exempted from the common ranke of women, and do speake of women as nature and experience do this day declare them. Nature I say, doth paynt them furthe to be weake, fraile, impacient, feble and foolishe: and experience hath declared them to be unconstant, variable, cruell and lacking the spirit of counsel and regiment. And these notable faultes have men in all ages espied in that kinde, for the whiche not onlie they have removed women from rule and authoritie, but also some have thoght that men subject to the counsel or empire of their wyves were unworthie of all publike office. For

2. Politicorum Aristotelis.

thus writeth Aristotle in the seconde of his Politikes: what difference shal we put, saith he, whether that women beare authoritie, or the husbandes that obey the empire of their wyves be appointed to be magistrates? For what insueth the one, must nedes folowe the other, to witte, injustice, confusion and disorder. The same author further reasoneth, that the policie or regiment of the Lacedemonians (who other wayes amongest the Grecians were moste excellent) was not worthie to be reputed nor accompted amongest the nombre of common welthes, that were well governed, because the magistrates, and rulers of the same were to muche geven to please and obey their wyves. What wolde this writer (I pray you) have said to that realme or nation, where a woman sitteth crowned in parliament amongest the middest of men. Oh fearefull and terrible are thy judgementes (o Lord) whiche thus hast

Reade Isaie the thirde chaptre.

abased man for his iniquitie! I am assuredlie persuaded that if any of those men, which illuminated onelie by the light of nature, did see and pronounce causes sufficient, why women oght not to beare rule nor authoritie, shuld this day live and see a woman sitting in judgement, or riding frome parliament in the middest of men, having the royall crowne upon her head, the sworde and sceptre borne before her, in signe that the administration of justice was in her power: I am assuredlie persuaded, I say, that suche a sight shulde so astonishe them, that they shuld judge the hole

Amazones were monstruouse women, that

worlde to be transformed into Amazones, and that suche a metamorphosis and change was made of all the men of that countrie, as poetes do feyn was made of the companyons of Ulisses, or at least, that albeit the owtwarde form of men remained, yet shuld they judge that their hartes were changed frome the wisdome, understanding, and courage of men, to the foolishe fondnes and cowardise of women. Yea they further shuld pronounce, that where women reigne or be in authoritie, that there must nedes vanitie be preferred to vertue, ambition and pride to temperancie and modestie, and finallie, that avarice the mother of all mischefe must nedes devour equitie and justice. But lest that we shall seme to be of this opinion alone, let us heare what others have seen and decreed in this mater. In the rules of the lawe thus it is written: Women are removed frome all civile and publike office, so that they nether may be judges, nether may they occupie the place of the magistrate, nether yet may they be speakers for others. The same is repeted in the third and in the sextenth bokes of the digestes: Where certein persones are forbidden, *Ne pro aliis postulent*, that is, that they be no speakers nor advocates for others. And among the rest are women forbidden, and this cause is added, that they do not against shamefastnes intermedle them selves with the causes of others, nether yet that women presume to use the offices due to men. The lawe in the same place doth further declare, that a naturall shamfastnes oght to be in womankind, whiche most certeinlie she loseth, when soever she taketh upon her the office and estate of man. As in Calphurnia was evidentlie declared, who having licence to speake before the senate, at length became so impudent and importune, that by her babling she troubled the hole assemblie. And so gave occasion that this lawe was established.

In the first boke of the digestes, it is pronounced that the condition of the woman in many cases is worse then of the man. As in jurisdiction (saith the lawe) in receiving of cure and tuition, in adoption, in publike accusation, in delation, in all popular action, and in motherlie power, which she hath not upon her owne sonnes. The lawe further will not permit, that the woman geve any thing to her husband, because it is against the nature of her kinde, being the inferiour membre to presume to geve any thing to her head. The lawe doth more over pronounce womankinde to be most avaricious (which is a vice intolerable in those that shulde rule or minister justice.) And Aristotle, as before is touched, doth plainly affirme, that whersoever women beare dominion, there must nedes the people be disordred, livinge and abounding in all intemper-

coulde not abide the regiment of men, and therfore killed their husbandes. reade Justine.

Arist. 2. Politic.

Lib. 50. de regulis juris.

what women may not be.

3. 16. lib. Digestorum.

Ad senatus-consul. Velleianti.

Lib. 3. de postulatione, Tit. 1.

Calphurnia.

De statu hominum Titul. 8.

Frome women power is taken away by the Civile lawe over their own children.

Dig. lib. 24. de donatione inter viris & fæminam. [sic] women be covetous, therfore unmete governors.

Lib. 1. Digest. de legib. & senatuscon. Titul. 3. Politic 2.

England and Scotland beware.

ancie, geven to pride, excesse, and vanite. And finallie in the end, that they must nedes come to confusion and ruine. . . .

But the question is: if women may succede to their fathers in offices, and chieflie to that office, the executor whereof doth occupie the place and throne of God. And that I absolutelie denie: and feare not to say, that to place a woman in authoritie above a realme, is to pollute and prophane the royall seate, the throne of justice, which oght to be the throne of God: and that to mainteine them *Num. 36.* in the same, is nothing els, but continuallie to rebell against God. One thing there is yet to be noted and observed in the lawe made concerning the inheritance of the doughters of Zalphead, to wit, that it was forbidden unto them to marie without their owne tribe, lest that such portion as fell to their lotte, shuld be transferred frome one tribe to an other, and so shuld the tribe of Manasses be defrauded and spoiled of their just inheritance by their occasion. For avoiding of which it was commanded by Moses, that they shuld marie in the familie or housholde of the tribe and kindred of their father. Wonder it is that the advocates *Our patrones for women do not marke this caution.* and patrones of the right of our ladies did not consider and ponder this lawe before that they counseled the blinde princes and unworthie nobles of their countries, to betray the liberties thereof in to the handes of strangiers. England for satisfying of the inordinant appetites of that cruell monstre Marie (unworthie by reason of her bloodie tyrannie, of the name of a woman) betrayed (alas) to the proude spaniarde: and Scotland by the rashe madnes of foolish governers, and by the practises of a craftie dame resigned likewise, under title of mariage in to the power of France. Doth such translation of realmes and nations please the justice of *Realmes gotten by practises are no juste possession.* God, or is the possession by such means obteined, lauful in his sight? Assured I am that it is not. No otherwise, I say, then is that possession, wherunto theves, murtherers, tyrannes and oppressors do attein by theft, murther, tyrannie, violence, deceit, and oppression, whiche God of his secrete (but yet most just) judgement doth often permit for punishment, as wel of the sufferers, as of the violent oppressors, but doth never approve the same as laufull and godlie. For if he wold not permit that the inheritance of the children of Israel shuld passe frome one tribe *NOTE.* to an other by the mariage of any doughter, notwitstanding that they were all one people, all spake one tonge, all were descended of one father, and all did professe one God, and one religion: If yet, I say, God wold not suffer that the commoditie and usuall

24

and the feventh Booke, beginning with the raigne of
King HENRIE the eighth.

Presentation of the Bible to Henry VIII

frute, which might be gathered of the portion of grounde limited and assigned to one tribe shulde passe to an other: Will he suffer that the liberties, lawes, commodities and frutes of hole realmes and nations, be geven in to the power and distribution of others, by the reason of mariage, and in the powers of suche, as besides, that they be of a strange tonge, of strange maners and lawes, they are also ignorant of God, ennemies to his truth, deniers of Christ Jesus, persecutors of his true membres, and haters of all vertue? As the odious nation of spaniardes doth manifestlie declare: who for very despit, which they do beare against Christe Jesus, whome their forefathers did crucifie (for Jewes they are, as histories do witnesse, and they them selves confesse) do this day make plaine warre against all true professors of his holie gospell. And howe blindlie and outragiouslie the frenche king, and his pestilent prelates do fight against the veritie of God, the flaming fiers, which lick up the innocent blood of Christes membres, do witnesse, and by his cruel edictes is notified and proclaimed. And yet to these two cruell tyrannes (to France, and Spain I meane) is the right and possession of England, and Scotland apointed. But just or laufull shall that possession never be, till God do chaunge the statute of his former lawe: whiche he will not do for the pleasure of man.

The spaniardes are Jewes and they bragge that Marie of England is of the roote of Jesse.

Note the law which he hath proclaimed in France against such as he termeth Lutherians.

[*Extracts*]

AN HARBOROWE FOR FAITHFULL
AND TREWE SUBJECTES

THE *note preceding the extracts from Knox's* Blast *explains the circumstances in which* An Harborowe *came to be written in* 1559. *Elizabeth had succeeded Mary in the very year which saw the publication of Knox's pamphlet, and the writer from whose work we have extracted the few pages which follow next was evidently not slow to see the convex edge of this Presbyterian boomerang, which now threatened the new Protestant monarch.*

In these pages we see the rising nationalist temper of England. 'God is English', *writes the author firmly, in one of his marginal rubrics; and the Reformation was, in fact, the form which this new cult of nationalism took in many of the northern countries. Protestantism to the Englishman meant independence of foreign domination, as originally expressed by the authority of the Pope, against which Englishmen (and often English sovereigns) had protested at intervals, even in the Middle Ages. When the Reformation had come in England it had, very significantly, taken at first the form of a political breach, made for political and personal reasons by Henry VIII. Doctrinal changes had not followed till later. In Elizabeth's time the principal significance of English Protestantism was still, for most people, the assertion of national independence, now threatened by the Catholic powers of France and Spain. For a few, on the one hand, it meant something more—security in their new possession of what had been formerly Church property; and on the other hand there were the Puritans, who aimed at the 'completion' of the Reformation by greater changes in doctrine, their interests coinciding mainly with those of the growing towns, and sometimes with that of the new owners of the Abbey lands.*

An Harborowe for Faithfull and Trewe Subjectes could be openly published in England, for the simple reason that it was a defence of the existing Government. It was nevertheless a novelty in those days for such an appeal to be necessary. Only the circulation of Knox's pamphlet and an awakening political sense could have made such a publication possible. Little known to-day, in a world which remembers at least the truculent title chosen by John Knox, this energetic reply deserves to be coupled with the Monstrous Regiment *as a landmark in the history of political literature. It should also be revered by all feminists and suffragette veterans as one of the first vindications of Woman.*

JOHN AYLMER

Published anonymously, An Harborowe *was actually the work of John Aylmer, later Bishop of London. Aylmer, who was one of the Protestant exiles on the Continent during Mary's reign, returned soon after the publication of* An Harborowe *to play a leading part in the shaping of Protestant policy under Elizabeth. He was a harsh persecutor of the puritans, and as such was greatly esteemed by Archbishop Whitgift. In this Aylmer's character contrasted strangely with that given him by Roger Ascham, who recorded his early success as the gentle tutor of Lady Jane Grey at about the same time that Ascham himself was practising his liberal principles in the education of the Princess Elizabeth.*

An Harborowe *has not been reprinted since its original publication, and we regret that lack of space makes it impossible to offer longer extracts from it. It will be noticed that France, not Spain, is the dreaded enemy at this stage—and much reproached for having made an alliance with the Turks. (Elizabeth herself, in later years, came to terms with Abd-el-Malek, the Emir of Morocco, on the basis of a common antipathy to Spain. Her Ambassador found him a 'good Protestant', which was doubtless some consolation.) In the reference to the Scots 'haver cakes' are oat-cakes and 'manchet' is the best wheaten bread. Compare Dr. Johnson's definition of oatmeal: the jibe has worn very well. 'Kie' is an old plural for cow, still used in Scotland.*

AN HARBOROWE FOR FAITHFULL
AND TREWE SUBJECTES

By John Aylmer

England hath hitherto taken greater losse by mens rule then by womens.

WHO loste olde Brytaine to Julius and the Romaines? men. Who loste it againe to the Saxons? men. Of whome wone it William conquerour? of men: who lost it to the Danes? men, who lost Normandie, Brytanie, Gascoigne, and Guine, and al our right in Fraunce? men, who lost Bulloigne, Bullenois and all the rest? a man. Who killed the Scottish King, when Henry .8. was in Fraunce? a woman or at the least her army? who brought in the light of gods worde into Englande? a woman, who lighteth now again the candle after it was put oute? a woman, whereby it is evident that we have, not yet so muche cause to complaine of losse by them, as by men. And in oure histories whiche we have before cited: wee maye see manye common welthes by women enlarged, or at the leaste well preserved, but fewe eyther muche weakened, or utterly destroyed. Onles you tell me of the destruction of Troye, which notwithstandinge, was rather thorowe the follie of Paris, then anye rule of Helena, and as for thys losse we have nowe, I doubte not, but as the olde fathers are wonte to saye, that as by a woman came death: so by a woman was broughte fourthe life. . . . Sticke not to helpe your natural cuntrey so muche as you can. God is benificiall unto you, be not unthankfull to his chefe minister. For like as the springes and brookes renne into the sea: so must all mens travail tourne to the defence of his countrey. If the springes should withholde their water: at the last the sea shuld lacke. So if every one of you hold back your hand: what shal become of your countrey & next of your selves? The

Philosophers say that the sonne draweth up the moistnes of the water in the sea, and thereof maketh the cloudes whiche after according to the wil of God, be caried over al the face of thearth to water it, & of that water, which cometh from the cloudes, riseth the springes and ryvers, so that neither the sea can be without the springes, nor the springs without the cloudes, nor the cloudes without the sea. Lo what a mutuall contribution here is in helping one another. In like maner if you yelde not to the defence of your countrie, parte of your frutes: it shalbe overrunne for lacke of helpe with your enemies, and what shall then become of you? If you yelde liberallie to your head, she shalbe hable by Gods grace to defend you with her souldiars, so that you may eare in hope, sow in suertie, reape with joye, and eate with plenty. Is not this sea of yours, your countey and quene, by many meanes sucked drie thynke you? Is it a Small charge to maynteyne a nomber of shyppes against the Frenche that they have no leasure to lande in Englande, and invade you? To maynteyne an armie in the borders, to keepe the countrey from burnynge and spoylynge? What saye you to the buyldynge of block houses by the seas side, the provision of harnes, gunnes, and weapons for the warre, to the kepinge about her, a great counsel of wise men to debate for your welth and safegard, to the sendinge embassadors hyther and thither, with a thousand more charges whiche wer to long to recken: From whence must thys come? but from the frutes of the earth, which by quietnes you gather: and without her defence you must lose. Oh you count it a great matter, to geve .3. or .4. shillings in the pound. Oh England, England, thou knowest not thine own welth: because thou seest not other countries penury. Oh if thou sawest the pezantes of Fraunce, howe they are scraped to the bones, and what extremities they suffer: thou woldest think thy self blessed (as in dede thou art) whiche haste rather fathers and mothers to thy governoures, then Kinges or Quenes. The husbandman in Fraunce, al that he hath gotten in his whole life, louseth it upon one day. For when so ever they have warre (as they are never without it) the kings souldiers enter into the poore mans house, eateth and drinketh up al that ever he hath, geveth their horse his corn, so longe as it lasteth, without paying a farthinge, and never departeth so long as there is any thing left in the hous. This was the maner: but this king hathe amended it with the wurse, for his souldiours come not thither, but his rakehels thofficers, which pare them even to the

How the french pezantes bee handled.

bones, the pore man never goeth to the market, to sel any thing:
but he paieth a tolle, almost the half of that he selleth: he eateth
neither pigge, gose, capon, nor hen: but he must pay as much
for the tribute of it there, as it might be bought for here: O unhappy and miserable men that live under this yocke. In Italy they
say it is not much better, the husbandmen be there so rich: that
the best coate he weareth is sacking, his nether stockes of his
hose, be his own skin, his diet and fare not very costly, for he
commeth to the market with a henne or two in one hande, and
a dosen egges in a nette in the other, whiche beynge solde and
tolde, he bieth and carrieth home wyth him, no Biefe or Mutton,
Veale or sea fishe, as you do: but a quarte of oyle to make sallettes
of hearbes, wherewith he liveth all the weke followinge. And in
Germanie thoughe they be in some better case then thother: yet
eat thei more rotes then flesh. For what cheare so ever they have
beside, they are sure of rotes and stinckinge hearbes, whiche they
call crowte. Thus these men live and thinke them selves happy:
if thei may have inough of this. Now compare them with thee:
and thou shalt see howe happye thou arte. They eat hearbes: and
thou Beefe and Mutton. Thei rotes: and thou butter, chese, and
egges. Thei drinck commonly water: and thou good ale and
beare. Thei go from the market with a sallet: and thou with good
fleshe fill thy wallet. They lightlye never see anye sea fish: and
thou hast thy belly full of it. They paye till their bones rattle in
their skin: and thou layest up for thy sonne and heir. Thou are
twise or thrise in thy lifetime called uppon to healpe thy Countrye,
with a subsidie or contribution: and they daily pay and never
cease. Thou livest like a Lorde, and they like dogges. God defende us from the feling of their misery. I am afraid our grutching
and groning, will make us to taste of this whip, as it must nedes
come to passe, if thy heade have not wherewith to defende the:
these will be the frutes of thy disobedience. We live in paradise.
England is the paradise and not Italy, as commonlye they call it.
For they have figges, Orenges, Pomgranates, Grapes, Pepons,
Oyle, and herbes: and we have Shepe, Oxen, Kie, Calves, Conies,
Fish, woll, Leade, Clothe, Tinne, Leather, and infinite treasures
more, which they lacke. We have plenty of all thinges: and they
scarcesitie of all thinges. Oh if thou knewest thou Englishe man
in what welth thou livest, and in how plentifull a Countrye: Thou
wouldest .vii. times of the day fall flat on thy face before God,
and geve him thanks, that thou wart born an English man, and

The husbandmans state in Italie.

The countrimen in Germani.

A comparing of the English man with other country men.

The frutes of England and Italy.

What will follow
oure grutching.

not a french pezant, nor an Italyan, nor Almane. If thou beiste
not thanckfull to God, and liberall to thy Quene and Country:
the poore pezante of Fraunce, shall enjoye thy wealthe: and feele
howe happye thou arte, and thou shalt taste of his miserye to
knowe howe unhappye he is. The Frenche shall teache thee to eate
rotes and Acornes: seinge thou canste not fynde in thy harte to
doe thy dutie, to them that mainetaine thys thy wealthe, Thou
muste learne to drincke water, if thou comest under his yocke,
and spare thy Barly and Ootes, for his greate horses. The Scottes

The folye of
the Scottes.

in spite of us, have made him their heade: but they shall tell me
or it be long, how wisely they have dealte, haver cakes will be
good manchet with them within a while. God that defended his

Josua.

children of Israel from the Amalechits, the Palestines, the Jebu-
sites, the Ammonites, the Moabites, and all the rest of their
enemies defend us from the slavery and misery of that proude
nacyon, that cruel people, and tirannous rulers. Furthermor for
the savegard of your country, if you be called to the warres,

An exhortacion
to manlines in
the warres.

grutche not nor grone not at it: go with good willes and lusty
courages, rather to mete them in the field, then to tarry til they
come home to you, and hang you at your own gates. Play not
the milk soppes in making curtsy, who shal go first: but shew
your selves true Englishe men in readines, courage, and boldnes:
and be ashamed to be the last, feare neither french, nor Scot. For
first you have God, and al his army of angels on your side: you

God is English.

have right and trouth, and seeke not to do them wronge, but to
defend your own right. Think not that God wil suffer you to be
foyled at their handes, for your fall is hys dishonour, if you lose
the victory: he must lose the glory. For you fight not only in the
quarel of your country: but also and chieflye in the defence of hys
true religion, and of his deare sonne Christe, not against men of
the same religion, which might make thevent doubtfull, but
againste his ennemies, Antechristes frendes, the Turkes confederates, ethnikes, Idolaters, and very helhounds. If there wer
nothing els to provoke gods fury and extreme vengaunce against

The french Turke.

that turkish Valesius the french tiraunte: but that he roigneth
him selfe in league wyth Christes sworn enemy the Turke: were
it not inough to kindle, yea to enflame the wrath of God againste
him? is he a king or a devel, a christian or a lucifer, that bi his
cursed confederacie so encourageth the Turke, that he nowe dare
be bolde to venter uppon Polonia, a Christian realme, whiche
hath received the gospel, and that way to come into Germany.

Oh wicked catife, and fierbrand of hell, which for thincreasing of his pompe and vayn glory (whiche he shall not long enjoye) wil betray Christ and his crosse, to his mortall enemy. Oh folish Germains which se not their owne undoing, whiche conspire not together with the reste of Christen Princes, to pull suche a Traytour to God and his kyngdome by the eares oute of Fraunce, and hange hym against the sonne a drying. The devill hath none other of his syde nowe, but him to mainteyne bothe the spirituall and the temporall Antechriste, the Pope and the Turke: GOD can not longe suffer this, though he wynke a whyle at his wretchednes, and suffer him to scourge us and other, until we knowe our selves: And after undoubtedly he will pull his feathers, he wyll coole his courage, as he did Nabucadnezer, and others whose example he followeth. Wherfore seyng he hath forsaken God lyke an Apostata, and solde him selfe to the devell: let us not doubte but God wilbe with us against him: when so ever he shall seeke to wrong us, and I trust wyll nowe in the latter age of the worlde shewe his myght in cuttynge of this proude Holophernes head, by the hande of our Judith: Oh blessed is that man that loseth his lyfe against such a Termagaunt: yea more blessed shall they be that spende their lyves against hym, then against his great maister the Turke.

The french is Christes enemy & the Turks Friende.

[*Extracts*]

COPIE OF A LETER WRYTEN BY
A MASTER OF ARTE OF CAMBRIDGE

PUBLISHED *on the Continent, probably at Antwerp, in the year 1584, this work was known as* Father Parsons' Greencoat, *on account of the colour of the original binding and the reputed authorship of Robert Parsons (or Persons), the famous Jesuit controversialist. The uninspiring title very easily gave way to that of* Leycesters Common-wealth, *under which it was three times re-published in 1641—the second, third and fourth editions being printed in England.*

Leycesters Common-wealth, *to call it by this shorter and more familiar name, was a terrible indictment of Elizabeth's favourite, Robert Dudley, Earl of Leicester. It contained the first printed account of the story—popularly accepted—that Leicester had murdered his wife (Amy Robsart); and this was but one of the crimes charged to him. Secretly circulated in England, the attack on such an unpopular figure as Leicester gained currency in spite of every effort to suppress it, the destroyed copies being replaced by manuscript versions. There were also contemporary editions in French and Latin.*

The method used is that of a dialogue between a gentleman, a lawyer and a scholar. In this it resembles the Conference about the next succession to the crowne of Ingland, *which Father Parsons wrote and published ten years later, discussing the rights of various claimants to the English throne (a subject of which the latter part of this anonymous work treats similarly). The balance of evidence favours Catholic authorship (though this has been queried) but there is no proof that Parsons was the writer, and the Jesuit Father was said to have disowned it.*

Internal evidence against the authorship of Parsons may be found in the digression—remarkable for the period—in which the writer preaches religious toleration. Parsons, like his friend Cardinal Allen (see the two extracts which follow in this selection), seems to have been far too vigorous an exponent of the Counter-Reformation to have advocated any such policy. Militant Catholicism was not conscious of playing a losing hand in Elizabethan England—certainly not in 1584, four years before the débâcle of the Invincible Armada. Yet clearly here was a writer who favoured religious toleration; and the evidence (as elsewhere in this work) indicates that he was a Catholic. For toleration is like democracy, with which it is intimately connected: whilst it can only be made effective by those in authority, it is most needed by those in opposition—and it is normally a plea of persecuted minorities before it is eventually implemented by a majority. The writer's example of Flanders was unfortunate, as that country was soon to be the scene of a ferocious persecution by the Spaniards. The 'Familians' to whom he refers were the Familists (Familia Caritatis), *a German sect then strong in Protestant parts of Europe, and in England, where they were the fore-runners of the Quakers.*

In the first of the two extracts which follow there will be found the gist of this early plea for toleration—the absence of which was for a long time to be the cause of religious persecution and political turmoil. The second extract published here to some extent sums up the indictment of Leicester, the principal theme of this unknown writer.

COPIE OF A LETER WRYTEN BY A MASTER OF ARTE OF CAMBRIDGE [etc.]

Commonly known as Leycesters Common-wealth

Anon.

GENTL.
Examples of tolleration in matters of Religion.

Germany.

I AM of your opinion (quoth the Gentleman) in that, for I have sene the experience thereof, and al the world beholdeth the same at this day, in al the countries of Germanie, Polonia, Bœmland, and Hungarie: wher a litle bearing of th'one wyth th'other, hath wrought them much ease, & continued them a peace, wherof al Europe besides, hath admiration and envie. The first douzen yeares also of her Ma. reigne, wherof your Ladie of the Court discoursed before, can wel be a witnesse of the same: Wherein the commiseration and lenitie that was used towards thos of the weaker sorte, wyth a certaine sweet diligence for their gaining, by good meanes: was the cause of much peace, contentation, and other benefit to the whole bodie.

The breach & reunion againe in Fraunce.

We see in Fraunce, that by over much pressing of one parte onlie, a fyre was inkindled not manie yeares since, like to have consumed and destroyed the whole: had not a necessarie mollification bene thought upon, by the wisest of that kinges Councell, full contrarie to the wil & inclination of some great personnages, who meant perhapes to have gained more by the other. And since that tyme, we see what peace, wealth and reunion, hath insued in that countrie, that was so broken dissevered & wasted before. And al this, by yeelding a litle in that thing, which no force can master, but exulcerat rather, and make worse: I mean the conscience and judgement of men in matters of religion.

Flaunders.

The like also I could name you in Flaunders, wher after al thes

36

broyles and miseries, of so manie yeares warres (caused principaly by to much streyning in such affaires at the beginning) albeit, the king be never so strycte-laced, in yeelding to publyque lybertye, and free exercyse on both partes: yet is he descended to this at length, (and that upon force of reason,) to absteine from the pursute and searche of mens consciences, not onlie in the townes which upon composition he receiveth, but also where he hath recovered by force, as in Tornay, & other places: wher I am informed that no man is searched, demaunded, or molested for his opinion or conscience, nor anie acte of Papistry or contrarie religion required at their handes: but are permitted to live quietlie to God & them selves, at home in their own houses: so they performe otherwise, their outward obedience & dueties to their Prince & country. Which onlie qualification, tollerance, & moderation in our Realm (yf I be not deceyved, wyth manie more that be of my opinion) would content al divisions, factions, & parties among us, for their continuance in peace: be they Papistes, Puritanes, Familians, or of what soever nyce difference or section . . .

*   *   *   *

And to seeke no more examples in this case, we know into what favour and special grace Sir Edmond Dudley my Lord of Leycesters good Graundfather was crept, with king Henrie the seventh, in the later end of his reigne: and what intollerable wickednes & mischiefe he wrought againste the whole Realme, and againste infinit particular persons of the same, by the poolinges & oppressions which he practised: wherby though the king receyved great temporal commoditie at that tyme, (as her Ma. doth nothing at al, by the present extorsions of his nephew:) yet for justice sake, & for meere compassion towardes his afflicted subjectes, that complained grevouslie of this iniquitie: that moste vertuous and wise Prince K. Henrie, was content to put from him, this lewde instrument, and devillishe suggestour of new exactions: whom his sonne Henrie, that insued in the Crown, caused presentlie before al other busines, to be called publiquelie to accompt, and for his desertes to leese his head. So as where the interest of a whole Realm, or common cause of manie, taketh place: the private favour of anie one, cannot stay a wise and godlie Prince, (such as al the world knoweth her Ma. to be) from permitting justice to have her free passage.

The punishment of Edmond Dudley.

Truelie it should not (quoth the Gentleman) for to that end were Princes first elected, & upon that consideration do subjectes

Gentl.

paye them both tribute and obedience: to be defended by them from injuries and oppressions, and to see lawes executed, & justice excercised, upon and towardes al men, wyth indifferencie. And as for our particular case of my Lord of Leycester, I do not see in right and equitie, how her Ma. may denie this lawful desire and petition of her people. For yf her highnes do permit and commaund the lawes daylie to passe upon thieves and murderers, wythout exception, and that for one facte onlie, as by experience we see: how then can it be denied in this man, who in both kindes hath committed more enormous actes, then may be well recompted.

*Leycest.
Theftes.*

As in the first, of theft, not onlie by spoyling and oppressing almoste infinit private men: but also whole townes, villages, corporations, and countries, by robbing the Realme wyth inordinate licences, by deceyving the Crown wyth racking, changing and imbezeling the landes, by abusing his Prince and soveraine in selling his favour both at home and abrode: wyth taking bribes for matter of justice, grace, request, supplication, or what soever sute els may depend upon the Court of the Princes authoritie: wyth setting at saile and making open market, of what soever her Ma. can give, do, or procure, be it spiritual or temporal. In which sorte of trafique, he committeth more thefte, often tymes in one day: then al the wayekeepers, cutpurses, cousiners, pirates, burglares, or other of that arte in a whole yeare, wythin the Realm.

Leycest. murders.

And as for the seconde, which is murder, you have hearde before somewhat saide and prooved: but yet nothing, to that which is thought to have bene in secret committed upon divers occasions at divers tymes, in sundrie persons, of different calling in both sexes, by most variable meanes of killing, poysoning, charming, inchaunting, conjuring and the like: according to the diversitie of men, places, opportunities and instrumentes for the same. By al which meanes, I think, he hath more blood lying upon his heade at this daye, crying vengeance against him at Godes handes and her Ma. then ever had private man in our countrie before, were he never so wicked.

*A heape of
Leices enormities
that would be
redie at the daye
of his trial.*

Wherto now, yf we ad his other good behaviour, as his intollerable licenciousnes in al filthie kinde and maner of carnalitie, wyth al sorte of wives, friendes and kinswomen: yf we ad his injuries and dishonours, done hereby to infinit: yf we ad his treasons, treacheries and conspiracies about the Crown: his disloyal behaviour and hatred against her Ma. his ordinarie lying, and common perjuring him self, in al matters for his gaine, both great and smal: his rapes and moste violent extorsions upon the poore: his abusing of the Parliament and other places of justyce, wyth the Nobylytie and whole communaltie besides: yf we ad also his open injuries which he offereth daylie to religion, and the Ministers therof, by tything them, and turning all to his own gaine: together wyth his manifest and knowen tyrannie practized towardes al estates abrode, throughout al Shires of the kingdom: his dispoylinge of both the universities, and discouraging of infinit notable wittes ther, from seeking perfection of knowledge and learning, (which otherwise were like to become notable) especialy in Gods word (which giveth life unto the soule,) by defrauding them of the price and rewarde proposed for their travaile in that kinde, through his insatiable Simoniacal contractes: yf, I say, we should lay together al thes enormities before her Majestie, and thowsandes more in particular, which might and woulde be gathered, yf his day of tryal were but in hope to be graunted. I do not see in equitie and reason, how her highnes sitting in throne, and at the Royal Sterne, as she doth, could denie her subjectes this moste lawful request: considering, that everie one of thes crymes aparte, requireth justice of his own nature: and much more al together ought to obteihe the same, at the handes of anie good and godlie Magistrate in the world.

[Extracts]

THE YEELDING UP
OF THE CITIE OF DAVENTRIE

*E*NGLISH *intervention against the Spaniards in the Netherlands, during the reign of Elizabeth, was the true prototype of many similar situations which have occurred since, when such preliminary sparring has frequently preceded a major conflict (e.g. the Balkan Wars before 1914 and the Spanish Civil War before 1939).*

Sir William Stanley, who had been brought up a Catholic and had served with the Spanish forces under Alva, against the rebels in the Low Countries, was nevertheless employed later in Ireland, for fifteen years, in the war of extermination which Elizabeth's Government was then waging against the Catholic Irish. With such a record he was considered reliable when he returned to the Netherlands, this time as a leader, under Leicester, of the English 'expeditionary force' sent to assist the Protestant rebels against Spain.

Sent to Ireland again for reinforcements, Sir William returned with some 1,400 men, mostly Irish and Catholics; and with their assistance he betrayed the city of Deventer in January, 1587, going over to the Spaniards with the city and his whole regiment. This extract from the writings of William Allen (created Cardinal later in the same year) is a defence of Stanley's action, printed at Antwerp with the bold (but somewhat hopeless) intention of influencing English opinion in favour of Stanley's treachery.

Cardinal Allen was one of those numerous Catholic exiles who ceaselessly worked abroad for the religious conversion of England or for a dynastic revolution which would give power to the Catholics again. (Allen was concerned with both the religious and the political objective, and conscientiously intrigued with whatever foreign power or dynasty seemed to be most likely to assist effectively).

The Copie of a Letter . . . concerning the Yeelding up of the Citie of Daventrie was published in 1587, and so far as we are aware has not been reprinted since that time. It takes the form of an address to the forces who had revolted, and (like the pamphlet which follows) makes an interesting comparison with that of John Knox in its insistence that revolt may be right and honourable. The unfavourable comparison of the morals of the English forces with those of the Spanish troops was not a happy one. The army which the Duke of Alva had brought to Flanders from Spain had included among its equipment a good supply of courtesans, carefully graded for the various ranks. (See Grose's Military Antiquities, *1801, vol. I, pp. 227–8.)*

THE YEELDING UP
OF THE CITIE OF DAVENTRIE

By William Allen

AND I pray you, Gentlemen, (to geve you domestical exam- *Examples of our owne countrie.*
ples,) what disgrace, or shame was it, for al the chiefe
Lordes of our countrie, to revolt from King John, in his *King John forsaken.*
dayes? & absolutly to denie him ayde, & assistence,
even in his lawful warres, until he returned againe to the obedience of the Sea Apostolike, and were absolved from the Censures
of the same, which he had justly incurred? Or for the English
Nobilitie, & specially for the renowmed Stanley, one of this Sir *Richard the third lawfully forsaken.*
William his house, and name, to revolt from King Richard the
Tyrant, and to yeeld him selfe, and his charge, to Henrie the
seventh? what dishonour was it, for the Nobilitie of England, in *Jane the usuper forsaken.*
our memories, to forsake Jane the pretended Quene: & Northum-
berland, the father of him, whom nowe you have forsaken, & to
yeeld the Towre committed to their custodie, and them selves, to
the lawful, and most Religious Quene Marie? Notwithstanding
what unjust bandes of oth, or promise soever they had made,
of feare & pusilanimitie, to the said usurper, & Hæretical Quene
before? In al these, & the like, there is neither sinne, nor shame,
nor scandal committed. For that to revolt, is of it selfe, lawful
or unlawful, honorable or otherwise, according to the justice,
or injustice of the cause, or difference of the person, from or to
whom, the revolt is made. Wherin, when the right from the
wrong is evident, & in the Capitaines, or souldiars conscience,
& in al godlie mens sight cleare, & undoubted, there nedeth
no more discussing of the matter.

Howe Catholiques should enforme their consciences for the justice of the warres.

To conclude breifly. In these warres, & al others, that may at any time fal for Religion, against Hæretikes, or other Infidels, everie Catholike man, is bound in conscience, to enforme him selfe, for the justice of the cause. The which when it is doubtful, or toucheth Religion (as is said) he ought to imploy his person, & forces, by direction of such, as are vertuous, and intelligent in such cases: but specially by the general Pastour of our soules, being Christes vicare in earth. Whose soveraigne authoritie, & wisdome, derived from Christ him selfe, may best instruct, and warrant a christian souldiar, howe farre, when, and where, either at home, or abrode, in civil, or foraine warres, made against the enimies, or Rebelles of Gods Church, he may, and must breake with his temporal soveraigne, and obey God and his spiritual Superiour.

A necessarie and a sure rule.

Againe (Gentlemen) by this your retiring your selves, from the service of Gods, and the churches enimies, you have not only provided wel, for your consciences, honour, & salvation: but also for the encrease of your knowledge, and experience in art militare, and of the exact order, & discipline to be observed in the same, being nowe to serve, under so vertuous, valerous, fortunate, famous, and victorious a General, as hath had fewe peers, in these latter ages. And in companie of so manie valiant, and expert Capitaines, and souldiars, of diverse Nations, as no where in Europe, better can be founde. Which your selves (my maisters) may more easely consider, by comparing your late General, my Lord of Lecester, his vertues, & famous factes (scilicet) unto the glorious exploytes, & victories, atchived by the Duke of Parma his Highnesse. Or the disorder of the English irreligious, and licentious companies, to the religious discipline, of the Catholike campe. Between which, I doubt not, but you finde a mervelous difference, and shal do dayly, more and more, to your infinite contentment. Would to God, by your honorable example, al others our deceived countriemen, would beginne to thinck earnestly, howe to discharge them selves of that dangerous, & infamous service of Hæretikes, and Rebelles, and render them selves, into this most just, and godlie course, that you are happely entred into. Which they should the rather speedely resolve upon, for that they can not be so ignorant, of the times lately past, or the present dayes, but they must nedes have marked, howe God him selfe, fighteth for the just causes, of his Catholike Majestie, and generally for al Catholike Armies,

Other commodities, of retiring to the Kings service.

The noble Duke of Parma.

A necessarie consideration.

against Hæretikes, and Rebelles. Wise men have noted, that though God for our sinnes hath suffered, and stil doth permit Hæretikes, to keepe great broiles, in al partes (almost) of the world, for a time: yeat he ever hath put them, in fine, to confusion: geving the victorie, lightly in al battailes, and encounters, to the Catholikes. And that oftentimes very miraculously, defeating (as in the warres of the Machabees, & elswhere in old time) great numbers, with a very fewe, & for one Catholike, a thousand Hæretikes slaine: and many glorious victories obtained without any bloudshed.

God geveth the victorie ever to Catholikes.

For Luther, & Zwinglius his time, I referre you, to the recordes of Germanie, and Swizerland, which set downe the overthrowes of Hæretikes in the filde. The fightes in Fraunce, where the Catholikes, ever have had also the victorie, be in al our memories mervelous. But of al others those of Flauders are most memorable. Where, besides the conflictes at Grunning, Mock, Mounts, Rosandal, Zeriksea, Northorne, Amerone, Antwarpe, Luart, Gemblowe, & the like, in every of which (the Lord God of Hosts mercifully fighting for his owne cause, & the Catholike Kinges right) verie few Catholikes, without any losse of men, in manner, slewe and defeated manie thousandes, of wel appointed souldiars: the same most just God of revenge, hath notoriously put to rebuke and confusion, al such forrein Princes, and people, as came to ayde his enimies. And sometimes, by his just judgement, hath brought them to ruine, even by those same Hæretikes, & Rebelles, that called for them, and for whose protection, they came into that countrie. As we have seen both in the case of the Almaine, & French succourses. And the like lucke seemeth to approch unto our English forces: except our Lord (which I hartely pray for) cal them from that unjust, and infamous service of Hæretikes. Who having the perpetual curse of Christ, & his holie Church, lying heavely upon them, can no more escape speedie destruction, then others, who unluckely have folowed that side, have done before them. Which I speake of charitie, love, & compassion of my deare countriemen: being assured, that if they perish in bodie (as it is to be feared, they shal do in that service) they shal lose their soules. . . .

Divers unbloudie victories, geven to the King Catholike, in these warres.

God hath destroyed al the Heretikes partakers miraculously.

[*Extract*]

AN ADMONITION TO THE NOBILITY AND
PEOPLE OF ENGLAND AND IRELAND

*T*HESE *extracts from writings attributed to William Allen are from a pamphlet published in 1588—the year of the Spanish Armada's defeat. Allen had been created Cardinal at the request of the Spanish king, for political reasons. As an English Catholic exile who supported the cause of Philip II against Elizabeth, he was intended to serve as head of a Catholic 'fifth column' in England and a link with the forces of the Most Catholic Monarch which were intended to invade this Protestant outpost.*

Accordingly the Pope (Sixtus V) had written to Philip on August 7th, 1587, that he had that day 'held a consistory and made Allen Cardinal to satisfy your majesty; and though in proposing him I put forward a motive which was very far from likely to excite suspicion, nevertheless it is reported that throughout all Rome there arose forthwith a universal cry: "Now they are getting things into order for a war with England." Therefore your majesty should not lose time . . .' After the assumed success of the invasion Allen was to be made Archbishop of Canterbury, Lord Chancellor of England and Papal Legate.

The Admonition *may not actually have been written by the new Cardinal, though it bore his signature. If, as has been claimed, the inspiration of this invective should be traced to Father Parsons, we have further reason for doubting that Parsons was the author of that plea for toleration in a pamphlet at which we have already glanced. The* Admonition *was an uncompromising declaration of 'Holy War' on Elizabeth and the Protestants, and it was intended to distribute this pamphlet widely after invading England.*

It is interesting to compare the author's invective with that of John Knox, who tackled a similar theme from a different angle, but with much the same vocabulary of abuse. Just as the Catholic Mary Tudor represented all that was monstrous in the eyes of Knox, so her Protestant sister was, to this Catholic writer, 'an incestuous bastard, begotten and born in sin, of an infamous courtesan, Anne Bullen, afterwards executed for adultery, treason, heresy and incest . . .'; and a list of crimes follows (of which we have selected a few examples) presenting a formidable indictment. The ill-repute of Leicester is once more fully exploited.

Both Knox and this Catholic writer (the latter with the full approval of the Church, and of the English Cardinal, even if he was not the actual author) urge eloquently the right of subjects to depose an evil ruler; so that Catholic and Presbyterian may be said to agree on one vitally important point—that is to say, in rejecting that 'Divine Right of Kings' upon which the successors of Elizabeth were to stake their crowns. Though English Protestants did not respond favourably to Knox's Blast, and most English Catholics remained unmoved by the appeals of the emigrés at Rome and Rheims, we may assume that something was done to shake the complacent security of the Tudors. But it was the Stuart dynasty which was eventually to feel the full impact of those new political philosophies which religious controversy was helping to shape.

At least one contemporary writer—evidently another English Catholic in exile—was aware of this new danger. In 1600 there appeared, 'printed at Collen' (Cologne), 'A Discoverye of a Counterfecte Conference held at a counterfecte place, by counterfecte travellers, for thadvancement of a counterfecte tytle'. This was a reply to the pamphlet by Parsons (mentioned in a previous note) wherein the Jesuit priest had discussed the claims to the English throne and put forward the same case for the deposition of Elizabeth that is to be found in the Admonition. *This Catholic critic of Parsons saw in all such arguments a dangerous precedent that could be used by the other side against a Catholic monarch, and instanced the revolt of the Netherlands—'that prodigiouse republic or colourable commonwealth in Holand & Zeland, framed and cloke togither in a hoche-pot with the baser sorte of a rout & rable of artificers & handy crafts men', who had committed 'malipert rebellions and enormities more than hethenish against their soveraign'.*

Though the whole edition of the Admonition *(published in 1588) was probably among the ill-fated cargo of the Armada galleons, and mostly destroyed with them, the writings of the Catholic exiles were not, in many cases, quite ineffective. They were certainly taken seriously by the Government; and even that artful politician, Lord Burghley, who was all-powerful in England, on two occasions appears to have turned journalist and published anonymously his replies to the squibs of the seminary priests. No modern edition of the* Admonition *is available, and the original is very rare.*

'Delators' in the text means professional informers. 'Promoting' is denouncing or accusing.

AN ADMONITION TO THE NOBILITY AND PEOPLE OF ENGLAND AND IRELAND

By William Allen [?]

Bᴜᴛ howsoever she be dissended or possessed of the croune, her manifolde wickednes hath ben, so heinous and intollerable that for the same she hathe bene in person justly deposed by the sentences of thre sundrie Popes, wherunto yf we adde the two former censures condemninge her incestuous nativity and generation, we shall finde that she hathe ben condemned by five declaratorie juditiall sentences of Gods Churche.

And to beginne with the highest and most heinouse crime of all against God and his Churche, she is convicted of many damnable heresies, and open rebellion against Gods Churche and See Apostolike, for which she is so notoriously knowne, termed and taken for an heretike, as well at home as abrode, that she was glad to provide by a special acte of parliament, that none should call her heritike, Schismatike, Tyrante, usurper, or infidell, under paine of highe treason.

She usurpeth by Luciferian pride, the title of supreme Ecclesiasticall government, a thinge in a woman, in all mens memory unheard of, nor tollerable to the mastres of her owne secte, and to Catholikes in the world most ridiculous, absurde, monstrous, detestable, and a verie fable to the posterite.

She unlawfully intruded herself, as before I have said, in to possession of the croune of England, and the annexed dominions, not by any dissent of inheritannce or other lawfull title, but only by enforced unjust lawes partly made by her supposed father beinge then an excommunicated person, and partly coacted by

46

herself and her complices in the beginninge of her pretended raigne, beinge indede taken and knowen for an incestuous bastard, begotten and borne in sinne, of an infamous curtesan Anne Bullen, afterwarde executed for aduoutery, treason, heresie and inceste, amongest others with her owne naturall brother, which Anne, her said supposed father kepte by pretensed mariage, in the life of his lawfull wife, the most renonmed and blessed ladie Queene Katherine, daughter of Castill and Aragon, as he did before unnaturally knowe and kepe bothe the said Annes mother and sister. . . .

She hathe caused the Preists of God violently to be plucked from the aulter in the middest of the soveraine action, and to be caried in scornefull manner revested through the streates, and exposed to all the ungodly villanie, irrision, furie, and follie of the simple and barberous people: a thinge certes that above all other kindes of irreligiosity most deservethe and sonest procureth God vengeance. *Impious scornefulnes.*

She hathe suppressed all the religious houses of bothe sexes, so manie as were restored after her fathers former horrible spoile, dispersed the professed of the same, and robbed them of all their landes and possessions. *Suppression of Monasteries.*

She hathe by unjust tyrannicall statutes injuriously invaded the landes and goodes of Catholike Nobles and gentlemen, that for conscience sake have passed the seas: and molested, disgraced, imprisoned, and spoiled, many at home of all degrees, because they wolde not give othe and agreement, to her Antechristian, and unnaturall proude challenge of supremacy, nor honor the Idoll of her prophane communion borde, whereby sum provinces, be in manner wholly bereaved of theire just gentlemen in administration of the lawes, & the people excedingly anoied by losse of so good lordes, and so great houskepers, for lacke of whom, the poore dailye perishe. *Oppression of Catholike Gentlemen, and extorsion.*

Besides all which sacrileges abhominations and extorsions against God his Churche and her owne people, she passingly hath indaungered the kingdom and cuntrie by this great alteracion of religion, which thinge ys never without inevitable perille, or rather sure ruine of the commonwealthe; as also she hathe done by great contempte and abasinge of the auncyent Nobilitie, repellinge them from due government, offices, and places of honor, thrustinge them to shamefull and odious offices of inquisition upon Catholike men, to the great vexation and terror *Destruction of the Nobilitie.*

47

of their owne consciences, forcinge them through feare and desier of her favor, and of her base leaders, to condemne that in others, which in theire hartes and consciences themselves like of, and putting into their houses and chambers, traitors, spials, delators, and promoters, that take watche for her of all theire waies, wordes, & writinges; by which the principall be alredy ruined moste lamentablie, and the rest stande in continuall thraldom daunger and dishonor: so jelous be all tyrants and usurpers, of their state, and so lothe they are to be seconded by any other then of theire owne creation.

Norfolke, Northumberland, Westmerland, Dacres &c.

She hathe in steade of the forsaid, and to their shame and despite, advaunsed base and unpure persons, inflamed with infinite avarice and ambition, men of great partialitie briberie and iniquity, to the highest honors and most proffitable offices of her courte and cuntrie, repelling from all publike action, charge and authority, under colour of religion, the wisest, Godliest, lernedst, and sincearest of all sortes of men, to the speciall annoiance and dishonor of the whole state.

Newe Nobilitie.

She hathe intruded the very reffuse of the worst sorte of mortall men, infamous amorous Apostats and heretikes, to all the spirituall dignites and prefermentes in the realme, who by their insatiable covetousnes and concupiscence, have made lamentable havoke, waste, and destruction of the anncientest (welneare) and honorablest spirituall states in Christendom, herself not alitle helpinge to the spoile of the same.

Newe Clerglie.

She hathe laid the cuntrie wide open to be a place of refuge and sanctuarie of all Atheystes, Anabaptistes, heretikes, and re-bellious of all nations, and replenished sundrie the coste townes and other, with innumerable strangers of the worst sorte of male-factors and sectaries, to the great impoverishinge of the inhabi-tantes, and no small perill of the whole realme: this beinge taken to be certen, that the number and qualetie of them is suche, that when time may serve and favour them, they may give a sturdy batail to the inhabitantes of the realme.

Harboringe strangers.

She hathe not spared to oppresse her subjects (never havinge just warres with any kinge or cuntrie in the world) with mani-folde exactions not only by ordinarie meanes of more frequent and large subsedies (for which only ende she hathe had more parliaments and more often prorogations therof then ever any lawful prince had, in so many yeares) but also by sundrie shame-ful guiles of lotaries, lawes, decrees, & falles of money and suche

Polinge the people.

AN ADMONITION
TO THE NOBILITY
AND PEOPLE OF ENG-
LAND AND IRELAND CON-
CERNINGE THE PRESENT VVARRES
made for the execution of his Ho-
lines Sentence, by the highe
and mightie Kinge Ca-
tholike of Spaine.

By the CARDINAL *of Englande.*

Aᵒ. M. D. LXXXVIII.

Title page: An Admonition to the Nobility

like deceites: and hathe imploied the riches of the realme to sett up and susteine Rebells and Heretikes against their naturall princes, to the great dishonor of our nation, damage and daunger aswell of our marchauntes, as of all other travaylers; a publike piracie and robberie bothe by sea and land, therwith authorisinge by her letters of marte, and otherwise permittinge, divers wicked persons to spoile whom they liste, without sparinge, sum peece of the gaine retorninge to sum of her owne cheif councellers and officers.

Sellinge of Lawes.

She dothe for monye and bribes, to the enrichinge of herself and servantes, by licenses, dispensations, pardons, and permissions, abolishe or frustrate many proffitable lawes: as she dothe to the same ende multeplie sundry frivolous actes, with great forfets to the transgressors, wittingly forbearing (as yt may be thought) the execution of the same, that after oblivion of the observation therof, her courtiers and other loste Cosines and compagnions (whom her excessive avarice will not suffer to rewarde of her owne) may make pray by promotinge the poore people, & so live and fede on the carcas of the commonwealthe: yea even sucke out the verie bludd of poore aflicted Catholike mens consciences, who besides those sacrilegious mas mulctes, and the new made spoiles and intollerable extorsions, for not comminge to their damnable Idolatry of the communion, (which for the love of Gods lawe they often incurr and susteine, to the utter lamentable ruine of them & their posterity) be faine by great importable giftes to procure at her officers handes, sum little ease and release of the intollerable feares and miseries that they live in. By which wicked trafique and other pittifull pillage of the people, sum of her creatures are growne so great and insolent, that all states & degrees within the Realme stand in awe and daunger of them.

Leycester.

In which sorte, besides others whom we nede not note, she hath exalted one speciall extorsioner, whom she tooke up first of a Traitor & woorse then naughte, only to serve her filthy luste, wherof to have the more fredom and intrest, he (as may be presumed, by her consent) caused his owne wife cruelly to be murthered, as after warde for the accomplishement of his like brutishe pleasures with an other noble dame it is openly knowne he made awaie her husband; who now of an amorous minion advaunsed to highe office, degree, & excessive welthe, is becum her cheife leader in all her wicked and unwonted course of

The Erle of Essex.

regiment, her instrument of the destruction of the nobilitie, by many indirect meanes, & of the ruining, abacinge, disgracinge; disauthorisinge divers aunceyent howses names and persons of renoume; besides innumerable of the communalty perished most pittifulie in sundry provinces for the feeding of his infinite avarice and other his unsatiable companions & reteinors, livinge only of briberie, spoile, and roberie: wherby, and throughe the favoure of the pretended he hathe this many a yeare overruled the chamber, courte, counsell, parliament, portes, fortes, Seas, Shipps, borders, men, munition, and all the cuntrie; hathe had still at commaundment all officers justices, Benches, Barres & Sessions, hath had the sale and monopolie of all lawes, offices, licenses, forfettes, Byshoprickes, benefices and Colleges, hathe made suche traffique, choppinge & chaunginge with his mistris, aboute the treasures, prerogatives, landes, and commodeties of the croune, that so & by diverse unspeakable trecheries, he hathe enabled and fortefied himselfe farr above the measure of any English subjecte, and hathe bene the principall disturber and destroyer of the provinces rounde about us, to the impoverishment of the people at home, and decay of all trafique abrode, with extreme perill of the lande.

With the forsaid person and divers others she hathe abused her bodie, against Gods lawes, to the disgrace of princely majestie & the whole nations reproche, by unspeakable and incredible variety of luste, which modesty suffereth not to be remembred, neyther were it to chaste eares to be uttered how shamefully she hath defiled and infamed her person and cuntry, and made her Courte as a trappe, by this damnable and detestable arte, to intangle in sinne and overthrowe the yonger sorte of the nobilitye and gentlemen of the lande, whereby she is become notorious to the worlde, & in other cuntryes a comon fable for this her turpitude, which in so highe degre namely in a woman and a Queene, deservethe not onlie deposition, but all vengeaunce bothe of God and man, and cannot be tollerated without the eternal infamie of our whole cuntrie, the whole world deriding our effeminate dastardie, that have suffred suche a creature almost thirtie yeares together, to raigne bothe over our bodies and soules, and to have the cheif regiment of all our affaires as wel spirituall as temporal, to the extinguishinge not onely of religion but of all chaste livinge and honesty.

Her dishonest lyfe.

[*Extracts*]

A REPETITION SERMON

IN an age when the expression of political opinions was heavily restricted and personally dangerous, many devices were evolved to cover such expressions in some innocuous guise. The pulpit afforded such a means to those who exercised the use of it; and sermons, afterwards printed and distributed as pamphlets, were among the vehicles of opinion which helped to mould thought, particularly in the seventeenth century.

This sermon, by Thomas Lushington, was preached at Oxford in 1624. Carefully woven into a surprisingly merry and epigrammatic discourse on a serious religious theme there are innuendoes relating to the popular clamour at the time for a war with Spain. Lushington was of the Court faction—the Royalists of later years—and his sharp jab at Parliament brought him trouble; for already the authority of Parliament was formidable, and members were touchy about attacks on their prestige which would pass unnoticed to-day.

Lushington, a man of obvious brilliance, did not make much mark on the history of his time. But he was mentioned with respect by Clarendon, who has recorded the applause with which this sermon was greeted by the congregation (applause in church being, apparently, a much more venerable custom than applause in Parliament, which was recorded as a novelty many years later). Perhaps the most effective contribution made by Thomas Lushington was an indirect one, for his pupils at Oxford included Sir Thomas Browne.

There were several editions of this sermon up to the middle of the eighteenth century, but for some 200 years it appears to have escaped notice. Its sharp jabs at the priests (i.e. the Catholic clergy) and the 'enthusiasts' of the sects are still easy to follow; but many of the shots fired in all directions hit targets which are no longer so easily visible.

The word 'garb' for news appears to be from the French gerbe (sheaf or bundle). 'Bethlem Gabor' was Gabriel Bethlen, Prince of Transylvania, who fought for Protestantism and Hungarian independence against the Hapsburgs. He was a Calvinist, but sufficiently tolerant to collaborate with a Jesuit in translating the Bible; and he is rightly described in the Encyclopaedia Britannica as 'one of the most striking and original personages of his century'.

For purely practical reasons the photostats used here were from the edition of 1741; but the earliest available editions only differ from it slightly in the spelling, which is remarkably modern.

A REPETITION SERMON

By Thomas Lushington

MAT. XXVIII. 13.

His Disciples came by Night and stole him away while we slept.

WHAT'S the best News abroad? So we must begin: 'Tis the Garb (*les novelles*) the grand Salute, and common Preface to all our Talk. And the News goes not as Things are in themselves, but as Mens Fancies are fashioned, as some lust to Report, and others to Believe: The same Relation shall go for true or false, according to the Key wherein Mens Minds are turn'd; but chiefly as they stand diverse in Religion, so they feign and affect different News. By their News ye may know their Religion, and by their Religion fore-know their News. This Week the Spanish Match goes forward, and Bethlem Gabor's Troops are broken; and the next Week Bethlem Gabor's Troops go forward, and the Spanish Match is broken. The Catholique is of the Spanish Match, and the Protestant of restoring the Palatinate; and each Party thinks that the Safety of the Church and Success of Religion depend upon the Event of one or other, and therefore they cross and counter-tell each others News. Titius came from London Yesterday, and he says that the new Chapel at St. James's is quite finished: Caius came thence but this Morning, and then there was no such Thing on Building. False News follows true at the Heels, and oftentimes outstrips it.

Thus goes the Chronicle-News, the Talk of the factious and pragmatick; but the Christian News, the Talk of the faithful, is spent in Evangelio, in hearing and telling some good News of their Saviour: And now all the Talk is of his Resurrection: The Christian Currant goes, News from Mount Calvary, the sixteenth Day of Nisan, in the Year thirty four, old style; as the three holy Matrons deliver it at the eighth Verse of this Chapter. But since, there are certain Soldiers arrived, and they say there was no such Matter as the Resurrection, 'twas but a Gull put upon the World by his Disciples; for it fares with spiritual News as with temporal, it is variously and contrarily related, till the false controuls the true. And as our modern News comes neither from the Court nor the Camp, nor from the Place where Things are acted, but is forged in Conventicles by Priests, or in some Paul's-Assembly, or such like Place, and the Divulge committed to some vigilant and watchful Tongue: So it is with the News of the Non-Resurrection; it came not from Mount Calvary, but the Priests are the Authors of it, at the eleventh Verse; and at the twelfth, they frame and mould it to the Mouth of the Watch. The Divulgers, Men of double Credit, they know the Truth, for they are of the Watch, and they will not lye, for they are Soldiers; nay, they will maintain it, for they are Knights, Milites, Knights of the Post, they are hired to say, saying, (and they did say) His Disciples came by Night and stole him away whilst we slept.

The Words are so plain, they need no opening. May it please you that I make three Cursories over them; One for the Soldiers, another for the Disciples, and the third for our Saviour. In the Two former we will beat the Point *pro* and *con*, and in the latter reconcile it, for that's the Fashion also. No Error so absurd but finds a Patron, nor Truth so sound but meets with an Adversary, nor Point controverted, but the opposite Tenet may be reconciled; be they distant as Heaven and Hell, as incompatible as Jews and Christians, yet they shall meet with a Moderator; and a cogging Distinction shall state the Question on the absurder Side. First then for the Soldiers, whose Cursory hath no Parts, that's not the Souldiers Manner, but yet is sprinkled with Absurdities, that's the Manner of the Watch. They speak partly as they fight, voluntarily, and partly as they watch, supinely, and thus they begin their Talk.

'Ye Men and People of Judah and Jerusalem, this Jesus of Nazareth was a very Juggler, a neat Compiler of Impostures, pretended Title to the Crown of Judah, made himself the Messias and the Son of God, brought such strange Opinions as would turn the whole World out of Byass; having no Proof from Sense or Reason for his Novelties, he would needs confirm them by Miracles; and in the World's Eye he seemed to do Wonders, though his Works were indeed but meer Delusions, wrought by Slight of Hand, *hocus pocus*. All which was so manifestly discover'd, that to stop the Current of such false Coin, my Lord President was forced to nail him to the Cross for a Counterfeit. His Master-trick was that of the Resurrection, whereof he forespake in his Life-time: For he was no ordinary Dealer, but would make his Cunning to survive his Person, and durst fore-say so. To put this Piece in Execution, he entertain'd a Rabble of Ruffians, whom he termed his Disciples, as all Plotters have Partners: These he instructed in the Game while he lived, and they were to play it when he was dead. The List of his Disciples consisted of Men and Women; for in all crafty Carriages, there lies a Woman's Part. The Men were to perform all Manner of Fact, and the Women, whose Activity lies in their Tongues, were to report the Miracle.

'The High-Priests and some of the Sanhedrim being wise to apprehend, and wary to prevent the dangerous Consequences hereof, procured a Warrant from the President to seal up the Tomb, and place a Watch there; and we were the Parties appointed to guard it. The Charge we underwent required good Service; for his Disciples were common Night-walkers like their Master, notable Cutters, and carried as much Courage as Cunning; such tall Fellows with their Weapons, that they made it but a Sleight, either to withstand or assault a whole Multitude, and durst do any thing in their Master's behalf. The other Night, when we apprehended him in Gethsemane, we were most of the lustiest Fellows in Jerusalem, and pretty well appointed; yet they stood to it stoutly, made a tall Fray, and sometimes put us to the worst. At the first Onset we were all knock'd down, and at our Recovery, Rabbi Malchus, a Follower of the High-Priest's Company, and our Captain, was singled out by one of their Side, a Sailor he seemed, who with his Whinyard lopt off one of his Ears; and had the Blow lit right, it would have cleft him down to the Twist: Nay, they were all Bravos, and their bloody Mind was seen upon Judas Iscariot, one of their own Company, who because he was our Bloodhound to scent their Master out, they persecuted the poor Wretch till they had paunch'd him; for not far from their Walk he was found hang'd with his Guts about his Heels. And for their bloody Pranks that Way, the Place begins to bear the Name of Aceldama, the bloody Field.

'For the Exploit of his Resurrection, they had the Assistance of their Fellow She-disciples, Night House-wives too; for they were hovering about the Sepulchre from the Dead of the Night till the Morning, and were as the Counter-Watch, to give Notice of some Advantage to the Disciples, who lay not far off, somewhere above Ground, while their Master was under it. All the Day-time they stir not, for Fear of Passengers frequenting to and fro in the Gardens and Walks about Mount Calvary, it being both Sabbath and Passover: But in the Night they took their Opportunity by this Means. We had been extreamly overtravell'd, both to apprehend and guard him; first, to the High-Priest, next to the President; from him to Herod, and back again; then to his Arraignment, then to his Execution, and ever since at his Grave: So turbulent the Man was, that his very dead Body would not lie still, and be quiet. This Over-watching, seconded with the Darkness of the Night, and Coldness of the Air, cast us into a heavy Sleep; thereupon the Women gave the Watch-word to the Disciples, who immediately do exhumate his Body; and while they translate and bury it elsewhere, the Women trot into the Town, and bruit it abroad, that their Master is risen.

' And the credulous City is partly inclined to believe the Legerde-main; they are willing to frame their Faith, and build their Salvation upon a flying Gull, raised by three Way-going Women, gadling Gossips that came from Galilee; one of them notorious, so devilish, that there came seven Devils out of her; how many staid behind, God knows: It is like she was so full, there was Room for no more; and by her ye may guess at her Companions. Consider of it; the Matter is of Moment, a main Point of State, that concerns your own Nation: We are but Strangers, and no farther interested than for the Truth's sake to speak it; and therefore be advised whether ye will rely upon the Word of a Woman, or upon the Faith and Reputation of a Soldier.'

Here the Soldier puts up, and sheaths his malicious and blasphemous Tongue, more sharp and deadly than his Sword, and gives our Saviour a Wound more mortal far than those upon the Cross: They did but put him in a Trance, suspend his Life for a Day or two, at the most but kill his Humanity; but This would murder his Divinity, and dead his Im-mortality; it would nullify the Gospel, and frustrate all our Faith: For, if Christ be not risen (saith St. Paul) then is our Preaching vain, and your Faith is also vain. And therefore I come to my second Cursory: For his Disciples stole him away by Night.

Herein we will deal Christianly and civilly, not give the Lie to the Soldiers, or foul words to the Watch: But yet we may say, that their Tale hath no Truth in any Point of it, but a meer Saying. Saying, say ye. They say not of themselves, but as the Priests taught them; they knew they said false; and therefore, our saying to the contrary will easily obtain. And therein we follow not the Random of their Roving, but take the Sum of their Saying, as it is here set down by the Holy Ghost, giving it Order and Parts. The Words then may easily be taken judi-ciarily, in Form of an Accusation, and then morally they are Calumny; the Soldiers either not heard, or not practised the Doctrine of John Baptist, Accuse no Man falsly. Or they may be taken popularly, in

Form of a Report or Rumour; and then morally they are a meer Gull or Slander. In what Sense soever, there are three Parties wronged in them; the Disciples, our Saviour, and the Soldiers themselves. The Disciples here are tax'd of Theft, that they should come by Night, and steal away their Master: Our Saviour of Impotency and Imposture, that he neither could nor did rise from the Dead, but was convey'd away by his Disciples: And the Soldiers of capital Negligence, that they were asleep. In the Cursory then for the Disciples, may ye please that I lay down three plain Contradictories to the Words of the Text, as they lie in order: First, the Disciples came not hither by Night. Secondly, he was not stole away. Thirdly, the Soldiers were not asleep. For Proof of each, whereof there are no cogent Demonstrations in Nature, *quid sint*; single voluntary Actions that leave no evident Effect, admit it not. We preach not before Jews and Infidels, to whom this Doctrine is scandalous and Foolishness; but the simple-hearted Christian, the willing Hearer, shall have rational Probabilities and perswasive Arguments, sufficient to convey Belief into a Heart illuminated, and prepared by Grace for it. For the first then, His Disciples came not by Night.

The Body moves not voluntarily, unless the Motion be grounded upon the Will; so that when the Influence of the Will upon the external Members is either intercepted or frustrated by any foreign Accident, the Body hardly admits of going and coming. The Heart, and first Mover of the Disciples, was now mated and set up by a Lease of impetuous Passions. All those Violents of the Soul which have mischiefs for their Objects, and are immediately distractive to the Patient that endures them, as Sorrow, Fear, and Despair, did now wholly possess them: Extream Sorrow for their Master's present Sufferings, as much Fear for their own future Danger, and their like Despair for their forehoped Happiness. Their Senses feel the Sorrow, their Fear torments their Fancies, and their Memory maintains their Despair; their whole Soul so assaulted, that there wanted nothing but a Fever to make them quite frantick. And Peter came near to that, so distracted, that for his Master's sake, first he will need fight, then he flies away; anon again he follows after him, at length he forswears him, and in the End goes out, and cries. In this Mode he is carry'd up and down, till he lays a Clog on his Conscience, that would hold him Work enough without coming to Mount Calvary. The Case of his other Fellows might be as bad, or worse, although the Scripture be therein silent. Thus far they go all with Peter, that they sleep, and fly, and follow afar off.

But when their Master was past all Recovery, then each Passion play'd his Part to hinder all Humour from coming to Mount Calvary. Their Sorrow contracts, and closeth them up in Jerusalem: Sorrow loves to be private and lurk in a Corner. Fears keep them within Doors: Fear dare not go abroad, especially in the Night; if she do, it is to fly a Danger, not to invite it. And to Despair all Business must yield: Despair will not stir in her own behalf, unless to do herself a Mischief, but of any other she is quite careless. To say then they came by Night, makes it but the more unlikely. They could not watch one Hour with him in Gethsemane, when it concerned his Life, while there was yet Hope to vindicate him from the Cross; and can they now watch with him a whole Night when he was dead and buried? If they were for a Night's Exploit, they would have done it in the Night before, when there was a fairer Opportunity, and greater Security. They now had no more Means this Night, but more Danger. When they went to Gethsemane, they had but two Swords in all, and were there disarmed of them; but one Coat apiece, and some stript of that; no Weapon to assault, nor Armour to defend. Fit Furniture, and fair Voyage for poor Fishermen to make to Mount Calvary in a dark Night, to affront the Roman Watch. And to what End? If their Master could rise again, what need they come hither? If not, they did him no Wrong to abandon him.

But why mention we the Resurrection? they came not thither, not to a Thought of it. He had indeed foretold them of it, but they understood it not: They could not prosecute what they never apprehended; could they hope to make others believe what they could not imagine? Could others grant that feazable, which they esteemed impossible? Or had they once Belief, yet they forsook it when they forsook their Master. They were beaten from it in Gethsemane, where but one of the Jews received any Loss, and he but one of his Ears, and that restored again; but they all lost every one his Faith, they lost their Saviour, and their Souls to boot. They were now as faithless as their Fellow Judas, as faithless in their Master as he was to him. The Resurrection quite forgot, not only the Thing itself, but their Master's Mention of it: And therefore they embalm his dead Body, and do entomb it as forlorn. The Priests themselves believed more than the Disciples: They feared it, and therefore fortified the Sepulchre; but the Disciples did not so much as hope. And when he was risen *de facto*, they could not believe it, though the Women avouched it: ὡσεὶ λῆρος τὰ ῥήματα αὐτῶν, the Women's Talk seems an old Wife's Tale, when they tell the Disciples of the Resurrection. Thomas will not trust his own Eyes though he see, and his Ears though he hear him. Had they any By-intent, they would have been very forward to report and spread the Fame; but they stood mute at it, and began to spread themselves each Man what Way his Fancy led him: The Fame of the Resurrection did not fright them. And how came the News abroad? who told it to the High-Priests? not his Disciples, nor the Women, but the Soldiers here themselves. But why stand we to defend the Disciples in a Fact never committed? no such Thing done as they objected. He was not stole away at all: My second Contradictory.

Nor by the Disciples, nor by any unless Men were mad, or weary of their Lives. The Advantage of the Act could no way recompence the Danger. The Laws so strict for meddling with Sepulchres, that they could expect no less than to incur the Crime of Sacrilege; which may be seen at large in the Digests *de Sepulchro violato*: which Laws, though since compiled, yet for the most part were then and there in Force, the Jews being under the Roman Jurisdiction. And though they should plead that they did only translate the Body, not abuse it, yet they could not avoid the Objection of *dolus malus*, and so incur an arbitrary Censure, which would be laid very heavily upon them, Things running as they did against our Saviour. What fair Interpretation could they look for on his Behalf, when he himself was charged with Treason, for asking a Penny to pay Tribute? Or if some had the Will to steal him, yet none had the Power or Means to perform it. The Watch there, termed Soldiers, were of a middle Nature between Soldiers and Hangmen; Speculatores, they carried a Spear in their Hands, but a Halter at their Girdles; always ready for any deadly Service. They were σωματοφύλακες, Satellites, a Guard to the Governor; and Custodes, Goalers, Wardens for Prisoners; and Vigiles, Watchers for their Bodies who suffered: The common Executioners of corporal Punishment, whether it reached only to Sense, or forward to Life. To express their Roman Nature home, the Eastern Nation borrowed Language from the Western, the Greeks from the Latin, *Custodia*; and the Syriac, as Master Fuller observes, from *Quæstionarii*, Officers *ad quæstionem* & *inquisitionem*, Questioners or Inquisitors, Tormentors, or Serjeants of the Rack, to extort Confessions in criminal Examinations. At the Peril of their Life it was, if the Party under their Execution did not endure the Extremity of the Law: If the Prisoner excaped with no Punishment, or with less, or *in ultimo supplicio* recovered by his Life, or his dead Body otherwise disposed than the Laws ordained or permitted, then were those Soldiers to take the room of the Prisoners, to be wasted and spent out upon the same Punishment whereto the Prisoner was liable; *Ejusmodi pœna consumendi*, the very Words of the Law. Could any Man now imagine the Watch could now be either so careless, or such Cowards, as to let our Saviour be stole away? Men durst as well have fetcht him from the Cross as from the Grave.

But say, that they were such maimed Soldiers, as that they had neither Eye to Watch, nor Heart to Ward; yet the Sepulchre itself was so impregnable, that it alone would secure the Body. There could be no Burglary, nor breaking it up, no undermining; the Soil was Pick-ax Proof, a firm Rock spread out of the Roots of Golgotha, gabion'd and rough-cast with Flint. No removing of the Tomb-stone; that, besides its Weight and Sullenness to give way, was rib'd and clasped down with Iron Bars and Bonds; the Closure soulder'd with the Seal of the San-hedrim. Their ἠσφαλίσαντατὸν τάφον, and σφραγίσαντες τόν λίθον, their fortifying the Sepulchre, and sealing up the Stone, says it was so, in the latter Verse of the former Chapter. For though he should revive, yet the High Priests never meant he should rise more, either by his own, or by the Strength of others. The Watch was but a Stale to colour their Pretence, and to lead their Request to Pilate. The Women's, Who shall roll us away this Stone? was a Matter more than they imagined, a Task above the Strength of a Man. A whole set of Leavers could not lift it: No rolling it away but by the Force of an Angel.

And now look into the Grave, see the Remains of the Resurrection, the impartial Witnesses and silent Sayings, that he was not stole away. The Linen and Grave Clothes wherein he was involved, lined and loaden with a compound of Myrrh, Aloes, and Mastick, Gums and Spices of Arabia, Unguents and Balms of Gilead, a Sear-cloth both costly and massie, ὡσει λητρας [sic] ἑκατὸν, to the Worth or Weight of an Hundred Pounds, somewhat unwieldy to be handled; The Kerchief so wrapt and plaited, as though yet it had not been used; and yet so laid aside, as though he would have come again. What manner of Men would leave these Things thus? His Friends would not for shame have stript him, and carried him away naked. His Foes would have esteemed the Linen and embalming Compounds far beyond his Body. Friend or Foe, or Neuter, they durst not stay to flay the glewy Sear-cloth from his Skin, and give a diligent Folding to the Kerchief. But if notwith-standing he was stollen away, Why was not Search made to recover his Body? No Hue and Cry to pursue the Malefactors? No Proclamation out for their Attachment? Why were not the Women apprehended, or taken upon Suspicion? Why not so much as questioned? Questioned! about what? The Soldiers knew well enough he was not stollen away; for they sate by, and mark'd it; they were the Watch, and they did watch; they were not asleep; which is my last Contradictory.

Hitherto they talk like Soldiers, of coming by Night, and stealing away; now like Watchmen, in saying they were asleep. So sottish and unreasonable is Malice, that, to burn his Neighbour's House, he will set Fire on his own; to bring in an Accusation on Christ and his Disciples, they make Confession of a Crime in themselves: They gull and befool themselves, and say, that the Watch was asleep. It may be as Watchmen they durst sleep, 'tis ordinary; but they durst not so as Soldiers, their Discipline too strict, and the Penalty thereof too severe. He that forsakes the Watch, *capite punitur*, 'tis Death (saith Paulus) in Law 9. in Excubias, §. *de re militari*; and some good Captains interpret Sleep equivalent to Absence; whatever were the Letter of the Law, Practice made it so. And Polybius tells us, it was so put in Execution. If any Man of the Watch be found asleep, (saith he) ξυλοκοπεῖ, he is put to the Bastinado, a capital Punishment, and reach'd to the Head: For the then Bastinado was *Fuste cæditur*; and as they now pass the Pikes; a thousand to one but the Party died under it. A whole Squadron of Men being to do Execution, one Back-friend or other would dash out his Brains, as now one Pike or other would broach him through. The Roman Discipline extreme dogged, and so profess'd itself, especially towards the Watch. The Ban-dogs of the Capitol, because they bark'd not that Night when the Gauls surpriz'd it, had their Legs broken, and were split alive upon a two-fork'd Stake set up in publick; and in Memory thereof (saith Livy) some Dogs were yearly so used, for Example's sake to make Watchmen beware.

And the Rounders so impartial herein, that they would make Execution *ipso facto*. Epaminondas walks the Round, and finding one Soldier asleep, some of the Corrounders entreat for him: Well, saith he, for your sakes I will leave him as I found him, and therewithal he stakes him to the Ground with his Halbert: He found him in a dead Sleep, and so he left him. Some dim Prints of that Discipline are seen to this Day in our modern Wars, where sometime the Rounder will clap a Musquet-shot through a sleepy Head: But antiently they durst do no other; for to wink at the Fault, or delay the Punishment, was, in the Governor, *Patrimonii & æstimationis damnum*, a Loss of Lands and Honour; and in Under-Officers, *capitale supplicium*. They durst not then sleep wilfully, and they had no need to sleep, they were not overwatch'd. How the Day-watch stood, I have not yet read; but for the Night-watch, all the World knows it was divided into four equal Parts, each containing three Planetary Hours, or one Quarter of the Night, how long or short soever. And the Turn came about but every third Night; and then every third Hour they were relieved by putting in a fresh Watch. It was now past the Vernal Equinoctial, no one Night-watch sate full three modern Hours; so three Hours over in above three-score would bring no Over-watching. Seeing then they neither durst, nor did, Why yet do they say they were asleep? The Reason is, They are of the ragged Regiment, mercenary Soldiers, hired to it by the Priests, with a large Piece of Money. The Provant-man will undertake to say any thing, yea to do any thing for Money; for ten Groats a Week tug at a Wheel-barrow, and for a Stiver more, serve the Enemy; and for a Piece, pistol a Prince; suffer any thing for Money; for a Dollar take the Strappado; for a Brace, draw at a Decimation. Thus the Priests dealt with the silly Soldiers, as they did with Judas, only put them upon hanging. An old Trick of the Priests, and much in Use at this Day, seeing that now they practise it one upon the other; and so let them; good Speed may they have.

But for all this they might be asleep, whether our Saviour were stole away or no. Somewhat the begging Soldiers would have, and they shall, his stealing away we can by no Means grant. The Resurrection, an Article of our Creed, the very Groundsel of all our Faith: His Re-surrection the Pattern and Pledge of ours, the Tenure whereby we hold our Title to Salvation. But for their being asleep, we will not much contend: It is credible they were so, the contrary being neither implied, nor expressed in the Scripture. But yet their Sleep is no Proof of their Saying. They know the things were done just as they say, for they were asleep the while. A right Roman Reason, a Proof put from a Priest to serve a sleepy Soldier. If they were asleep, how could they say he was stollen rather than risen? Or, if they suppose him stollen, how knew they his Disciples did it rather than other Men? This must needs argue in them either Calumny to accuse a Party without Cause, or Levity to lay the Cause upon a wrong Party; either way Folly to alledge so senseless a Reason. All our Knowledge is either from Sense, or Reason: from Reason they could not have it, That hath made against them all this while; from any Sense they could not, for they were asleep. In Sleep all Sensation is intercepted. They could neither hear, see, smell, taste, nor feel the Disciples coming, or his stealing; if they did, they were not asleep.

If some one were awake, and perceived it, why did he not give an Alarm to the rest? If they understood it afterwards from others, why do they not produce authentick Witnesses? If the Disciples themselves confessed it, why were they not punished, and Order taken to stop the Rumour of the Resurrection? There is no Way now left, but to pretend the Spirit, as our Enthusiasts do, and to say, that while they slept, they had it in a Dream by Revelation. But that is refuted by Retortion of the same, for by Revelation every Christian knows the contrary; God reveals it unto him.

But why did the Soldiers produce this Reason? The Reason is, they took it upon Trust from the Priests. It is an old Error (let us not contend for the Age) to believe that the Priest cannot err. But why are the Soldiers got thus to argue against themselves? The Reason is, no Body else durst do it. In those Times, the Soldiers bore all the Sway, assumed all Power to make Kings and Emperors. But since the Priest hath done the like, putting the Soldier by. And now the Peasant thinks 'tis come to his Turn, under Pretence of his Privilege in Parliament: He would dispose of Kings and Commonwealths, and rather than return it to the Priest from whom he hath taken it, would cast the Course back again upon the Soldiers. Nothing now contents the Commonalty, but War and Contention; he hath taken a Surfeit of Peace, the very Name of it grows odious: Now to give the Soldier his Passport, we sum up four Exceptions against his Saying: First, it is not Verisimile, the Unlikelihood of it hath appeared in every Contradictory. Secondly, they were *ignari rerum*, had no Information of what they affirm; neither Eye, nor Ear-witness of what they say, for they confess themselves asleep. Thirdly, Their Saying is contrary to what they had said before in the Morning they told another Tale, at the eleventh Verse of this Chapter; if that were true, this is false; if that were not true, why should we believe this? Or who will trust Men in contrary Tales? Lastly, the Parties were corrupted, hired with a large Sum to utter their Saying, at the twelfth Verse. These two latter lie without the Text, and therefore I wholly forbear them, especially for the Point of Corruption: 'Tis a crafty Crime, and commonly hard to prove. We also forbear the Lie to the Soldier, because he abhors it. But to the Priests who put this Lie in their Mouths, and to their Disciple-Priests, who at this Day practise lying, and allow it to be lawful, we would mend the old Saying, A Liar should have a good Memory, and rather require in him a good Wit. His Memory serves but to avoid Contradictions of himself, but his Wit to prevent the Contradictions of others, that an Untruth seem not also unlikely. If therefore the Priests would have lied wisely, and with Credit, like Satan himself, the Serpent whom they served, they should, as they did formerly, have laid our Saviour to Satan's Charge, and have said, that the foul Fiend came by Night, and fetch'd him away; leaving out, whilst the Watch slept, and instead thereof have argued from the Descent of the Angel, and the Earthquake: This could not so easily have been discovered; but it might even as easily, where Faith had a

Fortification; human Reasons urged against it are but as Paper-shot.
Cardinal Wisdom working against God is but Dirt and Rottenness.
Our Counsels are confounded, when carried against Christ. And so
I come to my third and last Cursory, upon the Word of our Saviour.

Hitherto we have cleared the Disciples, but we must also give the
Soldier content. There is no such Difference, but the Matter may be
reconciled, and the Question stated on the Soldiers side. Said I not,
it was the Fashion? The Soldiers then are in the right, their Saying
very sound and Christian: A Disciple of his did come by Night and steal
him away, and the Soldiers were asleep. A Disciple of his, and his most
beloved Disciple, his human Soul, came by Night, was united to his
Body, raised it, and withdrew it from the Sepulchre by Stealth, while
the Soldiers were so between Sleeping and Waking, that they perceived
it not. Of this Cursory very briefly, as the Words lie in order, declining
all emergent Controversies, for that our present Quarrel lay only with
the Soldiers.

We term him a Disciple, who receives Knowledge and Chastisement
from another. As our Saviour was God, his Soul was ὃ μαθητὴς, the
truest and most proper Disciple that ever was: It had received both
Knowledge and Chastisement, as never Man had; Knowledge of all
Manner, both Divine and Human, infused and acquired: But whether
it had no Ignorance, we leave it to the Catholics. And all Manner of
Chastisement, both exemplary and satisfactory, for all Mankind; the
Chastisement of our Peace was upon it: But whether it satisfied for
Reprobates, we leave it to the Arminians. His Soul came, it could
move, for it was separate; the Soul was from the Body, though neither
from the Godhead: As all the rest of the Disciples, it forsook him on
the Cross, and now it came again: But it came not as it went, it went
by Violence and foreign Force, the Jews expelled it from him, although
he was also willing it should go; but it came purely voluntary, by a
domestick Agent: But whether by Virtue of the Godhead, or its own
motive Faculty, we leave to the School-men. It came then, not as poor
Lazarus's Soul came to Abraham's Bosom, carried by Angels, but single
upon its own Force, and without any Help of others: But whether
attended and waited upon by Troops of Angels, we leave it to the
Fathers. For the Time, it came by Night; not for fear of the Jews, as
Nicodemus came to him, but for love of his Promise, that he might
rise the third Day. He came the second Night, the Night second to his
Passion, but third to the Day of his Resurrection, some time between
Midnight and Morning; but at what Time we leave it to the Chrono-
logers. The Unde of its coming was from somewhere else, from a

distant Ubi, for it was not come before it came: From whence defini-
tively, whether from Heaven or Hell, we leave it to the Calvinists. The
Quo or Term of its coming was the Grave, he subsisted there; but the
End of the Comer, was the Re-union to the Body, to make his real
Presence there: But whether thereby he became Omnipresent, to be
every where while he was in the Grave, we leave to the Lutherans. His
final Intent, not to organize the Body, it was not dismembred, nor any
way corrupted, not so much as *in fieri*, no not dispositively; but to
animate those Members, and to raise the Body from the Grave; in which
Action both the Body and the Soul had their mutual Efficiency, each
co-elevating other to make up the Resurrection: But whether these two
Agents imply several Operations really distinct, we leave it to the
Nominalists.

The Manner of his Resurrection so miraculous and ineffable, that
bad Words express it best. In a moral Relation to the Jews, it is here
termed Stealing: Not to shew what our Saviour did in his Rising, but
to intimate what the Jews had committed by their Crucifying. Things
of a super-eminent Nature, are fain to borrow Words of an inferior
Signification, when they are related to a low Capacity; so God gives
himself Attributes, not as he is, but according to the Weakness whereby
Man apprehends him. And here the Action of our Saviour is set down,
not as it is done, but according to the Wickedness that the Jews had
done. The active Signification of Stealing belongs to our Saviour, but
the moral Evil of it reflected upon others. The Law saith, he steals who
fraudulently takes away something of another's, with Intent to get the
Thing itself, its Use or Possession. If this Definition be true, his Resurrection was Stealing. His Body was now *Cadaver puniti*, the Carcase of
one that had publickly suffered, and thereby forfeit to the State; no
Man might meddle with it farther than to bury it, nor that without
special Permission; it was now none of his, his Right and Possession
of it both gone; a *tradiderat*, he had made Delivery of it, dispensed and
passed it away to Pilate: Pilate disposed his Right to bury it, to the
Watch to detain it, and now it was theirs. When therefore he took it
from the Grave, he stole it: His Repossession of it defrauded all the
Præ-detainers. Said they not also he was a Deceiver? But whether the
Angel that rolled away the Stone, was necessary or ministerial, we leave
it to the Hermonists. By natural Relation his Body was his own, as
being the essential and proper Counter-part of his Soul, præ-coexistent
with it in one Person; but morally it was not so, or if it were, yet he
might steal it for all that. A Man may steal that which is his own, by
interverting that Right in it which hath been transferred to another;

and what kind of Theft this was, we leave it to the Lawyers. God forbid we should lay other Theft to our Saviour, than that he attributes to himself, in saying, He came like a Thief in the Night, (i.e.) secretly and unawares: So was his Conveyance from the Grave, close, without the Consent and Notice of those that were present; such a Carriage we commonly call Stealth. We steal away from a Room, when we depart without the Knowledge of the Company: But whether he could convey himself so closely, as to pass through the Tomb-stone, we leave it to the Philosophers.

Yet so close it was, that the Watch perceived it not, for they were asleep; they were set to watch it, but they did not. Not to watch, is all one with not to be awake, and that with to be asleep. We commonly call him sleepy that is negligent or careless of what passeth, as the contrary we term Vigilant: So the Watch was fast asleep, they never gave Heed to the Resurrection: That so far from their Belief, that they had no Opinion of it. But if Death be a Kind of a Sleep, he is soundly asleep that lies for Dead; and so did the Watch in the 4th Verse of this Chapter, ἐγένοντο ὡσεὶ νεκροὶ, for Fear of the Angel they fell a shaking, and became as dead Men. His Presence gave them a strong Dormitive, it wrought beyond Sleep. Sleep reacheth but only to a Ligation of Sense; but in them all Motion ceased, they were exanimate: But whether that Fit held them only by way of Syncope, or did determine in a Cataphora, or soporiferous Passion, we leave it to the Physicians. Fearful and cowardish Soldiers, more womanish than women! At the Presence of the Angel the Women stand upright, but the Soldiers fall in a Swoon. Help them good Women, unbutton the Soldiers, ye need not fear their Halberts. There's Work for you and your Spices, your Odours to comfort and recal their Spirits. Bestow that Charity on the dying Soldiers, which you intended on your dear Saviour; for he is risen, and needs them not, but they may benefit the Soldiers. The Soldiers, used to such Fits, they had one of them the other Night in Gethsemane; but whether these Dejections were Sins in the Soldiers, we leave to the Casuists. Thus they were κοιμώμενοι, laid as Men asleep; for it signifies rather the Reclination or Posture of one asleep, than the Affection of Sleep itself. He that lies still without Sense or Motion, whether he be in a Sleep, or Trance, or dead, we say κοιμώμενος; and we call the Church-yard κοιμητήριον, because the Dead lie there as if they were asleep, they stir not. And so we must all be laid; there's no Dormitory. Our Case somewhat like the Soldiers: We are appointed here to watch our Saviour; and as we do it, we are subject to the Soldiers Infirmity, apt to be cast asleep, and become as dead Men. Yet let us not be subject to their Fear, our Death is but like their Swooning, that's the worst. We are liable to rise again, and our Resurrection shall be like our Saviour's: His and ours make a mutual Aspect; his the Specimen, and ours the Compliment. What he practised on himself, he perfects in us: He will come again by Night, and steal us to Glory, while we lie sleeping in the Grave. Even so come Lord Jesus.

AREOPAGITICA

*W*ITH *the Civil Wars of the seventeenth century we enter on the Golden Age of pamphleteering. In a period of disputed authority and many opinions, vigorously held, it was natural that printing presses, long held under control by the central government, should at last have supplemented political and military warfare. A wordy battle raged from the beginning of the Long Parliament to the establishment of Cromwell's 'Protectorate'; and even this return to despotism could not silence the writers who had once known freedom, for they continued to publish, legally and illegally, and to find the means for distributing their wares.*

A few early periodicals belong to this time, but most of the political literature took the form of pamphlets. George Thomason, a London bookseller of the period, collected specimens of these pamphlets from 1640 to 1661, during which time he amassed some 22,000 tracts, which have since become the property of the British Museum—bound in two thousand volumes.

Pamphlet battles frequently involved two or more parties in long disputes, with an astonishing effect upon the titles used, which grew longer at each sally. A work by five Presbyterian divines who signed themselves 'Smectymnuus' (a composite of their initials) called for a 'remonstrance' by Bishop Hall. This in turn drew Milton to publish his 'animadversions' on the subject, to which Hall's son answered with a 'confutation'. Finally we have Milton's famous pamphlet incorporating all these titles: 'An Apology against a Pamphlet called a Modest Confutation of Animadversions upon the Remonstrant against Smectymnuus.'

Such pamphlets were not necessarily as dull as their cumbersome titles might suggest to the present-day reader. In Milton's case never; if Milton was ever dull, it was in his poetry—his controversial prose scintillates with a spirit that never finds a place in his verse. He was a master of invective, scholarly but not always 'refined', and enjoyed a quarrel as thoroughly as any man who ever lived.

It is unfortunate that John Milton's defence of Smectymnuus is too personal and un-political for inclusion here. Instead we offer some extracts from his famous tract of 1644, in defence of the freedom of the press. As a supporter of the Parliamentary cause, Milton was horrified to find that those he had so vigorously defended in the name of freedom were themselves behaving autocratically when they had the power to do so. It was an experience not new to history, and it has been repeated rather monotonously in all subsequent revolutions. But not every age has been so fortunate in its true champions of liberty—the few who can stand firm, as Milton did, when that cause is betrayed by its political leaders. Areopagitica *remains, in spite of its exaggerated nationalism, a splendid and stirring statement of the case for a free press.*

Indeed, it went beyond the intentions of the writer. For Milton (like those to-day who want freedom for all except those whom they hold to be 'fascists') did not himself apply his principles to Catholics and episcopalians. The cause as he states it was greater than the man and greater than his age. Milton's reference to God and 'his Englishmen' affords an interesting comparison with John Aylmer's astonishing marginal rubric.

AREOPAGITICA

By John Milton

LORDS and Commons of England, consider what Nation it is whereof ye are, and whereof ye are the governours: a Nation not slow and dull, but of a quick, ingenious, and piercing spirit, acute to invent, suttle and sinewy to discours, not beneath the reach of any point the highest that human capacity can soar to. Therefore the studies of learning in her deepest Sciences have bin so ancient, and so eminent among us, that Writers of good antiquity, and ablest judgement have bin perswaded that ev'n the school of Pythagoras, and the Persian wisdom took beginning from the old Philosophy of this Iland. And that wise and civill Roman, Julius Agricola, who govern'd once here for Cæsar, preferr'd the naturall wits of Britain, before the labour'd studies of the French. Nor is it for nothing that the grave and frugal Transilvanian sends out yearly from as farre as the mountanous borders of Russia, and beyond the Hercynian wildernes, not their youth, but their stay'd men, to learn our language, and our theologic arts. Yet that which is above all this, the favour and the love of heav'n we have great argument to think in a peculiar manner propitious and propending towards us. Why else was this Nation chos'n before any other, that out of her as out of Sion should be proclam'd and sounded forth the first tidings and trumpet of Reformation to all Europ. And had it not bin the obstinat perversnes of our Prelats against the divine and admirable spirit of Wicklef, to suppresse him as a schismatic and innovator, perhaps neither the Bohemian Husse and Jerom no nor the name of Luther, or of Calvin had bin ever known: the glory of reforming all our neighbours had bin compleatly ours. But now, as our obdurat Clergy have with violence demean'd the matter, we are become hitherto the latest and the backwardest Schollers of whom God offer'd to have made us the teachers. Now once again by all concurrence of signs, and by the generall instinct of holy and devout men, as they daily and solemnly expresse their thoughts, God is decreeing to begin some new and great period in his Church, ev'n to the reforming of Reformation it self: what does he then but reveal Himself to his servants, and as his manner is, first to his English-men; I say as his manner is, first to us, though we mark not the method of his counsels, and are unworthy. Behold now this vast City; a City of refuge, the mansion house of liberty, encompast and surrounded with his protection; the shop of warre hath not there more anvils and hammers waking, to fashion out the plates and instruments of armed Justice in defence of beleaguer'd Truth, then there be pens and heads there, fitting by their studious lamps, musing, searching, revolving new notions and idea's wherewith to present, as with their homage and their fealty the approaching Reformation: others as fast reading, trying all things, assenting to the force of reason and convincement. What could a man require more from a Nation so pliant and so prone so seek after knowledge. What wants there to such a towardly and pregnant soile, but wise and faithfull labourers, to make a knowing people, a Nation of Prophets, of Sages, and of Worthies. We reck'n more than five months yet to harvest; there need not be five weeks, had we but eyes to lift up, the fields are white already. Where there is much desire to learn, there of necessity will be much arguing, much writing, many opinions; for opinion in good men is but knowledge in the making. . . .

Methinks I see in my mind a noble and puissant Nation rousing herself like a strong man after sleep, and shaking her invincible locks: Methinks I see her as an Eagle muing her mighty youth, and kindling her undazl'd eyes at the full midday beam; purging and unscaling her long abused sight at the fountain it self of heav'nly radiance; while the whole noise of timorous and flocking birds, with those also that love the twilight, flutter about, amaz'd at what she means, and in their envious gabble would prognosticat a year of sects and schisms.

What should ye doe then, should ye suppresse all this flowry crop of knowledge and new light sprung up and yet springing daily in this City, should ye set an Oligarchy of twenty ingrossers over it, to bring a famin upon our minds again, when we shall know nothing but what is measur'd to us by their bushel? Beleeve it, Lords and Commons, they who counsell ye to such a suppressing, doe as good as bid ye suppresse your selves; and I will soon shew how. If it be desir'd to know the immediat cause of all this free writing and free speaking, there cannot be assign'd a truer then your own mild, and free, and human government; it is the liberty, Lords and Commons, which your own valorous and happy counsels have purchast us, liberty which is the nurse of all great wits; this is that which hath rarify'd and enlightn'd our spirits like the influence of heav'n; this is that which hath enfranchis'd, enlarg'd and lifted up our apprehensions degrees above themselves. Ye cannot make us now lesse capable, lesse knowing, less eagarly pursuing of the truth, unlesse ye first make your selves, that made us so, lesse the lovers, lesse the founders of our true liberty. We can grow ignorant again, brutish, formall, and slavish, as ye found us; but you then must first become that which ye cannot be, oppressive, arbitrary, and tyrannous, as they were from whom ye have free'd us. That our hearts are now more capacious, our thoughts more erected to the search and expectation of greatest and exactest things, is the issue of your owne vertu propagated in us; ye cannot suppresse that unlesse ye reinforce an abrogated and mercilesse law, that fathers may dispatch at will their own children. And who shall then stick closest to ye, and excite others? not he who takes up armes for cote and conduct, and his four nobles of Danegelt. Although I dispraise not the defence of just immunities, yet love my peace better, if that were all. Give me the liberty to know, to utter, and to argue freely according to conscience, above all liberties.

What would be best advis'd then, if it be found so hurtfull and so unequall to suppresse opinions for the newnes, or the unsutablenes to a customary acceptance, will not be my task to say; I only shall repeat what I have learnt from one of your own honourable number, a right noble and pious Lord, who had he not sacrific'd his life and fortunes to the Church and Commonwealth, we had not now mist and bewayl'd a worthy and undoubted patron of this argument. Ye know him I am sure; yet I for honours sake, and may it be eternall to him, shall name him, the Lord Brook. He writing of Episcopacy, and by the way treating of sects and schisms, left Ye his vote, or rather now the last words of his dying charge, which I know will ever be of dear and honour'd regard with Ye, so full of meeknes and breathing charity, that next to his last testament, who bequeath'd love and peace to his Disciples, I cannot call to mind where I have read or heard words more mild and peacefull. He there exhorts us to hear with patience and humility those, however they be miscall'd. that desire to live purely, in such a use of Gods Ordinances, as the best guidance of their conscience gives them, and to tolerat them, though in some disconformity to our selves. The book it self will tell us more at large being publisht to the world, and dedicated to the Parlament by him who both for his life and for his death deserves, that what advice he left be not laid by without perusall.

And now the time in speciall is, by priviledge to write and speak what may help to the furder discussing of matters in agitation. The Temple of Janus with his two controversal faces might now not unsignificantly be set open. And though all the windes of doctrin were let loose to play upon the earth, so Truth be in the field, we do injuriously by licencing and prohibiting to misdoubt her strength. Let her and Falshood grapple; who ever knew Truth put to the wors, in a free and open encounter. Her confuting is the best and surest suppressing.

[*Extracts*]

LIGHT SHINING IN BUCKINGHAMSHIRE

B^Y the year 1648 the struggle for power in England had become, in the main, a contest between the Parliament (predominantly Presbyterian) and Cromwell's New Model Army, which was mainly recruited from the independent sects. The year was to end with 'Pride's Purge', that drastic elimination of the Parliamentary majority, leaving only the 'Rump', or acquiescent minority, by the authority of which Charles I was tried and condemned to death in January 1649.

But already, within the ranks of the army, forces far more radical than the army leaders were appearing. The men who gave Cromwell power included many who demanded full democratic rights for the people and some who contemplated a drastic social revolution as well. The most important of the 'left' political movements arising from the Civil War were those led by John Lilburne and Gerard Winstanley—the 'Levellers' and the 'Diggers'.

This anonymous pamphlet has sometimes been attributed to Winstanley, a sample from whose work appears later in this volume. There is, however, no reason to suppose that Winstanley had any hand in this Buckinghamshire challenge. It is simply one of the many revolutionary tracts of the period, rather more radical in content than most of the Levellers' literature (which insisted mainly on political democracy and religious toleration), but having some resemblance in substance with the social revolutionary programme of the Diggers— discussed briefly on page 120. In case any reader should be disposed to laugh at the historical knowledge of this anonymous writer, I may point out that Mr. Hannen Swaffer informed Indian readers in India and the World (July 1947) that the Anglo-Saxon kingdoms were subdued by the Romans, who were driven out by Boadicea. . . .

No edition of this pamphlet has been published since the original one in 1648.

Our printer's reader has offered the explanation of a word in this pamphlet, the meaning of which had completely eluded us: 'harets'—probably an alternative spelling of 'heriot,' meaning a fine paid to the lord of the fee on the death of landholder or tenant.

LIGHT SHINING IN BUCKINGHAMSHIRE

Anon.

B
UT now the honest man that would have liberty, cries down
all interests whatsoever, and to this end, he desires common
right and equity, which consists of these particulars following.

1. A just portion for each man to live, so that none need to begge
or steal for want, but every one may live comfortably.

2. A just Rule for each man to go by, which Rule is to be found in
Scripture.

3. All men alike under the said Rule, which Rule is, To do to
another as another should do to him: So that eye for eye, tooth for
tooth, hand for hand, &c, and if any one stole, to restore double, &c.

4. The government to be by Judges, called Elders, men fearing
God, and hating covetousness; Those to be chosen by the people, and
to end all controversies in every Town and Hamlet, without any other
or further trouble or charge.

And in the Scriptures, the Israelites Common-wealth, is an excellent
pattern, if led up to that in Gen. 1. and Gen. 9. mentioned in the beginning.

Now in Israel, if a man were poor, then a publike maintenance and
stock was to be provided to raise him again: So would all Bishops-lands,
Forrest-lands, and Crown-lands do in our Land, which the apostate
Parliament give one to another, and to maintain the needlesse thing
called a King. And every seven years the whole Land was for the poor,
the fatherless, widows and strangers, and at every crop a portion
allowed them.

Mark this, poor people, what the Levellers would do for you. Oh
why are you so mad as to cry up a King? It is he and his Court and

Patentee-men, as Majors, Aldermen, and such creatures, that like Cormorants devoure what you should enjoy, and set up Whipping-posts and Correcting-houses to enslave you. Tis rich men that oppess you, saith James.

Now in this right Common wealth, he that had least had no want: therefore the Scripture call them a Family, and houshold of Israel. And in the 2. of the Acts, amongst those that received the Gospel, they were gathered into a family and had all things common; yet so, that each one was to labour and eat his own bread. And this is equity, as aforesaid: for it is not lawful, nor fit for some to work, and the other to play; for it is Gods command, that all work, let all eat: and if all work alike, it is not fit for all to eat alike, have alike, and enjoy alike priviledges and freedoms? And he that did not like this, is not fit to live in a Commonwealth. See Gen. 9. And therefore weep and howl, ye rich men, by what vain name or title soever, God will visit you for all your oppressions; you live on other mens labours, and give them their bran to eat, extorting extreme rents and taxes on your fellow-creatures. But now what will you do? for the People will no longer be enslaved by you, for the knowledg of the Lord shall enlighten them, &c.

And now (according to our knowledg,) we shall discover your pedegree from your King to your Gentleman, and it is thus:

William the Bastard sonne of Robert Duke of Normandy, with a mighty Army of his fellow-Tyrants, and Theeves, and Robbers, enters Sussex, kils the Inhabitants, the Brittains, and their King, that were in an Army to withstand his cruelty and defend their rights, robs and destroys all places and persons at his pleasure, setleth Garrisons of Normans to enslave the Brittains, takes all Land, and causeth them to hold it by Copyhold, to pay fines and harets at his pleasure, &c. It is too tedious to relate all Polls, Tolls, Taxes, &c. that he made our Forefathers pay, Let the Reader view the Chronicle.

But amongst all unnaturall, unreasonable, tyrannicall and cruel Laws he made, as that of Curfur, of Felony, That the childe must suffer for the Father, &c. And all his tyraunical Laws he caused to be in an Outlandish tongue. So that here we take this power to be that little horn in Dan. 7. 24 because we never heard, or read of the like cruelty that any Tyrant did the like, for to cause his cruel Laws to be in an unknown tongue. Now the poor people knew not when they offended or no.

2. For the execution of those Laws, the people to come to what place he will appoint, at four Terms and times in a year.

And 3. to buy their Laws at the Lawyers unconscionable rate, for he set up and devised the Lawyers. Now as we shall make it appear

Englandes Woife with Eagles Clawes

that this is the horn, so the Caterpillers, Lawyers, will prove the eyes: which Lawyers are as profitable as magots in meat, and Caterpillars in Cabages, and Wolves amongst Lambs, &c.

And amongst those, see their preferment (as its called) to suck the people; as Attorny, Counsellor, Barrester, Sergeant, and accordingly Fees to rob, and they take Oathes, and out of this rubbish stuffe are all our Creatures called Judges, and they likewise all to be sworn. And then places of preferment (so called) to tyrannize, and to be the head Tyrants Sycophants, Wolves, Lyons, Leopards, &c. as Dutchy-General, Attorney-General, Lord-lubber-keeper, Lord Privy-Seal, Lord-Treasurer, Lord Barons of the Exchequer, and I know not what great Catchpoles besides these; all to be sworn to their dread Soveraign Tyrant Beast &c. And so being right whelps brought up to rent, devoure, rob, spoil, tyrannize, &c. over the poor people; then their dread Tyrant, as he hath received power and dignity from the Dragon, or Devil, as aforesaid, doth shelter, breathe out, and all to be daggle them with it, with hairy skind robes, resembling the subtle nasty Fox with his dirty tail. And because the Lord Keeper, Privy Seal, and Treasurers long tailes should not draggle in the dirt, they must have another Sycophant slave apiece to carry it up for them, with their hats off, doing homage to their breech O height of all baseness! What, will they creep in one anothers arses for honour? Why, oh, his Majesties breath of Honour it may be blows out Thire, and therefore he holds up his gown that might blow him that holds it up, and makes him be called Sir. Likewise those men thus honoured, must have a gue-gaw silver Mace carried before them, with a Cross a top on it, to shew they have their Title from the Defender of the Popish Faith; the Lord Keeper having a fools-bable like a Purse carried before him: now all these Lawyers, Lyers, and twelve Judges; Besides with their cowtred Caps; and Serjeants with their womanish Coifs and Peticotes on their Shoulders, with their Barresters, Atturnies, &c. Howbeit, they rob and devoure the people, striving who shall most play the knave and couzen; so that he may clime up into high places of profit: for all those upholding their Kings Prerogative, their Tiranny is unquestionable, that is the reason that they maintain the King can do no wrong; that he is a God on earth, as God is God in Heaven, and that he is the life of the Law; all Writs, Warrants, Commissions, &c. His name gives the beeing to them ; that he is the fountain of our honour and magistracy: yea, and that he is supreme head, Ecclesiasticall and Civil; also that he is to be accountable to none but God, and all this the better to hide their tyrany; for they being all from him, and all their Commissions; if you question them, then you must question him from whom their power was derived; but they say, he is not to be accountable, &c. so that by this means they uphold all their Tyranny; and there is no way, but to take down the Kingly power and then they will down too, and not before: Now these Lawyers are the Eys of the Beast, for the twelve Judges sit in the tyranicall House of Peers, another sort of the Kingly creatures to advise them in all tyranny, and how to keep the Norman yoake about the peoples necks.

The next thing to shew is from whence came our Nobility and Gentry, even from that outlandish Norman Bastard, who first being his Servants and under Tyrants; secondly, their rise was by cruell murther, and theft, by the Conquest; thirdly, their rise was the Countries ruine, and the putting them down will be the restitution of our rights againe, these are called Dukes, Earls, Barons, Marquesse, Lords, &c. And from this Bastard is all our royall blood, therefore to be utterly dis-esteemed: O then behold, o England, thy vanity in Idolizing the King and his Children!

Thy Priests have guld, bewitched, cheated, and betrayed thee into these tyrants hands with their sorceries onely for their own filthy lucre and bellies sake, because they have the greatest part of the spoile for their preaching up the King to be the Supream head, Defender of the Faith, Gods anointed; and that if thou doest resist his power thou re-sisteth the ordinances of God; now all this is but as bridles in thy jawes, and blindes over thy eyes, that thou must be ruled by the Church, and they are thy enemies, and thou must beleeve them; and keep thy selfe a good Subject to thy Prince, the condition is good: and by all these and a thousand tricks more they doe but mould thee to slavery this five hundred yeares and more and by this means the King and his Creatures ride thee in thy Estates, and Persons, and Labours.

And the Priests over thy Conscience and soule, and keeps thee in all ignorance and malice; and for so doing thy Priests are thy Princes, and beare rule, and for their so bewitching thee, they come by their Im-propriations and fat Benefits; and it is for those fat Benefits that makes them turn changelings, either to King or Parliament, which will best furnish their kitching. Therefore shake off those locusts and be no more deluded by them, but hearken to the voice of God in the Scrip-tures, and his Saints, and pay no more Tithes to those Priests, nay cast off those abominable deceivers.

All Charters, Pattents, and Corporations was devised onely to up-hold the Kings Tyrany, Greatnesse, and interest; and because the people did rise in many parts for their Priviledges and Right; and he being in straights and knowing not how to uphold his tyranny devised a way to set the people one against another, by making some Free, some Forreigners, &c. and so deviseth these Patents and Charters in all populous Cities and Towns throughout the Realme to uphold his Interest.

Now as for these bewitching Charters, see how they run . . . Out of our Princely grace, bountie, meer motioned princely favour, Doe give and grant to this our Citie or Town, &c. To be a body Corporate, to consist of a Major, Bailiffs, and Burgesses, &c.

. . . We bequeath to the same body Corporate (and every business must be sworn, to be the Kings creatures) then out of that pack, they have power to choose twelve Aldermen for a Common-counsell, and they all be sworn again: Then out of this stuffe, all the Burgesses to choose a thing called a Major, and she all to be sworn to the Kings; then she shall be a Just-asse of Peace and Coram, and have a silver Hartichoak or toy called a Mase, carried before her; and she and her twelve Adermen following after in their Conie skin Gowns, as so many fools in a Mid sommer Aile: and those petty tyrants shall domineer over the Inhabitants by vertue of their patent, and enclose all, letting and setting of the poors lands too, and moneys, stocks of moneys to their own use, and claim a priviledge from their Charters and patents, that they scorn to be accountable to others, but to their Prerogative Masters; so that you see all tyrany shelters it self under the Kings wings: is it not time then to throw down the King, and bring his person to his answer: these Patents and Charters is the main wheele and prop that upholds the Kings tyrany; for by this means the Prerogative people, strives to uphold the King and Lords interests, to get favours of them, to hold up their own knavery and deceit; and doth choose such Burgesses for the Parliament, as will be for the King, as Caterpiller Lawyers, Coliers, or Lords of the Manor, Impropriators, or such like; and it is from those Patent Towns, that the House of Commons is filled with so many kingified Prerogative self interest, proud and cheating Varlets as now it is: and until those Corporations be thrown down, we can expect never any hope of freedome by a Parliament: see how Londons Common-Counsell stir up their Hackneys with Petitions and Mutineys, for a Treaty with our Conquered enemy, &c.

[*Extracts*]

TYRANIPOCRIT DISCOVERED

*T*HERE *appears to be no clue to the authorship of this remarkable pamphlet, perhaps the best written of all the revolutionary works during the Commonwealth and Protectorate. Published at Rotterdam in 1649, it was dated by Thomason August 14th, i.e. the day on which it came into the hands of the London bookseller. There was no subsequent edition. The author was evidently one of the radicals who had incurred the displeasure of Cromwell and his colleagues and taken refuge abroad. His lines burn with the zeal of the true revolutionary, who had seen one tyranny replaced by another, and social inequality untouched by a change in masters. But (as in the case of Winstanley, noticed below, and that of Lilburne toward the end of his life) this unknown writer had something in him closely akin to the Quakers. He tells his readers that he has 'not written any thing, through hate to any person; for I doe not hate Tyrants, but their tyrannies'. His chief concern is to expose the 'White Devil' (hypocrisy) which he finds much more formidable than the 'Black Devil' of undisguised oppression and petty theft, etc.*

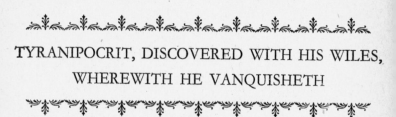

TYRANIPOCRIT, DISCOVERED WITH HIS WILES, WHEREWITH HE VANQUISHETH

Anon.

HEE that will seeke God without, and not within himselfe, may wel say with Simonides: The more hee seeketh, the lesse hee findeth what God is, for what God is in himselfe without us, that knowledge cannot help us; but the knowledge of God within our selves, and in his other creatures, that is all in all to us: but I intend to treat of practice, more then of knowledge, because Christ pronounced more woes against malicious, then hee did against ignorant sinners, and amongst others hee said: Woe bee unto him that knoweth his masters will, and doth it not, but what shal become of him, that knoweth the will of God in Christ, and hateth it; and what are al proud, tyrannical, hypocritical, impious Christians, but haters of God in Christ, for so long as they are so, and doe so: they doe grieve the Spirit of God in their hearts and consciences, and that is a great sinne, if it bee not impiety: then being it is so, woe be unto you, all you tyrannical, hypocritical Christians, you proud Christian Princes, and hypocritical Prelates, and all you superfluous, rich, uncharitable christians, ô you prophane Princes and dissembling Prelates, you will have the name of Christ, the more shame you ought to have of your wilfull and examplary sinnes, which you maintaine contrary to the rule of Christ. O thou white devil, I would faine uncase thee, and discover thy vile practices, that all men may see and know that thou art an ugly, odious devil, I meane thou that wilt winne honour by thy impious practises, thou that hast God in thy mouth, but wilt not cast the devil out of thy heart, thou that commandest and teachest others to doe that good which thou praisest in thy mouth, and hatest in thy heart: thou that bindest heavy burdens, and layest them on other mens shoulders, but wilt not touch them thy selfe with one of thy fingers: ô it is thou that stealest with a high hand, and yet with an impudent face, thou wilt outface the Law.

As for the sinnes of the blacke devil, they are better known to the world, which is ready to take notice of them: The Senate of Tyrants, and the Synode of Hypocrits, are ready to correct and punish him, according to the lawes of the place where he resideth, and in so doing, they do not amisse; but who shall correct and punish the white devil, who shall tell him that hee is running downe the hill to Hel? his owne conscience if hee had one, that might help him, but that is gone long since, and if he should sell his hypocrisie to buy him a conscience, that would spoile the white devil of all his glory. But tell mee thou proposturous impious world, if thou canst, who hath taught thee to punish the transgressors of the second Table of Gods Commandements more then the first? who hath taught thee to hang poore artlesse theeves and to maintain tyrants, and rich artificiall, proud, hypocritical, partial theeves, in their impious practices . . .?

. . . For this hypocritical doctrine to bee rich and godly, is meat and drinke alone for this world, and therefore hee that hath not this doctrine, let him not presume to mount the Pulpit, nor to preach to Kings, Princes, and other superfluous rich, and uncharitable persons, for without this doctrine, hee shall bee esteemed in those dayes, by such men, as an old Almanack, and hee shall have so good entertainement of them, as Christ had by the Gargasites: for if they doe not use him worser, yet they will intreate him to depart out of their countries, because hee is not for their profite. But suppose that riches doe not wholly separate a man from God, yet superfluous riches maketh his way to Heaven the more difficall and harder: for Christ said, It was hard for a rich man to enter into Heaven, but hee never said, it was hard for a poore man to enter into Heaven, and therefore extraordinary riches are stumbling-blockes, which should bee removed out of the way. But consider, if rich men doe not set their hearts on their riches, for therein consisteth the art of hypocrisie: for to carry fire in a mans bosome, and not to burne himselfe, to touch pitch and not to bee defiled therewith, and to have superfluous riches, and not to set a mans heart on them, is all on difficulty, if it bee not an impossibility: but doe not rich men set their hearts on their goods, when they have made a combination, that if any poore artlesse theeves doe steale the goods from them, which they have stolen from the poore before, that the poore theeves shall hang by their necks till they bee dead: What, will they hang men for that which they doe not care for, for a trifle which they doe not regard? I hope they will not say so for shame, that Christians will hang their Christian brethren for nothing. O preposturous dissembling white devil, thou art like unto none, but the devil thy father, or willfull sinne his mother. O hypocrit, hang thy poore neighbour freely, if hee doe steale thy idols from thee, yet say, and confesse the trueth, which is that thou lovest, thy stolen goods more, then thou lovest God in Christ, or Christ in thy poore brother, which is all one? and in so doing, although thou doe continue an uncharitable wretch, yet thou shalt quit thy selfe from hypocrisie, which is no small sinne. But to conclude this point, too much pelfe is a dispersing of the minde, and a dividing of the affections, and so it is a seperating of the heart from God; for God should have the whole desire of the heart, for a divided heart is not upright with God.

I would faine bee quit of this tyrannicall, hypocriticall, impious white devil, but hee is so full of deceit, and hee hath so many evasions, and so much sophistry to maintaine his impious practises, that I doe not know how to deale with him, for neither the law of nature, nor grace, nor Gods commandements, nor the rule of Christ, nor God within nor without him, nor Heaven, nor hell, nor love to good, nor hate to evill, nor any things else that can move impious persons to yeeld to reason: for God through nature hath formed all men alike, and generally hee hath given alike bodies and limbes unto every one, and yet partiallity, contrary to God and nature, doth crosse Gods intent concerning the maintenance of the creature, which nature, according to the will of God, hath impartially produced in the world, and yet in despight of God, nature and reason, which are contrary to partiallity, the impious world will make some men too rich, and others too poore, and yet the worldlings cannot show any reason why they doe so abuse both God and nature, and yet they will continue in their unnaturall, unreasonable, impious partiallity, against the knowledge of their owne consciences; for there is no man, if hee would enter into a serious consideration with God in his heart and conscience, but hee must needs know, that to give unto every man with discretion so neere as may bee, an equall share of earthly goods, is consonant to the law of God and nature, and agreeable to the rule of Christ. And for the trueth of this, I appeale to the consciences of all charitable and reasonable men, and let God, the impartiall judge of all the world, judge this cause, and decide this matter, and to enforce the trueth for what I say, concerning this matter, consider how God commanded the children of Israel to divide their land, and how hee was offended with them which did disposesse their neighbours, and in the primitive Church, the christians

had their goods in common, and wee should take notice of Lycurgus
with the Lacedemonians, and of the Gramanthians, and the Masegates,
and other people which have had an equallity, or a common and
equall share of worldly goods, so neere as they could, and so they have
lived and laboured together in peace and concord, as brethren should
doe. Now I beleeve that in those dayes, most men will grant that a
reformation is needfull, but the question is, who, or what shall bee
reformed: Tyrants and Hypocrits, and all impious persons, would
have a reformation: in the Church the hypocrit would have a conformity in ceremonies, and in the Senate-house, the tyrants will have
the rich artificiall theeves, to reforme or deforme the poore artlesse
theeves. O such a reformation would please both tyrants and hypocrits, and al impious persons, such a reformation would content
tyrannicall Princes, and hypocriticall Prelates. A reformation that will
subject reason to tyranny, that all the world will imbrace, but a reformation that would subject tyranny to reason, that is so odious to
the world, as a repenting sinner is to the devil. A reformation that
will establish tyranny and slavery, and make the rich richer, and the
poore poorer, that is the reformation that the devil would have, but a
reformation *sine* partiallity, that would give unto every man alike
meanes to live on, and that would cause all able persons to labour
according to Gods commandement, and agreeable to reason, and that
would maintaine and cherrish all old, weake, and impotent persons, so
well the poore as the rich, &c.

Such a reformation the seeming sanctified world hateth, and hee
that should propound such a reformation in our impious christian
world, hee should be esteemed of, as the Jewes esteemed of Christ, and
they said, that hee had a devill: and the world is now so impious, as it
was then: as for example, now at this present time are assembled at
Munster, the Agents of most of our supreame christian Rulers, and
what to doe? or to what end? not to destroy tyranny, but to order it
for the profite of some persons in this world, and for the damnation of
all mankinde in the world to come, for they will maintaine the causes
of evill, and yet they will seeme to take away the evill effects, for they
doe not intend to root out tyranny, but to divide it, and to part the
slaves, that every tyrant may abuse his slaves at his owne pleasure,
therein they are very circumspect, not for the universall freedome and
profite of all mankinde, but for the private profite of some: and how
hypocriticall tyrants shall share the world betweene them: They doe not
seeke to make the rich poorer, that so the poore might bee made richer.
They doe not care to cause an equallity of goods and lands, that so

young, strong and able persons might labour, and old, weake, and impotent persons might rest: they take no care to educate all mens children alike, and to give them alike meanes to live on, that in so doing they might breake the gall of murmuration, that so all mankinde might live in concord, and labour for their livings one so well as another, according as God, nature, and reason would have them: they doe not labour to subject tyranny to reason, but they would subject reason to tyranny, and so doe our Senators at London, and all the world over; but I shall have occasion to say more of this matter hereafter, and here will I end the first part of my triple intelligence. God the glory, and mankinde the profite, Amen.

It is said, *ubi fide, ibid amor*, let that bee as it is; this is certaine, where God is, there is love, & *Amor vincit omnia*, and hee hath all that hath God, for hee is in al, and over all, and will turne all to the best for them that doe love him, and keepe his loving commandement. I intend to write a little concerning faith and love, because I have observed the evill constructions, that presumpteous sinners doe seeme to make of that doctrine, which in the point of justification, doth preferre faith before love: I would not dispraise faith, but I would praise love, and prefer love above, and before all, because God is love, for when wee have done all that wee can to find God in his attributes, which are infinite, yet wee must reduce God to one, for hee is one simple uncompounded substance, and then what shal wee call him, Mercie, Justice, Power, &c. all those are in God, but God is one: the Apostle said, that God is love, and when Christ would expresse the wonderfull incomprehensible nature of God, he said, Behold, so God loved the world, that through love, hee gave his onely begotten Sonne to save the world, if the world would bee saved by him. As I take it in all the Bible, there is but one place that seemeth to approve of that doctrine, which teacheth justification by faith alone, and it seemeth at that time the Apostle did not so much desire to advance faith, as hee did to condemne them which would save their selves by their good workes, for neither faith nor good workes, can save any man: no man can bee saved, if the love of God bee not spread abroad in his heart, and that alone is sufficient to salvation, and if faith alone can accomplish salvation, the devil can say that Christ is the Sonne of God, a greater faith then some men have; but whether faith alone can justifie, I will not curiously dispute, for God never commanded man to search for any such needlesse knowledge.

But consider the effects and operations of faith and love: for the meer knowledge of vertues cannot please God, nor profite men. It is

the practicall more then the theoreticall part of vertues, that wee are
to labour to attaine, and therefore let us consider the operations of
faith and love, and compare them together, and then wee shall see how
much love doth exceed faith; for love respecteth both God and man,
but faith doth not so respect his brother, and therefore faith is not so
perfect as love is. Faith will love and honour God, if hope tell him that
God will save him, and bring him to Heaven, but Love will love God
although dispaire tell him, that God will cast him into Hell. True love
knoweth neither Heaven nor Hell; but faith is all for Heaven. Faith is a
marcenary, but love is a voluntary souldiour, that knoweth no why nor
wherefore, but saith with Christ, Behold, here I am, ready to do thy will,
O God. But consider the operations of faith and love concerning our
neighbours, for man may profite man, but no man can profite God, and
therefore if wee will doe good, wee must doe it to mankinde, and not
to God without man. Now for faith, that cannot help our neighbours,
for what can it help mee that another man hath faith? faith no doubt is a
comfortable thing for him that hath it, but anothers faith cannot help
mee; but if I bee poore, and want food and raiment, if my rich neighbour doe love mee, although hee doe not beleeve as I doe, yet love will
cause him to help mee; but if hee have faith to remove mountaines, and
goods to build Churches, yet if hee do not love mee, hee would not
help mee, except hee played the hypocrit, and then in helping of mee,
hee would hurt himselfe, but charity, although it bee poore and cannot
help, yet shee is willing to help, and love and charity are all one. I
know that a man may have a false love, as hee may have a false faith;
but a man may better prove his love, then hee can his faith, for love is
an inheirent quallity, which God gave to man in his first creation, but
faith is a second gift of God, and the accomplishing of it is in God alone,
for God can save a man although hee want faith to beleeve it: love is
naturall, and when it is fixed aright, then it is divine, which is, when
wee give unto God our good wils, and our neighbours our good
workes. Through love all things were created, and through love all
mankinde are redeemed, and through love all things are, and shall bee
preserved, and God is love, and when a man goeth to God with a
loving heart, then Promise, Law, Prophets, Gospell, Christ, and all
Doctors, have done all that, for which they were ordained, for in all
such willing hearts, God is all in all, for all things are from God,
through God, and to God, and God is love. But the devil and all impious men, hate love, because love is contrary to their nature, and
therefore they would overthrow love, by preferring of faith before her:
if they had opposed hate without hypocrisie against love, that could not

TYRANIPOCRIT,

Difcovered with his wiles, wherewith he vanquisheth.

---

*VVritten and printed, to animate better Artifts
to purfue that MONSTER*

ROTTERDAM,

Printed in the year of our Lord, 1649.

Title page: Tyranipocrit

have wronged love so much, but the devil striveth to set those two principall vertues at ods, thereby to despight God the more, because God is the authour and giver of them both.

But some say, that this justifying by faith alone, is Pauls doctrine, but if Paul were now alive, hee would find out another doctrine for presumptious sinners, which should teach them to worke out their salvation with feare and trembling, and for them that stand, to take heed least they fall; for that which is accidentall to one man, is incidentall to every man: For let occasion bee offered, and God withhold his preventing grace, or if God prepare the temptation, and then leave a man to himselfe, tell mee then, O thou proud earth-worme, what would become of all thy supposed strength? But it may bee, that thou art the eldest sonne, and hast alwayes beene at home with thy father, having not disobeyed him at any time, and therefore thou presumest that God is bound to keepe thee from falling, and it may bee hee wil; but consider how thou repinest at thy younger brother, whose fall was predestinated, to bee for the glorious mercy of God in Jesus Christ, and yet thou wouldest not rejoyce with his father, because hee had received him safe and sound. But tel mee how this lost sonne could bee so welcome to God, when hee had sinned so boldly. O this, or that sonne, so lost, and so found, was al predestinated sinners, and al such as God had prepared the temptations for them, through which they fell, and al repenting sinners, and al such as are accidentally overtaken by sinne, and al such as hate themselves, because they have beene made the instruments of sinne and Satan, &c. but al those which continually doe delight to walke in their wilfull sinnes of knowledge, and are so willing as the devil is, to bee made his instruments to sinne, al such are none of that lost, and found sonne.

This world is a warfare for some, and a plague for others: God is most wonderful with them that love him, for some of them hee causeth to fall accidentally, and that so hainously, that they through disperation, are ready to flie in the face of God, for in that sad condition, God permitteth the devil to open a mans conscience, and hee, to affright such a poore dispairing worme, bringeth along with him the quint-essence of hel, I meane dispaire: God deliver us from such phisicians, for when a man hath not the feeling of the favour of God in his apprehension, then disperation ceaseth on the conscience, and when the devil, dispaire, and a mans owne conscience, are all against one poore worme, let any one judge, if hee can, the miserable state, and poore condition of that man, when all those three at one time shal make warre within him, presenting to his consideration Heaven lost, hel wonne, the endless length of eternity, and above al, the separation from God, and that for ever, as our doctors doe affirme, and stoutly maintaine. Now if any one can tell of a greater hel, let him speake, for I know none: now beeing it is so, let no man presume of his owne strength, nor any special predestination, for they are both alike, deceitful: And therefore consider this al you proud tyrants, which have your dinners served in with trumpets, and wil have men kneele to you, and wil bee drawne in costly coaches, with six or eight horses, as though you triumphed over the poore people, which you have robbed of their necessary maintenance, to maintaine your selves in pride and gluttony, &c. but consider from these sayings of Christ, how a man may bee deceived in his faith.

Christ told the Jewes, That many should come from the East and West, and should sit downe in the Kingdome of Heaven, with Abraham, Isaac and Jacob, and the children of the Bride-chamber should bee cast out. Now in whose esteeme were those out-cast children? not in Gods esteeme, for then they had not beene cast out; but they were children in their owne esteeme, and therefore they were cast out. And hee said, Many will say unto mee on that day, Lord, have not wee prophesied, and cast out devils in thy Name? behold much faith to little purpose: yea, a faith to remove mountaines cannot profite a man, but to augment his misery. But consider who are the greatest beleevers: are they not our Princes and Prelates, that doe make warre, and kill the poore innocent people? The Emperour, if al were stated as the devil would have it, hee should bee the head of the tyrannical christian world, and the Pope of Rome, hee should bee the head of the hypocritical christian world, but now the Catholique, and the most Christian Kings, and the Defender of the Faith, and many more which are like them, wil share with those two hypocriticall tyrants. Behold, those have faith enough, but they have not much love, except the fruits of love bee tyranny, pride, hypocrisie, partiallity, voluptuousnesse, &c. for in maintaining and practising of such like impieties, they and their richest subjects, doe imploy most of all their wealth and power, not to build up, but to pull downe the Common-wealth: and for our merchants, they travel by Sea and Land, to make christian prosolites, chiefly our Indian merchants; but consider their practises, and the profite that wee have by their double dealing, first in robbing of the poore Indians of that which God and nature hath given them, and then in bringing of it home to us, that wee thereby may the better set forth and show the pride of our hearts, in decking of our proud carkases, and feeding of our greedy guts with superfluous, unnecessary curiosities, and although their dealing concerning the Indians goods, bee bad, yet they deale worser with their persons; for they either kill them, which is bad, or make them their slaves, which is worse: I know not what to say concerning such impious proceedings, with them poore innocent people; but concerning such merchants and their merchandise, I would that those which are permitted to speake, and to preach some part of the trueth, would say what they know concerning this matter, which is, That when Rome and Greece were wel ordered, although they were Heathens, yet they would not have permitted so many needlesse curiosities, to bee brought into their countries, to have spoiled their people and Common-wealth withall. Now such things as the poore Indians doe not know how to imploy for the devils profite, our merchants bring them home to us, and wee proud gluttons imploy them for his greatest glory, for wee cloath ourselves with their silke and gold, to show that wee are glad that the devil will use us to maintaine his proud kingdome withall, and some will have their meat painted, so well as their cloathes laced, with gold and silver, that so they may please the devil within and without, and it may bee that such persons have a golden faith, because they eat gold, and weare gold: And it seemeth that all rich, uncharitable persons, which have, and hold an extra-ordinary portion of worldly goods, more then their poore neighbours have, that they expostulate with the poore according to that which followeth. Come on, you poore villaines, what will you doe, for you see that wee rich hypocriticall tyrants, have gotten by fraud and force, the most part of the goods of this world into our impious power, and wee have made a law, as wee call it, that if any poore persons doe steale any of our goods, which we have taken from them, that they shall hang by their necks till they bee dead: but now you poore miserable wretches, if you will serve the devil and us, then wee will imploy you in his, and our service, but wee will not use you in any vertuous actions, for they are contrary to our natures, but as the devil doth use us, so wee will use, and abuse you: some of you shal serve by sea, and some by land, but most of you shall serve to maintaine pride and tyranny: some of you shall robbe the poore Indians for us, and some shall bring us new fashions out of France, and some shall flatter us, and kneele unto us, and blow trumpets when wee eat and drink, and some shall vexe and trouble honest men, because they will not bee our slaves, and serve the devil freely as wee doe, and some of you shal kill our neighbour Tyrants slaves, for if wee suppose that hee hath done us any injury, then wee will send some of our slaves to kill some of their slaves, and then one innocent shall kill another, for that is sport alife [sic] for the devil

91

and us, and some of the vilest of you, shall doe that for us, that God hath commanded us to doe our selves, which is, to till our land; but although God had no more wit then to command us to doe such base and vile labour, yet wee are wiser then to doe that which hee commanded us: no, our poore slaves shall doe that for us, and wee will proudly command them to doe it, and wee will pay them poorely for doing of it, and when they have done it, wee will esteeme of them, almost so much as wee doe of our hounds and horses, and yet wee will bee faithfull Christians, and wee will rule all Christendome, not according to the rule of Christ, but according to our partiall, tyrannicall, hypocriticall, impious rule, which wee have invented, and which wee doe intend to maintaine so long as wee can.

But Tyrants may say, that it is *Crimen læse* to speake of such matters, and therefore I will bee silent. And now concerning faith and love, I say and affirme, considering the presumptious sinners of this age, and the evill constructions that uncharitable persons make concerning justification by faith alone, that it is better to preach and teach that doctrine, which is best to keepe presumptious sinners, from sinning through security, then it is to preach and teach an uncertaine doctrine, of an absolute predestination in God of man, without man, which is contrary to Gods nature, for God cannot bee partial, neither can God do the works of a tyrant, as that doctrine would have him to doe, and above all, it may cause men to neglect the walking with God in their hearts and consciences, which is the summe of all pious Religion, but those doctors may, and I thinke they will say, that they doe not meane, that men should bee saved, or thinke to bee saved by faith without charitie.

To which I answer: If a mans intention bee good, God will, and doth accept his good will; but if a man have taught a trueth, if it bee not the most necessary trueth for his auditors, when hee shall come to know it, hee must then change his theame, and preach and teach that part of the trueth, which is most needfull for his auditors. Now the cause being so, let all doctors seriously consider without partiallity, or respect of persons, what doctrine in those dayes is most needfull to bee taught, wherein so many presumptious sinnes are not alone committed, but maintained; but if men should let predestination alone, and seriously preach to such persons that doctrine of repentance, and of working out of their salvation in feare and trembling, that might chance to take off the proud spirits of some of our gallant persons, which have their dinners served in with trumpets, &c. Now if such doctrine were well preacht, and that they were well put in minde, that God will cast downe the proud, and that hee will give grace to the humble, it may bee they would come to a serious consideration of the way of God with man, and so turne unto him, that hee might heale them. There is now, and a long time hath beene, a great caveling in the Christian world, concerning faith and good workes, and by which of them two a man may be saved; for wee marcenary Christians, God help us, desire salvation more then sanctification, for wee cry out with Paul's Jaylor, and Peters auditors, What shall wee doe to bee saved? but wee should rather say, Lord, what is thy blessed will, that wee may delight in it. But for faith and good workes, neither of them are ours, nor are they absolutely necessary to salvation, for Christ said one is necessary, and that is not faith nor good workes, but that *unum necessarium*, is to participate of Gods nature. It may bee that faith, or good workes, or predestination, or some other thing may bring a man to Heaven, but if the love of God in Christ, bee not shed abroad in his heart, hee will bee cast out as the devil was.

I grant that we ought to labour to have a faith, to beleeve that God is not partiall, and that God in himselfe hath predestinated all men alike, concerning their everlasting salvation, and we may beleeve that God wil save no man with his sins, nor damne him without them, and wee may beleeve that pride, hypocrisie, tyranny, &c. are wilfull sinnes, which God cannot pardon till wee forsake them, and wee may well beleeve that God cannot save a white devil, except hee become blacke, because that is contrary to his nature, and wee should have so much faith as Elias and Nathan had, to tell our Princes, as they did theirs, that our Princes trouble the Christians, more then the Princes of the Jewes, did their people: and that they kill many Uriahs, and cause their wives to bee whores, because they want meanes to live on, and wee may beleeve that such practises are contrary to God and nature, to reason, and the rule of Christ; and yet all this is done, because the devil and uncharitable, superfluous rich men will have it so. And wee should have so much faith, to know that all men are lyars, and therefore concerning our walking with God in our hearts and consciences, wee should wholly and alone depend and wait on God, for the direction of his Holy Spirit within us, for if any man can speake or preach well, that hee that taught him, the same must teach all men, for Christ sent his auditors to God in their consciences, there to bee taught of the onely teacher, which is the Holy Ghost: and wee should have a faith to tel all superfluous, rich persons, that they doe serve the devil of freewill, and they cause the poor to serve him by compulsion. Such a faith would please God, because it would profite men, and therefore let no man presume to speake of faith, if hee have not so much faith, as to strive to doe and say such things, for those are the practicall part of faith, which is the summe of al; but to labour to have a theoricall, mysticall, forbidden faith, to know what God is in himselfe, or what hee doth in himselfe without us, or his other creatures, such a faith is not alone unprofitable, but sinfull: but a faith to keepe Gods commandements according to the rule of Christ, such a faith wee ought to have, and practise.

Now to attaine to that *Unum necessarium*, that one which is onely needfull to salvation. A man must goe unto God with a willing minde, and in his desire hee must give himselfe wholly unto God, with a resolution to walke with God, and in all things to bee ruled by him, then all is done, for then God hath his desire in that man, for to that end God made the world, and all that is therein: now when man giveth himselfe so unto God, then is that *unum necessarium* attained, and consider that God doth not at all times worke that good in man, which man desireth, for then wee should have no strivings, but God accepteth any man that desireth to bee good, for the willing is ours, but the working is Gods, and therefore it is the delighting in good or evill, that maketh a man good or evill in Gods esteeme. And now to conclude the second part of this intelligence, God grant all mankinde such a faith, as may bee pleasing unto himselfe, and give us that love, which is himselfe. O God for Jesus Christ his sake: God the glory, and mankinde the profite, Amen.

Mundus vult decipi, the world will bee deceived, as the Munke said when hee went into his Cloyster, and therefore, said hee, I came here. *Zelum Dei, & nomen Christi Antichristus habet*: To bee zealous for God, and to have the name of Christ, that hath beene, is, and will bee, the manner of the tyrannicall, hypocriticall Christian world. O simulated sanctity, which art double iniquity, how impious art thou! thou art the mother and nurse of all impiety, thou art the root of hypocrisie, which is the destroyer of all vertues. O seeming sanctified holinesse, thou art too bad to bee named: I have observed some of thy wicked practises, concerning mankinde on thy working-dayes, and now through Gods grace, I wil enter into thy *Sanctum Sanctorum*, to see how thou dealest with God on thy Sunday, I doe not say rest-day, for on that day thou doest the devil double service, but first I would show how most of our doctors, both writers and preachers, doe abuse themselves and others, through partiality, concerning tyrants and tyrannies, for they all doe seeme to hate tyranny, and yet they flatter the Tyrants in their tyrannies, wherein they deale preposturously, because they preferre the bodies of tyrants before their soules, and the private, before the publique profit, for men should love the Tyrants, and hate their tyrannies, and therefore our doctors should sharply reprove the Tyrants, and not flatter them in their tyrannies, as they doe, and they should venter their lives, to draw tyrants from their tyrannies, counselling and perswading them, will they, nill they, to leave their tyrannies, and to become honest men, not fearing nor caring for their frownes nor favours; for through the converting of tyrants, the whole Common-wealth should bee bettered: and I would desire all men seriously to consider, if a man may bee silent at such sinnes of other men, as are committed to the dishonour of God, and the prejudice of the Common-wealth. I know what I should say concerning this matter, and all reasonable men know, that to be silent, is a consenting to a thing. O then consider how men doe faile concerning this matter: I know that the world doth chuse some men, and permit them to reprove some sinnes in some men, but if a man should prie into the well-ordered impieties of Tyranipocrit, then hee shall bee punished for want of a calling, and if they have called him, they will tell him that it was not to reprove them, but to pray for them, and to reprove other men, and the reprovers doe know their mindes, although they were silent, and so they doe silence trueth, and conceale iniquity in great persons, the one will not heare the trueth, and therefore the other wil not speake it: And if another doe speak of their partiality in that kinde, they will punish him for interrupting of them in their simulated sanctity. Thus it hath been, is, and will be, the proceeding of the impious world. *Usque ad finem*, and therefore if a man have no sins of his own to cast out, then let him weepe for, and fight against the sinnes of other men, but the world is, and will bee deceived in the esteemation of things, for those which practise tyranny in those dayes, they will bee called gracious Lords, and hypocrits will bee called Holy Fathers. I am so beset with hypocriticall partiallity, that I know not which way to turne mee, for I would have all visords taken away, so that all such as doe practise tyranny and hypocrisie, should be called Tyrants and Hypocrits, as reason would that they should, but partiality saith no, not so, for hee saith, that Kings, Princes, Prelates, and other impious persons, may doe the workes of Tyrants and Hypocrits, and yet they must not bee called hypocriticall tyrants. Now if those bee not hypocriticall tyrants, that have gotten so much pelfe, that they are growne so proud, that they will have their dinners served in with trumpets, and ride in Coaches drawne by sixe or eight horses, as though they triumphed over the poore which they have robbed, and will have men to kneele unto them, and force men to goe to warre, and kill one another: if those that oppresse the poor as tyrants, live idle like tyrants, build and fare like tyrants, and spend their goods and time, like tyrants, doing all the workes of tyrants and hypocrits, and yet bee gracious Lords and Holy Fathers, certainely then there is neither trueth nor falshood, but all is fantasies, imaginations, dreames, and illusions, &c. for if such will not, and therefore must not bee called Tyrants and Hypocrits, then there are no such things on earth, and therefore wee should not use the names of Tyrants and Hypocrits any more; but one day wee shall know how partiality and hypocrisie have deceived us in this matter.

O cursed partiallity, how many friends hast thou, that with thee, doe make warre against poore unregarded, simple trueth? and therefore all you Preachers and Teachers, labour to doe one impartiall thing for Trueths sake, make that which is sinne in one man to bee sinne in every man, if it bee done with alike will and knowledge: make pride, tyranny, and such like evils to bee sinne, or no sinne, if it bee no sinne, then teach poore men to bee rich and proud, but if it be sinne, then tell Kings Princes, and Prelates, and such like persons, that pride, tyranny, hypocrisie, &c. are sinnes in them, and that in them such sinnes are more displeasing to God, then they are in meaner persons. O plough no more with an oxe and an asse, doe not weare garments of lincy wolcy, bee wholly for God, or nothing at all for God. Set the sinnes of great ones before their eyes, because you know that they are great sinnes, so well as you doe set the sinnes of the poore people, for God is no respecter of persons: and you know that *Potentes potenter punienter*, Mighty men shall bee mightily punished, for the sinnes of Rulers, are double and intollerable sinnes: For wilt thou steale, that commandest another that hee shall not steale? Wilt thou bee idle, which commandest another to labour? Wilt thou bee proud, that teachest another to bee humble? &c. But those rich artificiall theeves, which doe not stand by the way side, and take mens purses, nor creep into windowes, but have gotten a more impious artificiall way of stealing, then the poore artlesse theeves have, such thinke themselves secure, and because the law and the hang-man are their slaves, that dare not hang them, therefore they make themselves theeves by act of Parliament, and yet they will bee called gracious Lords, and such are no theeves, for all that they robbe and steale, is their owne, by so good right as the Lion had to the whole Hart, and if need bee, they can produce sheepe-skins, wherein it is written, that such a countrey, citie, towne, or village, lands, houses, goods, &c. are all theirs: but let such artificiall theeves consider, that one day all uncharitable writings shall bee burnt, and it is to bee feared that such artificiall theeves, shall then burne with all their uncharitable writings, except their hearts here in this life doe so burne with love to their poore neighbours, that they doe restore again that which by fraud or force, they have taken from them, and that is all the worldly goods that the rich Tyrants have, more then their poore slaves, neighbours, and brethren have.

But now let us consider how wee Christians doe behave our selves on our Sunday, for that is the chiefest matter to bee treated of, in this last part of my Intelligence, and now I wish that our Christian Rulers would seriously consider, what manner Sabbath God in Christ, doth require of us: for if God had delighted in a ceremoniall Sabbath, hee would have maintained the Jewes Sabbath: but if Christ bee the end of the Law, then hee is the end of the ceremoniall Sabbath, for that was included in the Law; but God never delighted in ceremonies, for they are not consonant to his nature, for that which doth please God at any time, must please him at all times, and that is not ceremonies, but a new creature. God, for causes best knowne to himselfe, permitted ceremonies for a time, to the Jewes: And the Law was given by Moses, but grace and trueth came by Jesus Christ, and therefore Christ is the end of the Law, and of all ceremonies contained in the Law, and as Christ said, God is a Spirit, and will bee worshipped in spirit and trueth. Now beeing ceremonies are not consonant to Gods nature, and Christ taught us, that God is in us, and shall wee seeke him in ceremonies which are without us? God is in our hearts and consciences, where hee will bee found of us, if wee will there seeke him according to his promise, and shall wee seeke him in ceremonies contrary to the rule of Christ? I know not who changed the Jewes Sabbath into our Sunday, some say it was one of the Popes, which is like enough to bee true; but if one Pope brought it in, many Popes do maintaine it: But consider our demeaner on the Sundayes, but first take notice how wee doe order our Church affaires, before wee come to our Church worship. First wee ordaine, or chuse us Preachers and Teachers, as wee doe other officers, onely wee are a little more circumspect concerning their education, for commonly we chuse humane Artists, good Gramarians, curious Linguist, such as can orderly speake Hebrew, Greeke, and Latine, such as have beene brought up in humane Schooles, and have no experience in that honest simple life, of tilling the land, nor keeping of sheepe, but some of them are good Sophisters, that can tell us that hote is cold, and cold hote, that white is blacke, and blacke is white, &c. O Christian world! how contrary art thou to Christ? for hee thanked God, because hee had not revealed the mysteries of the Kingdome of Heaven to worldly wise men.

God destroyed the ancient language, because of that proud Babilonian builder Nimrod, and yet wee more impious then hee, learne strange languages to build Christ a Church withall, for in these dayes, hee that cannot speake strange languages, shall not bee thought fit to preach, nor to teach Christians, and are not such curious Artists and Linguists, worldly wise men? such as are not fit to preach the gospel of Christ, because arts and languages are enemies to humility, which is the summe of Divinitie: for, *Christianismus non cadit sub regulas*, but our Christianitie seemeth in these days to consist in rules and formes, for take those from us, and then a Turke, or a Moore, or any Barbarian, will bee so good a Christian, and much better then some of us.

Now consider that hypocrisie will bee alwayes seeming to doe good, which she hateth, but will never bee good, because that is contrary to her nature: now when wee have gotten us Prelates, then the worke is more then halfe done, for tyranny, hypocrisie, superstition, and ignorance, have builded us idolatrous churches to our hands. O Hypocrisie, how impious art thou! sixe dayes thou hast served the world, the flesh, and the devil, and yet thou art not satisfied with sinning, but on the seventh day, thou wilt bring thy sinnes to Church, that there thou mayest sanctifie them, and make them compleat impieties, for then thou cloathest thy selfe in a more prouder manner then at other times, because then thou wilt doe the devil more service, then on the working-dayes.

I have endeavoured to show, that all impious sinnes, are wilfull sinnes, and that pride, tyranny, hypocrisie, &c. are wilfull sinnes. Now for a man to seeme to pray unto God, for pray hee cannot, so long as hee will keepe such sinnes, as hee hath a power to leave, but will not, for such a one to ride or goe to Church, to mocke God, is the greatest impietie that can bee imagined, for God hath given man a power, to desire to bee good, and if hee cannot attaine his desire to bee good as hee desireth, then hee hath a power to hate himselfe, because of the great power of sinne, that is within him, and if hee cannot leave his proud heart, yet hee can leave his proud habeliments by which hee showeth his pride to the world, which are his proud cloaths, proud coaches, proud Shippes, proud houses, proud Churches, proud pictures, proud wife, children, and servants, &c. such things, men and women have power to leave, and such things must bee left, before wee begin to pray, or else in stead of praying, wee shall tempt God, for God will not help, but when all helpers faile: for God hath given unto man a free power to will, and till man hath used his willing power, in leaving such sinnes as are in his power to leave, God will not help him. God will deliver us from all those sinnes which wee have done, but not from those sinnes that wee desire to doe. God will pardon all our sinnes which are past, if wee doe not desire to have them acted againe, because it is the office of God in Christ so to doe; but there is no power in God nor Christ, to save a man with his sinnes. And now beeing that nothing is contrary to Gods nature but wilfull sinners, and pride is wilfull sinne, what doth a proud person in the Church? hath hee not sins enough already, but hee must church his pride, the more to augment his impietie?

O consider this, all you that are young and strong, and yet you are so loaden with pride, that when you will play the hypocrit with the tyrant, then you will bee drawne to Church in costly coaches, with pampered horses, when if you would leave your pride, one asse would carry you, if your owne legges would not beare you, but pride is a heavy sinne, and therefore proud persons had need of many horses to draw their pride and themselves together; but all proud persons have not coaches, and yet they doe their best to show their pride, for some have the feet of their boates so long, and the tops so wide, and therein so many emblems of pride, that it makes them to straddle, as if they had the pox, yea some have so many tokens of pride hanging on their stinking carkasses, that if they had any of Gods grace in them, they would bee ashamed to see themselves: And what hath beene said of the proud man, may bee said of all Tyrants and Hypocrits, and all wilfull sinners: O impious partiallity, how contrary art thou to God, and all goodnesse! young, strong, lusty, and able persons, which are well able to goe on their feet, must ride in coaches, and old, lame, blinde, and impotent persons, must craule on the way, and not have horses, nor asses, coaches, nor Sedans, to draw, carry, help, or ease them. O see, and consider, if you bee not starke blinde, if this partiall dealing of the worldlings, bee not contrary to the Law of God and nature, and the rule of Christ.

Some of the Grecians had a temple, into which none but merciful persons might enter: if there were such a custome concerning our Churches, then Tyrants should not bee admitted to come to Church, much lesse to have the chiefest roome in the church. O this partiall white devil, that in the Christian world ruleth and disposeth all things contrary to reason, hath need of some better-mouthed dogs to barke at him; But I have waited so long, that I am almost blinde with expecting, to see if any better barker would undertake this taske, but I saw that men loved to sleepe in a whole skinne, and it seemeth in these dayes, that men doe thinke it no sinne, to bee silent at other mens

99

presumptious sinnes, and therefore men will not, or dare not tell hypo-criticall tyrants, that they are impious white devils, then at length I re-solved to doe my best concerning that matter. But to the purpose, which is to drive our seeming holy persons from their sanctuary; because *simulata sanctitas est duplex iniquitas.*

O consider that it is bad enough to bee a blacke devil, and to stay at home with our sinnes, and not to bring them to Church, and so to make our selves impious white devils. O for an evill man to sacrifice, or seeme to doe any good, that is the greatest impietie that can bee imagined. When Cain will sacrifice, and yet murther Abel, and when Salomon will honour his mother, and yet kill his brother: when Judas will pretend for the poore, and yet sell his master: when Julian buildeth churches, and yet hateth Christ: when Periander will make good lawes for the Corinthians, and yet hee will observe no law himselfe: when King Henry the eighth will reforme Religion, and yet his owne manners were contrary to reason: when Alexander will bee free of his franckin-cense to the gods, and yet kill men. O what shall I say concerning Sauls obedience, Jezabels fastings, Jehus zeale, &c. when hee that buildeth like Crassus, and fareth like Lucullus, and yet speaketh like Cato, then beware the goose, for the Fox preacheth. I doe not name all those to defame the dead, but to show how odious hypocrisie is in Gods es-teeme, and how much better it is to bee a blacke devil, then a white one, for God can wash a blacke devil in the blood of Christ, and so cleanse him; but there is no helpe for a white devil: and above all other impious wights, none can be so vile as that inhumane monster, when tyranny and hypocrisie are joyned in one, which the devil doth on the sunday. for then hee calleth tyranny and hypocrisie to church, and there in the presence of God and the Congregation, it seemeth hee saith unto them: Come on, my two deare and best beloved children, Tyranny and Hy-pocrisie, I know that on the weeke-dayes you have done mee all the best service that you could, and now because I have no better jewels to bestow on you, then your owne selves, therefore in recompense for all the good service you have done, and shall doe for me, I will give you each to the other, and therefore cause Formallitie to proclaime the banes, which shall baine all the world.

There is a contract of Matrimonie betwixt Tyranny and Hypocrisie, and the devil, who is the father of them both, hath given his consent: now if any one can show any reason, why these two Imps of hell should not bee joyned in one, let him speake, if it bee not too late, for when they are joyned together, then trueth and reason must bee silent. Now when this needlesse ceremony is past, and none doth contradict the devils desire, then hee that preached to Eve in Paradise, and hee that taught Cain to kill his brother, and Judas to sell his Master, hee supplieth the place of a priest, and as it seemeth, hee saith unto them as followeth:

Thou Tyranny my sonne, and Hypocrisie my daughter, stand up and heare your charge: Thou Tyranny shalt confesse here before God and this Congregation, that thou doest take unto thee to bee thy wedded wife, my daughter Hypocrisie, to live with her, and to love, comfort, respect, and cherrish her, and to maintaine her against all sincerity, trueth, and reason. And thou Hypocrisie, promise Tyranny to doe the like for him: now take each other by the hand. Now the blessing of him that taught Cain to sacrifice, and Judas to preach, &c. bee with you, and remaine with you for ever.

And now thou TYRANIPOCRIT, for that henceforth shall bee thy name, for now I have joyned you in one, therefore you shall have but one name: now *vive* Tyranipocrit, live long and prosper, and hee that will not honour thee, let him not live on earth, and when hee dieth, let the infernall furies torture him. And now consider the great love which I doe beare unto you two, for I have many other children which must live, but because all the world is yours, therefore all other sinnes and sinners shall bee yours, and to order them for your, and my greatest profite: Partiallity shall rule, place and displace all thy whole traine of sinnefull servants, and for thy Privie-counsellers, thou shalt have atheistry, pride, security, artificiall theevery, hatred, malice, disdaine, uncharitablenesse, &c. and for my blacke children, which are whores, and knaves, gluttons, drunkards, swearers, Sabbath-breakers, artlesse theeves, and all poor prophane persons, they shall bee all your slaves, and wait and attend on Tyranipocrit, and his friends, and you may freely use, and abuse them at your pleasures, for these, although they bee my children, yet they are so unruly, and out of order, that I know not almost how to trust them, and many of those blacke ones, through Gods grace, many times doe quite forsake mee, and therefore I doe not care so much for them; but for you Tyranny and Hypocrisie, which I have now joyned in one, you and your privie-counsellers which I have named before, you seldome, or never faile mee, and therefore Tyranipocrit hearken thou unto mee, and in all things bee ruled by mee, and then I will teach thee how thou shalt commit and maintaine any impiety whatsoever, and that with a faire seemblant. First, thou must get an hypocriticall Painter, and cause him to paint Trueth and Justice, and then cause seeming Zeale, to hang up painted Trueth and Justice in the Church and Senate-house, and then cause Hypocrisie to write many faire sentences, taken out of the Holy Scripture, and are fit to maintaine tyranny through hypocrisie, and then bee sure that thou hang or bannish Tom tell trath: And I charge thee to bee very circumspect in all things, for the establishing of iniquitie, and as occasion shall serve, thou mayest convent tyrannicall Senates, and hypocriticall Synodes, but remember that I doe charge thee on my blessing, that whatsoever thou pretendest or reformest, that thou doe not molest or trouble the white devil, for then my whole kingdome would bee in danger of falling: but thou mayest reforme many things for my profite, so thou bee sure, that nothing bee the better for thy reforming, for it is a bettering and not a reforming, that hurteth my kingdome, I doe not care what forme tyranny bee put into, neither what fashion hypocrisie can set on tyranny, so I may have the substance, I doe not care for the show: and therefore cry out aloud for new formes, that in them you may commit new impieties, and hypocrisie shall carry all things so in the clouds, that through her jugling, the people shall say, that good is evill, and evil good, which is the highest degree of impietie.

And if at any time Tom tell Trath should chance to open his mouth, you must deale very circumspectly with him, and first turne him over to hypocrisie, that shee may deale with him, as Tyranny had dealt with her before, which is, to convert him through gold and preferrement; but if hee bee obstinate, and will not hearken to her hypocriticall perswasions, then turne him over to Tyranny, and hee shall call a Counsell of Warre against him, and if hee will not recant, then hatred shall condemne him, envie shall judge him, and cruelty shall execute him, and infamie shall proclaime his rebellion, because hee would not honour and obey Tyranipocrit. And I charge thee, that in all thy impious practises, that thou make a show of piety and charitie, in giving some thing for Gods sake, to honour the devil withall, for when thou hast robbed a hundred or more, then cause ostentation thy almner, to feed some few poore people at thy gates, and that in a proud detestable manner, not fit for men, much lesse for Christian brethren, and when you have convented Parliaments, then make a great show of zeale, for the welfare of all mankinde, but give partiallity with hypocrisie leave to rule and dispose all things, and bee sure that in all your conclusions, you doe subject reason to tyranny, and not tyranny to reason, and if you cannot make it seeme good by Logick, Sophistry shall help you, for this is a generall knowne maxime: Take away the cause, and the effect will follow, but you shall strive to take away the effects, and yet maintaine their causes, for you shall hang the poore artlesse theeves, and maintaine the rich artificiall theeves, which cause the poore to bee theeves: And labour to have a uniformity in ceremonies, for concord in formes, and discord in manners and conditions, that can never hurt the devils kingdome, for if you maintaine rich tyrants, then they will make poor slaves, make the rich richer, and then they will make the poore poorer, and then what formes soever you have, the devil doth not care; for then the rich with their too much, and the poore with their too little goods, shall both serve sinne and the devil: the rich of free-will, and the poore by compulsion, make it so, that pride may abound in the rich, and misery in the poore; for if you should make and main-taine an equallity of goods and lands, as God and nature would have, as justice and reason doth crave, then the gall of murmuration would bee broken, and then mankinde might live in love and concord as brethren should doe, for then the devils kingdome would fall, or con-sume away to nothing, then tyranny and oppression would cease, and the Kingdome of Christ would flourish, and then mankinde might rightly sing the 133. Psalm: O how happy a thing it is, And joyfull for to see, Brethren together fast to hold, The band of amitie, &c. where now like a company of impious apes, they maintaine the causes of discord, and yet they ride, or goe to Church, and there sing and pray for concord. O impious impietie! for they seeme to pray unto God, that hee will force them to doe that which they hate, for they tempt God, to have him to doe that for them, which hee hath given them a power to doe themselves, but they will not, neither will they cease from tempting God in that impious manner, for they know that they doe hate that which they seeme to pray for; for they know, that if every man had an equall portion of goods and lands, then every man might live as God commanded all men, by the sweat of their owne browes, and not as they doe now, by the sweat of other mens browes, for now every poore man must bee a slave to the rich, and if the rich man bee the deeils slave, what a miserable slave must the poore man bee, that must bee a slave to him, that is a slave to the devil?

But it is not fit, that the devil should ruine his owne kingdome, and therefore I charge thee, Tyranipocrit, and all thy friends and coun-sellors, which are many and evill, that if any man dare to prate of an equallity of goods and lands, amongst such false Christians as inhabit Europia, let him die without mercy, because hee is a dis-turber of the tranquilitie of Tyranipocrit, and therefore hee is not for the devils profite, for the devils kingdome is established through iniquity, and yet it hath a show of equitie, which is the mysterie of iniquitie.

I cannot tell you all the impious sport, which they had at this cursed wedding, all other feasts are nothing comparable in all impieties, to this feast. That feast of Ahasuerus, of Balshazar, of Lucullus, Crassus, Herod, and such like, the feast at Paris, where so many thousands of innocents were slaine, was not so impious as this feast. But when the alsion dayes were ended, the devil would not neglect his time, and then it seemeth that hee in his diabollicall manners, told them that for the present, that hee had done them, and they had done him all the best service that they could doe each other, for which hee gave himselfe, and them many thankes, and he said, that the joyning of Tyranny and Hypocrisie, did please him better then any thing that ever hee did, for a greater impietie for the destruction of mankinde, was never plotted in hell: but yet to secure their estates, hee would returne to hell, there to consult with his infernall counsellers, and so hee committed all the whole impious crue, to their owne wicked wils, for they are so bad, and as much displeasing to God, as the devil can bee, and hee commended and committed unto them all the deadly sinnes, and hee charged them, upon paine of his displeasure, not to repent, And hee charged them to maintaine partiallity, and in all things to bee ruled by him, for hee would invent strange prerogatives for some persons to sinne by authoritie, &c. so when hee had given them their charge, and blessed them, hee seemed to leave them for a season.

Now how there can bee so much tyranny in the Common-wealth, when there is so much sinceritie in the Church, and both are ruled by one spirit, how this can accord and stand together, that is a mysterie above my capacitie, and it seemeth to bee so strange a paradox, that it is able to make a man mad, if hee consider it seriously, as hee ought; for it is so impossible, that tyranny and sincere religion should accord with each other, as it is to cause God and the devil to bee of one minde; but all is not gold that glistereth, nor all of the church, that are in the church, for Hypocrisie can counterfeit sinceritie, and faith in the mouth, may bee infidelitie in the heart, and when the devil seemeth to bee an Angell of Light, then there is much zeale, but no piety. Tell mee why in those dayes Zacharias is not slaine between the Temple and the Altar: why is not John beheaded? Steven stoned? Peter crucified? &c. Is this world better then that world was, wherein those men suffered? No certainely: but our Zachariasses are better daubers then that Zacharias was, for ours can better reprove the blacke, then the white devil, and a blacke devil is not so cruell as a white devil, neither hath hee so much power, if he were so cruell, and it seemeth that our Teachers had rather have money and good words, then either stones, roopes, or swords, and it seemeth although they speake so much of faith, yet when it comes to bee proved, concerning the right reproving of Tyranipocrit, when they consider what power hee hath gotten, which is so great, that hee that hath not his marke, must neither buy nor sell, O then faith in them is at a low ebbe: for then they stagger, and cannot tell whether faith or its object, bee a reallity, or an imagination, and if they have a wavering faith, yet they doe not know how to resolve, And although they have heard that God is a defender of trueth, yet considering how simple Tyrants in former times have dealt with such as have maintained the trueth against them, and their tyrannies, how much more, thinke they, shall those bee tormented, that shall now oppose Tyranipocrit, hee unto whom the devil hath given and resigned his whole power and authoritie. O Tyranipocrit! hee sweepeth off the starres of Heaven with his hypocriticall tayle; for those which tyranny cannot subdue, hypocrisie will seduce.

Now when I thinke of the inhumane cruelties, and vile impieties, which have beene committed in the Christian world, since the joyning of Tyranny and Hypocrisie, then I thinke that the devil did himselfe a notable piece of service, when hee joyned them in one. When I thinke how Vladislaus King of Hungarie, through the Popes instigation, broke his faith with the Turke, through which the King, the Cardinall, and thirty thousand more, lost their lives. When I thinke how worse then barbarians, the French-men dealt with the Waldenences, and so did the Spaniards with the Moorians, and how the English hunted the poore Irish: and how Duke d'Alva persecuted the Belgians: and how in the Low-countries, Predestination got the vantage of Free-will: and how Rochel was circumvented by the Reformadoos, and how in England the Presbiterians doe cast out the Bishops, their tyrannicall brethren, &c. When I consider those, and many more such cruell changes, and no bettering, but all to establish tyranny in other formes and fashions, then I think O white devil, O Tyranipocrit, how impious art thou: O thou old serpent, thou dost change thy old hide, but thou wilt not leave thy old tyrannicall nature. And if tyrants must make us slaves, what doe wee care what names they have, call them Kings, Bishops, Senators, Souldiers, &c. Tyrants, if they will exercise tyrannicall power, it makes no matter what names they have, if the King call his slave a subject, and the slave call his tyrant a King, what are wee bettered by that? call your selves and us, what you will, so you doe administer Justice indifferently, without any respect of persons, because justice exalteth a Nation: and what can bee more just then to give unto every man that which God, nature, and reason, hath alotted him? O to give unto every one with discretion, so neer as may bee, an equall portion of earthly goods, to maintaine him in this life, that is the greatest actuall justice that man can doe.

This is perfect charitie, & *Charitas non excidit, nec potest quidem*: and therefore if wee will worke by any other rule, wee must erre, and the more wee doe strive to doe justice, before this equall foundation bee first laid, the further wee shall bee from either doing or knowing what justice is; for hee that doth justice partially, is an enemie to justice. The rule of God in Christ, is to love thy neighbour as thy selfe, *ergo* if thou doest love to bee rich, then thou must labour to have thy poore neighbours so rich as thou wouldest bee. I need not reiterate this matter so often, if men would confesse the trueth, for all reasonable men doe know, that this is the right rule; but selfe-love, and an evill, long-continued custome, pride, the devil, Tyranipocrit, partiallity, the world, and all impious persons, in this cause doe make warre against God and nature, Christ and reason, against trueth and justice, against their owne consciences, and the welfare of mankinde here and hereafter. O partiallity and hypocrisie, how doe you deceive men through new formes, and respect of persons. When the new tyrants which have droven out the old, are in all things so bad or worse then the old tyrants were, onely they have, or doe pretend to have a better faith, and a new forme of tyranny, and in all their other practises, they are worse then their predecessors, then it seemeth that the devil is growne young againe, or else hee did cast out himselfe, that so hee might returne againe with more power, to commit more strange impieties. And therefore all you which have cast out any old Tyrants, consider seriously what you have yet to doe, and so neere as you can, make and maintaine an equallity of all goods and lands, for that is your dutie, which if you will not perform, you are worse then the old tyrants, because you did pretend a bettering, which they did not. . . .

. . . But for Kings and Queenes, Lords and Ladies, gentle-men and gentle-women, Holy Fathers, gracious Bishops, learned Divines, such as command and teach others, for such to bee slaves to sinne and the devil, to help him to maintaine his proud impious kingdome, that is the greatest shame in the world. O consider that you are Christian rulers, and therefore your lives and manners should best accord with the life and manners of Christ. O search diligently all the whole Historie of Christ, and see if you can finde that hee had such things done unto him, as you will have done to you, or if hee did cause such things to bee done to others, as you cause to bee done to others: See if hee had his dinners served in with trumpets, or if hee had his Cup-bearer to kneele unto him, or if hee had so many vaine titles of honour, or so many proud blasoones of armes, or if hee had his coach drawne by sixe or eight horses, or if hee had so many thousands a yeere to spend, more then his poore neighbours, and so in all other things concerning his and your deportment. O if you could finde a History that would conforme Christ to you, for you will not bee conformable unto him, except you change your manners, surely such a book in these dayes, would bee more esteemed then the Old or the New Testament; But if you cannot finde such a History, then leave your pride, and follow Christ in humility, if you will bee Christian Rulers; but if you will not leave your pride, and all your wilfull sinnes beside, then resigne your ruling power, which you have usurped over Christians, to others, whose lives and manners doe better accord with the life and manners of Christ, then yours doe.

Now for the trueth concerning this matter, let any man confute mee, if hee can, if not, then let all reasonable men labour to effect, that which God and all good men doe affect: and for equallity of riches, I suppose that evill-minded men will say, that it is impossible that every man should have, and hold a like portion of earthly goods. To which I answer as I have done before: That if the Rulers of this world, cannot make all the poore rich, yet they can the richest poorer, for their sinne is not so much, in that some men are too poore, as it is in that some are too rich. The Magistrates duty is, equally to divide and share such goods, as God hath given them a power to dispose of, and when they have done that, then they have done their duty. O impious world, thou art not so much to bee blamed, because there are abuses, but because thou maintainest them. Doe thou take away the superfluous riches from the rich, and divide them amongst the poore: first limit the goods of the rich at ten, twenty, thirty, fourty, or a hundred pounds a yeere, and then share their overplus amongst them that have lesser meanes, then thou hast left the other, and then see if the poore have more goods then the rich: now if one have so much as another, then it is done, if not, then make a new division againe and againe, so long till thou hast made them all alike rich, and yet that is not enough, but once in a yeere, or oftener, thou must examine every mans estate, to see if they have not made their goods uneven, and if they have, then thou must make it even againe.

This is not so hard to bee done, and this is plaine english, and very good reason, and this would easily bee done, if all men did love their poore neighbours as themselves, and if all our Judges, Lawyers, Projecters, Procters, Plotters, and all such like creatures, and if all Magistrates in every towne, would imploy themselves and all their power, to make and maintaine this law, and once in a yeere to make all even, as they doe now to make it uneven.

O how many old and new Courts of Injustice are there in England, and all to deceive trueth, with a fained show of justice, and who but the devil, hath profite by our Court-holders? They call them Courts of Justice; but God knoweth if there bee one just court in all the land, for till that just foundation bee laid, all rules and ordinances whatsoever they bee, are nothing else but tyrannical injunctions, for the rich theeves doe make a combination, and call it a Law, to hang a poore man if hee doe steale, when they have wrongfully taken from him all his maintenance; yea, those impious theeves which doe robbe the poore, doe make lawes, as they call them, to hang the poore people, when they themselves doe deserve double hanging.

But now I would speake to them, which I feare will not much regard it, I meane our Divine Philosophers, and would desire them to consider seriously what they have to doe: for, as I have said before, it is not enough for them to preach and teach trueth, but they must preach and teach the most necessary trueth, and they must reprove all persons according to their sinnes, without any partiallity, so well the King, as the begger, and Tyranipocrit, as the poorest slave, and if hee doe not, but willingly permit partiallity through feare or favour to sway his affections, as they use to doe, and so to bee silent at the sinnes of great men, and yet condemne the poore for smaller offences, then all the trueths which they have taught, will bee reckoned unto them for lies, like Sauls obedience, and Jehus zeale, for they did some of that which God commanded them. For Saul hee killed the poore Amalekites, but hee would not kill their proud King, and Jehu hee murthered Ahabs sonnes, and burnt Baals priests, &c. for so much was for his owne profite, but Jeroboams calves and Tyranipocrit, Jehu taketh no care to root them out. ô you Divine Philosophers, you doe know what I should say concerning this matter, and you know how to comment upon the Histories of these men: ô then apply them to your selves, and therefore strive to doe all your duty, which is to reprove impartially, and to discover the white devil, which is Tyranipocrit freely, and then no doubt, but you shall have of the world so good entertainement, as Zacharias the sonne of Barachias had, and he was slaine betweene the temple and the altar.

And for our Potentates, I doe assure them, and if they have any consciences, they doe know it better already then I can tell it them, that the best service that they can doe, is to give unto every man with discretion, an equall portion of temporall goods, and when that is done, then they may goe to Church and sacrifice, if they will, but not before: this is the right rule, and this is the fulfilling of the law of love, which is the law of God in Christ: this is perfect charity, & *charitas non excidit, nec potest quidem*, charitie cannot erre, for when it is in distresse, then it looseth its selfe in God: ô consider this, all you proud, hypocriticall, uncharitable persons, which doe carry your impious sinnes to Church, to sacrifice with them there: ô remember that, *Cor vel solum orat, & vita innoxia plusquam os*, the object of charity should bee our neighbours misery: ô then, what doth an uncharitable, superfluous, rich person in the Church, before hee have parted his goods with the poore: ô hypo-criticall impiety, thou detainest the meanes which God hath ordained to helpe the poore in this life, and yet thou ridest to church, and prayest, or rather temptest God to helpe the poore miraculously, for thou hast, and wilt hold the meanes wherewith they should bee holpen, and although they doe know that simulated sanctity, is a double iniquitie, yet they doe sticke to that other saying, which is, *qui nescit simulare, nescit vivere*; hee that doth not know how to dissemble, doth not know to live: ô Christian world, how contrary art thou to Christ! nothing can bee more rediculous to the world, then the rule of Christ. Who will give his coat after his cloake, and turn one cheek to bee smitten, after the other? Who will sell all to follow Christ? &c. but if wee may have wealth and honour to bee Christians, if wee may rule for gaine, and teach for hire, and have our lusts for lawes, and play the tyrant sixe dayes, and the hypocrits on the Sunday, &c. such a christianitie pleaseth the world: wee will bee christians of our owne making, and wee will have Christ in formes and fashions, in health, wealth, and liberty, at times, and in places, &c. ô consider wherefore at this present time, the world is so out of order, is it for want of Lawes or Lawyers? No certainely: for the world had never more Politicians, and worldly wise men, then it hath now; but because they will not doe that which God in their hearts and consciences, tels them is right: therefore they with their too much wit, and too little wisedome, spoile all the world, and all this is, because superfluous arts are more esteemed, then needfull labour, and because a painted trueth, or a faire lie, is more regarded then simple trueth, and because in these dayes men have too much faith, and too little love, and because the white devil pleaseth the im-pious world, much better then the blacke, and because all impious per-sons doe hate God in Christ, and yet they will not forsake his name, although they hate his nature, for they will have Christ, not as a Lord to rule them, but as a slave, so they will rule him, which is the greatest injurie that man can offer unto God, for to keepe Christ in a mans mouth, and to hate him in his heart, and to doe all things contrary to his nature: what greater impiety can there bee imagined? and yet so or worse, doth Tyranipocrit deale with Christ, and therefore all you which have most power on earth, strive with all your might, to cast out Tyranipocrit, with his Viceroy, Partiallity, or never expect that God will blesse your proceedings. God is an all-sufficient helper, but hee will not bee mocked, neither will hee helpe, where there is no need of his helpe: First wee must doe all that wee can in every respect, to helpe our selves and all mankinde, with that power which God hath given unto us already, and when in all things wee have done all that wee can, then wee may freely goe unto God for more power. Wee cannot call againe yesterday, nor measure eternitie, nor undoe that which is done, such things are for God, and not for us; but to give our goods to the poore so long, till they are so rich as we are, that is for us, and that God doth require of us. And now I will review and consider what I have treated of in this Treatise, and so conclude.

The chiefest matter, and the principall points of the same, are those: That no predestinated sinnes, can hurt man concerning his eternall salvation, except man will, and that all our thoughts, words, and workes are predestinated, and that in Gods esteeme there is no sinne, but an evill will, and the desire of an evill heart, that would, if hee could, doe something contrary to the nature and revealed will of God in Christ, and that Gods predestination is no forcing power, but a prescience and a disposing of man, so, and according as hee hath in this life delighted in good or evill, and so as hee hath, or doth desire to bee used as an instrument for God, or the devil; for it is contrary to the nature of God, to force the desire of man, neither doth God give more grace unto one man to bee saved, then hee doth to all, and every man, for if hee should, then God must bee a partiall respecter of men, which were blasphemy to affirme. And concerning our passive Religion, I have not erred in that, because for that I have not propounded any rule: for, *Christianismus non cadit sub regulas*; and therefore let every man leave all his wilfull sinnes, and then let him goe to God in the power of Christ, which is in every mans heart and conscience, and there hee will, if they will, through his Holy Spirit, teach them which way hee will have them to follow him, and what hee and wee in us, will have him to doe for us, and with us.

And concerning our actuall Religion, I have showed wherein that consisteth, which is, To give an equall portion of worldly goods unto every man, and now I say againe, as I have said before, that before any good can bee done in church, or common-wealth, that Partiallity must with an unanimous consent, bee put to death, and hee must bee buried in an oblivious grave, and wee must borrow Pope Pauls great stone, and lay that upon his vile carkeise, so that hee may never rise againe, to doe any more mischiefe in the common-wealth.

And for my Intelligence, I have partly showed the great dammage, that mankinde doe sustaine by their marcenary dealing, concerning divine matters: and concerning faith and love, I have done the like, and I have partly showed what an impious sinne it is, for an evill man to doe, or seeme to doe good: and for the Sabbath, because wee are Christians, I would have six days more added unto it, that so it might bee a compleat Sabbath.

Those are the principall heads of this subject, and now I say, that I thinke that it is bad, for a Preacher to take wages of those, which hee in the Name of God ought to reprove. It is worser to preferre any thing before love; but it is worst of all, to teach evill men to doe good. And now if any one will quarrell this doctrine, I am a poore Artist, and a poorer Sophister, yet when all false glosses shall bee out of date, and no language shall bee understood, but that of the heart, when Partiallity shall have no power, and respect of persons shall not know the King from the begger: when gold and glory shall not bee regarded, and when men shall have nothing but their consciences, to cloath them withall; when wee shall all appeare naked, before the Judgement-seat of God in Christ, then this poore contradicting, and contradicted labour of mine, shall answer for it selfe.

And now for a farewell, according to that knowledge which God hath given unto mee, concerning his way with mankinde in Jesus Christ: I say, that sinne is no longer sinne, then it is delighted in, and to delight in any thing but God, that is sinne. Hee that loveth God without man, hee hateth God in man: and hee that loveth God, and not man, hee hateth them both. The prayer of the mouth, is good: of workes, better: of the heart, best of all. It is bad for a poore man to sinne, worse for a rich, but worst of all for a Ruler. Hee that sinneth through feare, doth ill: through favour, worse: through malice, worst of all. Hee that seeketh places to worship in, and times to pray at, is a locall-worshipper, and a time-server. Hee that teacheth a partiall God, and an artificiall Religion, erreth in both alike. Hee that saith, that the mercy of God endureth for ever, and yet that it may faile a man in this life, if hee seeketh it, maintaineth an absurd paradox. Hee that maintaineth that God hath predestinated young children to damnation, is an uncharitable person. They that will not teach the most necessary trueth themselves, nor permit others that would, are worse then that dog, that would not permit the horse to eat the hay. Hee that goeth to church to learne the will of God, doth well, but hee that is, what hee may bee if hee will, hee hath chosen the better part. Hee that teacheth an absolute predestination in God of man, without man, hee cannot honour God, nor comfort man. Hee that teacheth a partiall God, loveth partiallity, and that is his god. Hee that doth not endeavour to discover hypocrisie, hee seemeth to bee an hypocrit himselfe. Hee that commandeth and teacheth another to bee good, and yet himselfe will bee evill, hee is that impious Tyranipocrit. Hee that will hate mee for any trueth that God hath herein revealed through me, if hee would truely forsake the world, the flesh, and the devil, and his *ego sum*, then it may bee hee would bee of another minde.

Now I take God to witnesse, that I have not written any thing, through hate to any person; for I doe not hate Tyrants, but their tyrannies, and now I say with Cicero: *Non nobis solum nati sumus, ortisque nostri partem patria vendicat, partem parentes, partem amici.* But to passe by parents, countrey, and friends, I will conclude with them noble Grecians, which said: I will maintaine the trueth against all men. So help mee God.

Verax parit odium, Deo soli gloria.

[*Extracts*]

THE POOR MAN'S ADVOCATE

*F*ROM *an elaborate plan of state socialism, such as would scare even the back benchers of the present Parliamentary Labour Party, we are only able to include here the Epistle Dedicatory and the final address to the House of Commons.*

The author, Peter Chamberlen, was one of a long family of surgeons who made a great deal of money out of an invention which they kept secret for three generations—the short forceps for midwifery. Like most of the Chamberlens, our present author combined skill and success as an accoucheur *with inventiveness and an itch for writing, also for dabbling in politics. The altruistic sentiments expressed in* The Poor Man's Advocate *are a little hard to reconcile with the monopoly (on which the Chamberlens so largely depended) of a secret instrument so vitally important to humanity. But there is no reason to suppose that Peter Chamberlen was insincere in his plea for a scheme which might have provided an answer to the vast social problems of his time. Most of the other schemes advocated by the Chamberlen family have, in fact, been subsequently put into effect.*

The Poor Man's Advocate *and the pamphlet which follows (Winstanley's* True Levellers Standard*) were both published in April 1650 (1649 old style). There was no subsequent edition of this pamphlet. There is a shrewd prophetic hint in the writer's suggestion that unpaid soldiers will fall upon their masters; this was very soon to happen.*

The significance of 'linsey wolsey' (elsewhere referred to as 'lincy wolcy') is made very clear on page 117. As a mixture of wool and flax, it was symbolic of confused thought or double-mindedness.

THE POOR MAN'S ADVOCATE

By Peter Chamberlen

The Epistle, to the Representatives of all the Authority, and Power of England. The High and Honourable House of Commons Assembled in Parliament.

Ye choyce men of England

I CANNOT but honour, whom the Lord hath been pleased to honour. I am commanded to love you: give me then leave to be jealous of you. Love lyeth not in flattery for the Law saith, thou shalt not hate thy Brother, but freely tell him of his faults. If any man say he hath none, he deceiveth himself, and the truth is not in him.

Ye are many, and there was one Judas amongst the Apostles. I know him not: but he that beareth the bagg will certainly betray you. He that perswadeth you to sell that precious oyntment, which cost so much blood, whose Odor might perfume all the Nation with the sweet savour of charity, doth he do it that he loveth you, or because he hath the bagg? Such you have declared have been amongst you. If any yet remain, give him this sop, and discover him.

Note the man that dippeth with you in the Dish, whose Lips still ready for the guilty sop of new Assesments, or sauc't with Birdlime Gelly of DELAY, kisseth you with the seeming tendernesse of Bulbegger caution, and blindeth your wayes with a prudential Forehead of politick Diversion.

That is, he that doth and will betray you, give him the power of DELAY, and you shall yeild your selves to staves and Clubmen; to the rabble of multitudes and Tumults. Your Antidote is to refuse no reasonable Proposition offered to you because the Person hath a name, or the thing a defect: but seperate the good from the bad, and amend what is amisse: so shall you gather up the Wisdom of the Nation, and have the blessing of a multitude of Councellors. (Safety.) Wisdom cryeth out in the streetes: she is not lockt up in Cabinets.

I confesse you are all above me, and see over me: but I am under you, and see under you. Yea, I see you are supplanted and blown up, if you prevent it not.

Taxes will eat up the grasse under your feete. How came the Son of Solomon to lose his Kingdom.

None more fond of a King then the English, yet they departed from him to ease their purses, and their Consciences. If they forsooke their King (I spake it to some of your House in the beginning of this Session) will they not forsake their fellow Subjects for the same causes?

Few honest men will engage to be Taxers, and knaves will tax none (willingly) but your friends: nor will Collectors gather from others, unlesse compell'd: nor Clarkes discharge any but your bribing Enemies. So you still spurre the free horse, and necessitate your friends against you. Will your Enemies then be for you? I write this feelingly, as not only cloyd with Taxes, but overcome with the infinite abuses in them. Now when no more Taxes are to be had, must not the Souldier fall upon his Masters?

But what is the end of Taxes? Are you not still advanc't into a Debt? For which you are perswaded to sell all you have? And when you have sold all, and are in Debt, shall you not then be bankrupt?

Keep your Lands and keep your Credit.

Sell your Lands and sell your Credit.

Be pleased to remember the first occasions for money. Was it any more then an Army of 30000. which afterwards grew to 50000? Were not the free wil-Offerings of the Times sufficient for the day? With new Occasions, were not new Taxes and Delinquencies to above 40. Millions? most of which might have been spared, might but the Giver and Receiver, the Borrower, and the Lender have clapt hand in hand, (as was Petitioned,) or the Souldier have been suffered to have been of Age to receive his own money without standing at the end of a long Shuffle-board Table of Committees, or a Committee of Gurdians? But Hocus Pocus. All is gone. The Souldier still in Arreare, so as to sel publique faith for 4s. in the pound, debts still unpaid, and you are kept so bare, that you may not have present Credit for your own money without a pawn, nor that without new Taxes. Yet the Jugler saith, you have the Crownes in your pockets.

Had the Army been all this while as great as at present, for England

and Ireland at 1.560.000 *l.* per An. And all Subsidies, Loanes, Taxes, Revenues, & Contributions, &c. put into a bottomles bagg. We could not be in 8 years time more indebted then 12.480.000 *l.* and we pay interest for half so much, besides the debt that payes no interest.

Some men can eat their Cake and have their Cake. Your Debts are nigh as many, as if you never had had Taxes, nor they received interest. I am sure I speak the complaint of many of your Members, and I think I speak the sence, grievance, and vindication of the whole House. And if money be thus made the great Lord of the Land, shall not you and we all be tyed up at last in a Usurers bag, and sold to Ishmalites, to Pharao, the Pope, the Spaniard, the Turk, or any that will give most money for us.

It is high time you should find a Remedy, and this it is. Keep whol the publique stock. Provide for the poor, and they will provide for you. Destroy the poor, and they will destroy you. And if you provide not for the poor, they will provide for themselves.

The businesse sounded well, in the late Kings eares about 16. yeares past. Then was not such a stock to begin the work. Nor such a Debt as now to clog it. All difficulties are in beginnings. The King liked it, and (not knowing our distance) recommended it to Bishop Laud, which I took as a providence to desist from it.

This is the best Elixir: The Philosophers stone, that is so cheap, yet multiplies such Treasure.

Though you would pardon all, and take the debts upon you, proclaiming (with the Apostles.) Let him that stole, steale no more. Set but 200000. Poor at work, and if they clear but 20 *l.* a head, (as that's the least the meanest Hine can do that payes his Rent.) The year will bring about 4000.000 *l.* to the publique Treasurie, beside all other profits herein mencioned. Hasten this work of God, and establish the Honour of your memories in the hearts of all men. They are not weary of you, but of your Taxes and Delayes. Nor care they to change faces, but conditions.

And with this joyfull work proclaim a Jubile of Conscience, but let it not usher in a babel of sin.

How much blood and expences had been saved, had honest men distinguisht between Libertie of sin and Libertie of Conscience, between punishment of sin and punishment of Conscience? Tye up sin, leave Conscience free. Let no man here presume above his senses, God only judgeth the heart.

He that breaketh the Law, is judged by the Law, and there the senses are sufficient. He that dispiseth the Gospel, is judged by the Gospel;

but that's discerned by the spirit. God loves not linsey wolsey. He appoints no Gospel Censures for legal Transgressions, nor legal Censures for Gospel sins: The Magistrate for the Law, the Church for the Gospel.

Herein if we are guided by the supream Authority and Power of all the world, and the fundamentall Lawes of Nature written to Moses by God, we may all agree concerning the Authority, Power, and Lawes of England, unlesse we must ever continue *penitus toto divisus, ab orbe*, out of the World. *Verbum sapienti.* I am not tedious, unlesse displeasing, And can there be displeasure in love? the Christian love of him that is,

YOUR HONOURS IN ALL HUMBLE CHRISTIAN DUTY,

3 April 1649   *PETER CHAMBERLEN*

*   *   *   *

TO THE SUPREAM AUTHORITY OF ENGLAND.
THE HIGH AND HONORABLE
HOUSE OF COMMONS
ASSEMBLED IN PARLIAMENT
THE HUMBLE PETITION OF OFFICERS AND SOULDIERS, CITIZENS AND COUNTRIMEN, POOR AND RICH: AND ALL SORTS, WITH ALL THE DISTRESSED AND OPPRESSED PEOPLE OF ENGLAND

Sheweth, That

IT being the work of Nature, Reason and Christianity, by which we shall be judged in the last Day, (Mat. 25.) And the very bottom of all Pretences in all States, Councels, and Corporations, To Cloath the Naked, Feed the Hungry, Visit the Sick, and Relieve the Oppressed: All former Laws, Statutes, Commissions and Consultations having been of small effect hitherto: Houses of Correction being more apt to make Men (from being poor) to becom Vagabonds and Beggars, by taking from them the Repute of so much Honesty as to be trusted with Employment, and conveying into them a further Impudency, or desperateness, (as by experience is manifest,) and many having of late years perished for want of Necessaries: The Lord having now put into your Hands a present Opportunity of adding this great work to all the mighty works which he hath done by you.

May your Honors be pleased (all due respects being first had to your great Losses, Damages, and constant Vigilancy, out of the Kings Revenues, Bishops, Deans, and Chapters Lands, and Moovables; Delinquents Estates, and Offices) to grant to your Petitioners (or so many of them as shall be thought fit) and to all the poor of England, the rest of all the Premises. 2. And all that remaines due upon publick Accounts. 3. All, or so much of the Commons, Wasts, Forests, Chaces, Heaths, Moors, &c. as is due unto the poor. 4. All Mines not wrought on at present, all drowned Land, Lands deserted of the Sea or the like, they agreeing for what is due to any Owner. 5. The sole benefit of all Manufactures, Engines and Inventions either by Sea or Land, by your Petitioners brought into Use in England. 6. All parish-Collections, and concealed or abused Charities; with power to search all Records, Wills, Church-Books, and Books of Accounts, to that purpose, gratis: to be as a publique Treasure of the Land, for all publique Designs, in one common joynt Stock.

And some of your petitioners will put in sufficient security. 1. To provide all necessaries for the Army, so long as the Army shall be thought necessary. 2. To joyn with the Army when occasion requires, and to obey all civill Commands of the State, as well for suppressing of Insurrections at home, as opposing Forces from abroad. 3. To pay all the Arrears of the Army within 5. years. 4. To maintain all publick Ministers of State: And to continue pay (during life) to so many of the Kings Servants, as in your wisdoms shall be thought fit. 5. To receive all the rest (if they desire it) and all the poor of England (prisoners and others), and to feed and cloath them and set those that are able on work, those that are not able into Hospitals, and little Children into Schools and Nurseries. 6. To receive all Fraudulent persons, Theeves and Robbers (not guilty of murther) into houses of labor, till they have earned and paid double the Damage they have done. 7. To take off all Taxes within one year, except Customs. 8. To pay all the Debts of the publique Faith which remain due at 6. per Cent, within 10. years. 9. To pay all the Kings debts due before this Parliament, within 20. years. 10. To set up a publique Banck, as in Amsterdam, Venice, and other places. 11. To erect an Academy for all Exercises for the education of youth. And if your Honours shall think good, to grant the Fishings, Customs, and Revenues of the Navy, &c. then your Petitioners will undertake to maintain a constant Navy at Sea, and to secure the Merchants at 1. per Cent, a month, for the narrow Seas. 2. To take off the Customs from unwrought Materials and Commodities, and Food and Ammunition imported, and lay them upon unwrought materials and Commodities, and Food and Ammunition exported. 3. To take off all Customs from Manufactures Exported, and lay them upon Manufactures Imported.

Thus may your Honours be eased of great burthens and Molestations: Be free to other great Affaires: Vindicate the Integrity of your Proceedings above others: Stop the mouths of your Enemies: Take away all Taxes and Groanings of the People: Do all the great works of Charity: Reconcile all Parties: Gain all the Peoples Love: Enfranchise their Spirits: Make Trade free: Establish the Peace of the Nation; Establish your own Peace before God and Man: And bring down the Blessings of God abundantly upon all your Faithfull Endeavors.

[Extracts]

THE TRUE LEVELLERS STANDARD ADVANCED

GERARD *Winstanley is by far the most interesting of the seventeenth-century revolutionaries. In spite of the title of the pamphlet from which these extracts are taken, Winstanley was not one of Lilburne's 'Levellers' (see page 74). In this statement of 1649 he is merely 'cashing in' on the name of the Levellers, better known in his own time, and since, than his own 'Digger' movement, and distinguishing his own movement at the same time as the 'true' Levellers, because of their more radical programme. Though signed by various 'Diggers', there is little doubt that the pamphlet was mainly, if not wholly, Winstanley's work.*

Winstanley's conception of society as it should be was far reaching in its revolutionary idealism. He saw freedom not merely as a political redistribution of power, but as implying also a redistribution of work and wealth, with the abolition of poverty. Like the 'Single Taxers' over 200 years later, Winstanley saw the origin of poverty and social inequality in the inequitable distribution of landed property, the origin of most material wealth. His method, as indicated in this pamphlet, was that of 'direct action,' combined with a moral appeal to the conscience of the community.

Eduard Bernstein, in his Sozialismus und Demokratie in der grossen englischen Revolution, *pointed out certain affinities between the Diggers and the Quakers. (The Diggers, like the early Friends, refused to take off their hats to their social 'superiors'. They declared it their aim to 'conquer by love'. Bernstein also notes Winstanley's motto, in his last publication: 'The inward Testimony is the soul's strength', and the fact that he then addressed his audience as 'Friends'). But the story that Winstanley, like Lilburne, ended by becoming a member of the Society of Friends is no more than a conjecture without any proof attached to it.*

THE TRUE LEVELLERS STANDARD ADVANCED, OR THE STATE OF THE COMMUNITY OPENED, AND PRESENTED TO THE SONS OF MEN

By Gerard Winstanley and Others

A Declaration to the Powers of England, *and to all the Powers of the World, shewing the Cause why the Common People of* England *have begun, and gives Consent to Digge up, Manure, and Sowe Corn upon* George-Hill *in* Surrey; *by those that have subscribed, and thousands more that gives consent.*

In the beginning of Time, the great Creator Reason, made the Earth to be a Common Treasury, to preserve Beasts, Birds, Fishes, and Man, the lord that was to govern this Creation; for Man had Domination given to him, over the Beasts, Birds, and Fishes; but not one word was spoken in the beginning, That one branch of mankind should rule over another.

And the Reason is this, Every single man, Male and Female, is a perfect Creature of himself; and the same Spirit that made the Globe, dwels in man to govern the Globe; so that the flesh of man being subject to Reason, his Maker, hath him to be his Teacher and Ruler within himself, therefore needs not run abroad after any Teacher and Ruler without him, for he needs not that any man should teach him, for the same Anoynting that ruled in the Son of man, teacheth him all things.

But since humane flesh (that king of Beasts) began to delight himself in the objects of the Creation, more then in the Spirit Reason and Righteousness, who manifests himself to be the indweller in the Five Sences, of Hearing, Seeing, Tasting, Smelling, Feeling; then he fell into blindness of mind and weakness of heart, and runs abroad for a Teacher and Ruler: And so selfish imagination taking possession of the Five Sences, and ruling as King in the room of Reason therein, and working with Covetousnesse, did set up one man to teach and rule over another, and thereby the Spirit was killed, and man was brought into bondage, and became a greater Slave to such of his own kind, then the Beasts of the field were to him.

And hereupon, The Earth (which was made to be a Common Treasury of relief for all, both Beasts and Men) was hedged into Inclosures by the teachers and rulers, and the others were made Servants and Slaves: And that Earth that is within this Creation made a Common Store-house for all, is bought and sold, and kept in the hands of a few, whereby the great Creator is mightily dishonored, as if he were a respecter of persons, delighting in the comfortable Livelihood of some, and rejoycing in the miserable povertie and straits of others. From the beginning it was not so.

But this coming in of Bondage, is called *A-dam*, because this ruling and teaching power without, doth dam up the Spirit of Peace and Liberty; First within the heart, by filling it with slavish fears of others. Secondly without, by giving the bodies of one to be imprisoned, punished and oppressed by the outward power of another. And this evil was brought upon us through his own Covetousnesse, whereby he is blinded and made weak, and sees not the Law of Righteousnesse in his heart, which is the pure light of Reason, but looks abroad for it, and thereby the Creation is cast under bondage and curse, and the Creator is sleighted; First by the Teachers and Rulers that sets themselves down in the Spirits room, to teach and rule, where he himself is only King. Secondly by the other, that refuses the Spirit, to be taught and governed by fellow Creatures, and this was called Israels Sin, in casting off the Lord, and chusing Saul, one like themselves to be their King, when as they had the same Spirit of Reason and government in themselves, as he had, if they were but subject. And Israels rejecting of outward teachers and rulers to embrace the Lord, and to be all taught and ruled by that righteous King, that Jeremiah Prophesied shall rule in the new Heavens and new Earth in the latter dayes, will be their Restauration . . .

*　　*　　*　　*

They have by subtile wit and power, pretended to preserve a people in safety by the power of the Sword; and what by large Pay, much Freequarter, and other Booties, which they call their own, they get much Monies, and with this they buy Land, and become landlords; and if once Landlords, then they rise to be Justices, Rulers, and State Governours, as experience shewes: But all this is but a bloudy and subtile Theevery, countenanced by a Law that Covetousness made; and is a breach of the Seventh Commandement, Thou shalt not kill.

And likewise . . . a breach of the Eighth Commandment, Thou shalt not steal; but these landlords have thus stoln the Earth from their fellow Creatures, that have an equal share with them, by the Law of Reason and Creation, as well as they.

And such as these rise up to be rich in the objects of the Earth; then by their plausible words of flattery to the plain-hearted people, whom they deceive, and that lies under confusion and blindness: They are lifted up to be Teachers, Rulers, and Law makers over them that lifted them up; as if the Earth were made peculiarly for them, and not for others weal: If you cast your eye a little backward, you shall see, That this outward Teaching and Ruling power, is the Babylonish yoke laid upon Israel of old, under Nebuchadnezzar; and so Successively from that time, the Conquering Enemy, have still laid these yokes upon Israel to keep Jacob down: And the last enslaving Conquest which the Enemy got over Israel, was the Norman over England; and from that time, Kings, Lords, Judges, Justices, Bayliffs, and the violent bitter people that are Free-holders, are and have been Successively. The Norman Bastard William himself, his Colonels, Captains, inferiour Officers, and Common Souldiers, who still are from that time to this day in pursuite of that victory, Imprisoning, Robbing, and killing the poor enslaved English Israelites.

And this appears cleer, For when any Trustee or State Officer is to be Chosen, The Free-holders or Landlords must be the Chusers, who are the Norman Common Souldiers, spred abroad in the Land; And who must be Chosen? but some very rich man, who is the Successor of the Norman Colonels or high Officers. And to what end have they been thus Chosen? but to Establish that Norman power the more forcibly over the enslaved English, and to beat them down again, when as they gather heart to seek for Liberty.

For what are all those Binding and Restraining Laws that have been made from one Age to another since that Conquest, and are still up-held by Furie over the People? I say, What are they? but the Cords, Bands, Manacles, and Yokes that the enslaved English, like Newgate Prisoners, wears upon their hands and legs as they walk the streets; by which those Norman Oppressors, and these their Successors from Age to Age have enslaved the poor People by, killed their yonger Brother, and would not suffer Jacob to arise.

O what mighty Delusion, do you, who are the powers of England live in! That while you pretend to throw down that Norman yoke, and Babylonish power, and have promised to make the groaning people of England a Free People; yet you still lift up that Norman yoke, and

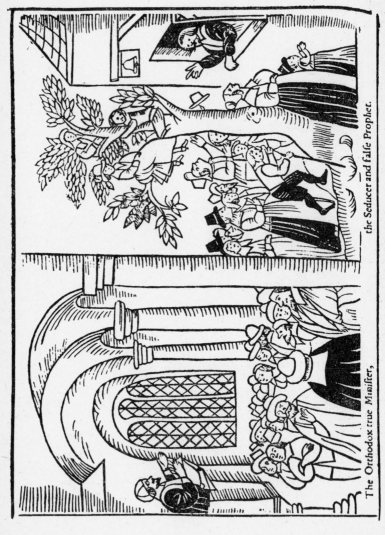

The Orthodox true Minister,

the Seducer and falſe Prophet.

A Glaſſe for the Times

slavish Tyranny, and holds the People as much in bondage, as the Bastard Conquerour himself, and his Councel of War.

Take notice, That England is not a Free People, till the Poor that have no Land, have a free allowance to dig and labour the Commons, and so live as Comfortably as the Landlords that live in their Inclosures. For the People have not laid out their Monies, and shed their Bloud, that their Landlords, the Norman power, should still have its liberty and freedom to rule in Tyranny in his Lords, landlords, Judges, Justices, Bayliffs, and State Servants; but that the Oppressed might be set Free, Prison doors opened, and the Poor peoples hearts comforted by an universal Consent of making the Earth a Common Treasury, that they may live together as one House of Israel, united in brotherly love into one Spirit; and having a comfortable livelihood in the Community of one Earth their Mother. . . .

The common People are filled with good words from Pulpits and Councel Tables, but no good Deeds; For they wait and wait for good, and for deliverances, but none comes; While they wait for liberty, behold greater bondage comes instead of it, and burdens, oppressions, taskmasters, from Sessions, Lawyers, Bayliffs of Hundreds, Committees, Impropriators, Clerks of Peace, and Courts of Justice, so called, does whip the People by old Popish weather-beaten Laws, that were excommunicate long ago by Covenants, Oaths, and Ordinances; but as yet are not cast out, but rather taken in again, to be standing pricks in our eys, and thorns in our side; Beside Free-quartering, Plundering by some rude Souldiers, and the abounding of Taxes; which if they were equally divided among the Souldiery, and not too much bagd up in the hands of particular Officers and Trustees, there would be less complaining: Besides the horrible cheating that is in Buying and Selling, and the cruel Oppression of Landlords, and lords of Mannours, and quarter Sessions; Many that have bin good House-keepers (as we say) cannot live, but are forced to turn Souldiers, and so to fight to uphold the Curse, or else live in great straits and beggery: O you A-dams of the Earth, you have rich Clothing, full Bellies, have your Honors and Ease, and you puffe at this; But know thou stout-hearted Pharaoh, that the day of Judgement is begun, and it will reach to thee ere long; Jacob hath bin very low, but he is rising, and will rise, do the worst thou canst; and the poor people whom thou oppresses, shall be the Saviours of the land; For the blessing is rising up in them, and thou shalt be ashamed.

And thus you Powers of England, and of the whole World, we have declared our Reasons, why we have begun to dig upon George hill in Surrey. One thing I must tell you more, in the close, which I received *in voco* likewise at another time; and when I received it, my ey was set towards you. The words were these: Let Israel go free.

Surely, as Israel lay 430. yeers under Pharaohs bondage, before Moses was sent to fetch them out: Even so Israel (the Elect Spirit spread in Sons and Daughters) hath lain three times so long already, which is the Anti-type, under your Bondage, and cruel Task-masters; But now the time of Deliverance is come, and thou proud Esau, and stout-hearted Covetousness, thou must come down, and be lord of the Creation no longer: For now the King of Righteousness is rising to Rule In, and Over the Earth.

Therefore, if thou wilt find Mercy, Let Israel go Free; break in pieces quickly the Band of particular Propriety, dis-own this oppressing Murder, Oppression and Thievery of Buying and Selling of Land, owning of landlords, and paying of Rents, and give thy Free Consent to make the Earth a Common Treasury, without grumbling, That the yonger Brethren may live comfortably upon Earth, as well as the Elder: That all may enjoy the benefit of their Creation.

And hereby thou wilt Honour thy Father, and thy Mother: Thy Father, which is the Spirit of Community, that made all, and that dwels in all. Thy Mother, which is the Earth, that brought us all forth: That as a true Mother, loves all her Children. Therefore do not thou hinder the Mother Earth, from giving all her Children suck, by thy Inclosing it into particular hands, and holding up that cursed Bondage of Inclosure by thy Power.

And then thou wilt repent of thy Theft, in maintaining the breach of the eight Commandment, by Stealing the Land as I say from thy fellow-creatures, or yonger Brothers: which thou and all thy landlords have, and do live in the breach of that Commandment.

Then thou wilt Own no other God, or Ruling Power, but One, which is the King of Righteousness, ruling and dwelling in every one, and in the whole; whereas now thou hast many gods: For Covetousness is thy God, Pride, and an Envious murdering Humor (to kill one by Prison or Gallows, that crosses thee, though their cause be pure, sound, and good reason) is thy God, Self-love, and slavish Fear (lest others serve thee as thou hast served them) is thy god, Hypocrisie, Fleshly Imagination, that keeps no Promise, Covenant, nor Protestation, is thy God: love of Money, Honor, and Ease, is thy God: And all these, and the like Ruling Powers, makes thee Blind, and hard-hearted, that thou does not, nor cannot lay to heart the affliction of others, though they dy for want of bread, in that rich City, undone under your eys.

[Extracts]

KILLING NOE MURDER

*I*N January 1655 *all pretence of democracy or constitutional government came to an end. Cromwell began to rule without a Parliament—a despot more absolute than even the Tudor sovereigns.*

It was indeed a masterly stroke on the part of Edward Sexby to dedicate a pamphlet, the object of which was to incite the reader to assassinate Oliver Cromwell, to the 'Protector' himself. Only the dedicatory letter is reproduced here, as it is certainly the best part of the pamphlet, and the rest of it is something of an anti-climax after this brilliant beginning.

Sexby, formerly a colonel under Cromwell, was one of the many for whom the 'Protectorate' meant final disillusionment. Of these some (including many of the 'extreme left') went full circle in their revolt against Cromwell, and finished up as Royalists. Colonel Sexby, a Fifth Monarchy man, was among these; and his famous pamphlet, written under the pseudonym of 'William Allen', was published during this phase of his career, in the year 1657. Travelling in various disguises, Sexby circulated Killing Noe Murder *himself in England, finding it well received among Cromwell's numerous enemies, both Royalist and Revolutionary. Authorship of this pamphlet was also claimed later by a certain Colonel Titus, and it is probable that he collaborated with Sexby in the writing of it.*

KILLING NOE MURDER
BRIEFLY DISCOURST IN THREE QUÆSTIONS
[DEDICATORY LETTER]

By 'William Allen'

i.e. Edward Sexby (*and possibly* Silius Titus) *for whom this was a pseudonym*

And all the people of the Land rejoyced: and the City was quiet, after that they had slain Athaliah with the Sword. 2. *Chro.* 23. 21.
Now after the time that Amaziah did turn away from following the Lord, they made a Conspiracie against him in Jerusalem, and he fled to Lachish: but they sent to Lachish after him, and slew him there. 2. *Chro.* 25. 27.

To his Highnesse, OLIVER CROMWELL,

May it please your Highnesse:

How I have spent some howers of the leasure your Highnes hath been pleased to give me, this following Paper will give your Highnes an accompt. How you will please to interpret it I can not tell, but I can with confidence say, my intention in it is, to procure your Highnes that justice no body yet does you, and to let the people see, the longer they deferr it the greater injury they doe both themselves and you: To your Highnes justly belongs the honour of dying for the people, and it cannot choose but be an unspeakable consolation to you in the last moments of your life, to consider, with how much benefit to the world you are like to leave it. 'Tis then onely (my Lord) the titles you now usurpe will be truly yours, you wil then be indeed the deliverer of your Countrey, & free it from

128

a Bondage little inferiour to that from which Moyses delivered his. You will then be that true Reformer, which you would now be thought. Religion shalbe then restored, Liberty asserted and Parliaments have those Priviledges they have fought for. We shall then hope that other Lawes will have place besides those of the Sword, and that Justice shalbe otherwise defind then the will & pleasure of the strongest, and we shal then hope men wil keep oathes again, and not have the necessitie of being false, and Perfidious to preserve themselves, and be like their Rulers. All this we hope from your Highnes happie expiration, who are the true Father of your Countrie for while you live we can call nothing ours, and it is from your death that we hope for our inheritances. Let this consideration arme and fortifie your Highnesses minde against the feares of death, and the terrours of your evil Conscience, that the good you will doe by your death, wil something ballance the evils of your life. And if in the Black Catalogue of High Malefactours, few can be found that have lived more to the affliction and disturbance of mankind, then your Highnes hath done: yet your greatest enemies wil not deny but there are likewise as few that have expired more to the universall benefit of mankind then your Highnes is like to doe. To hasten this great good is the chief end of my writing this Paper, and if it have the effects, I hope it will, your Highnes wil quickly be out of the reach of mens malice, and your enemies will only be able to wound you in your memory, which strokes you will not feel. That your Highnesse may be speedily in this security is the universall wishes of your gratefull Countrey. This is the desires and prayers of the good and of the bad, and it may be is the only thing wherein al Sects, and factions do agree in their devotions, and is our onely common prayer. But amongst all that put in their Requests and supplications for your Highnesses speedy deliverance from al earthly troubles, none is more assiduous, nor more fervent than he, that with the rest of the Nation hath the Honour to be

May it please your Highnesse:
Your Highnesse present Slave and Vassall,
W. A.

[*Extract*]

A PLEA FOR LIMITED MONARCHY

THE year 1660 saw the end of the Protectorate. Oliver Cromwell had died in 1658, to be succeeded by his son Richard, who had no control over the army—the only political organisation which his father's reforms had left in existence.

Out of a brief chaos the commander of the English forces in Scotland, General Monk, emerged as the popular champion of a 'free Parliament', and was soon master of the country. The Long Parliament of 1640 met again, for the last time (complete with the members expelled in 1648) to dissolve itself at last, having arranged for the calling of the 'free Parliament' demanded by almost all parties.

It was in the middle of this upheaval, in 1660, that this pamphlet appeared. It was attributed to Sir Roger l'Estrange by William Oldys, who (besides being an eminent antiquarian) came of a Royalist family, his father being a great collector of books who moved in the same circles as l'Estrange. Halkett and Laing's Dictionary of Anonymous and Pseudononymous English Literature (Revised Edition, 1928) accepts l'Estrange's authorship, which has nevertheless been queried; and the British Museum compromises by cataloguing the edition in the Thomason Collection as anonymous, that in the Harleian Miscellany (which is the edition used here) being attributed to Sir Roger. . . . It may be noted that the earliest edition known includes 'with additions' in the title, implying some previous lost edition of this pamphlet.

Against L'Estrange's authorship it has been urged that it was too moderately written for this fiery Royalist, also that he never claimed it. The obvious reply appears to be that the circumstances made moderation advisable, and that L'Estrange might not have cared to admit authorship of a moderate statement that could have been used so effectively against him when he was later defending Stuart attempts at absolute Government.

Whether the writer of the 'Plea' anticipated or actually influenced Monk's decision is problematic. What is certain is that Monk was actually negotiating with Charles II before the new Parliament (the 'Convention', as it was called) had settled the terms on which it would accept a Stuart Restoration. The Restoration which followed was, in fact, accomplished on Charles's own terms, as defined in his 'Declaration from Breda', and was arranged single-handed by Monk, with overwhelming popular support.

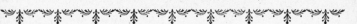

A PLEA FOR LIMITED MONARCHY, AS IT WAS ESTABLISHED IN THIS NATION, BEFORE THE LATE WAR; IN AN HUMBLE ADDRESS TO HIS EXCELLENCY, GENERAL MONK, BY A ZEALOT FOR THE GOOD OLD LAWS OF HIS COUNTRY, BEFORE ANY FACTION OR CAPRICE, WITH ADDITIONS

By Sir Roger L'Estrange [?]

Optima Libertas, ubi Rex, cum Lege, gubernat

SIR,

FINDING, by several Letters, published in your Name, that you profess a more than ordinary Zeal to popular Government; and not knowing any Thing herein, that can so mislead you, but the glorious Pretence of a Free State (a Notion, which hath even intoxicated many, otherwise, great and worthy Persons) I held it my Duty, first, to acquaint you, how necessary it is to distinguish betwixt the Form and Essence of a Commonwealth; the Mistake whereof (each for the other) hath proved so fatal in our Times: Next, to examine, whether those that surfeited of our kingly Government, and longed for Novelty, have not, indeed (like the Dog in the Fable) lost the Substance of Liberty and Happiness, in Pursuit of the Shadow.

Our fierce Champions of a Free State will not, I presume, maintain, that it is subject to no Violations, lest woeful Experience confute, and force them to confess, either that a Commonwealth may degenerate, or, at least, that this never was a Commonwealth: And, as they must renounce their Senses, so they must deny the Faith of Story, which proves, that Republicks have been sometimes invaded with Usurpation, some-times debauched and embased with Oligarchy, mostly, by Reason of their Weakness and Divisions, subdued or forced to truckle under their neighbouring Princes; always tormented with Faction. Neither, in-deed, do they themselves offer any Argument but such, as, in Effect, beg the Question, by presupposing great Unity in the Coalition, great Probity in the Intention, and great Purity in the Exercise; which, doubtless, being admitted, we should so little need to differ about Forms, that, perhaps, we should scarce need any Government at all. The stoutest Assertors of Monarchy must, likewise, acknowledge, that it, being but Earthen-ware (tho' the finest and strongest) is subject to divers Accidents; for nothing under Heaven is perfect. And, when we constitute Governments, we must not think to build Babels against the Deluge, but imbank against Floods, and inclose the best we can against Trespassors. This being premised, let us consider these two Governments, not Metaphysically, in Notions abstracted from their Subjects (a Pastime which our Platonics much delight in) but morally and reasonably, as concrete and adapted to Times, Places, and Persons, viz. our own.

I might, perhaps, decide the Question in few Words, by alledging the manifest Inclination of the whole People, now, to Monarchy; for, As no Man can be wronged with his Consent, so neither is any to be obliged against his Will; and how should a Government, founded upon Inequality and Force, ever subsist without it? Or, a State, which is the meer Adjective of an Army, become a Substantive; Beginnings of this Kind being so ominous? As reasonably might I object Matter of Title and foreign Pretence; for the same Estate with a Flaw in the Convey-ance, or clogged with Statutes and Judgments, is not surely of like Value, as if it had descended clearly from the Great-Grandfather, and were free both from Claims and Incumbrances; and one that hath little, yet owes nothing, is likelier to thrive than he who owing vast Sums (which he resolves never to pay) dares not walk the Streets for Fear of Serjeants; but my Intent is only to shew, that our former Government (as it excellently complied with the Laws, Genius, and Interest of this Nation) so it comprehended all the Benefits of a Com-monwealth in great Perfection; and this I shall do as briefly as I can.

To shew how it complied with our Laws and Constitutions, let it suffice that (Monarchy, in these Nations, being more antient than Story or Record, more venerable than Tradition itself) our Laws were, as it were, under that Climate, habituated to that Air and Diet, grafted into that Stock; and though they have (God be thanked) forgot their

Norman, yet they will hardly learn Greek, much less Utopian: That, in the late Protector's Times, our Lawyers, with one Voice, importuned him, rather to assume the Stile and Power of a King, to which they found all our Laws were shaped, than retain that of a Protector, unknown to the Law; that nothing hath rendered our Architectors of a Commonwealth more obnoxious, than that their infinite Discords, in other Things, generally agreed in the Necessity of subverting all our Fundamentals, in order to their Design; which hath likewise obliged all sober Men and true Patriots (even the chiefest Pillars of the Parliament's Cause, in the late War) to unite themselves with the Royal Interest, as not enduring to hear of those violent and dangerous Alterations, which they see a Republic must introduce.

For its Compliance with our Genius consider, that as our English Nature is not, like the French, supple to Oppression, and apt to delight in that Pomp and Magnificence of their Lords, which they know is supported with their Slavery and Hunger; nor like the Highland Scots, where the Honour and Interest of the Chief is the Glory of the whole Clan; so doth it as little or less agree with the Dutch Humour, addicted only to Traffic, Navigation, Handy-crafts, and sordid Thrift; and (in Defiance of Heraldry) every Man fancying his own Scutcheon: Doth not every one amongst us, that hath the Name of a Gentleman, aim his utmost to uphold it? Every one that hath not, to raise one? To this End, do not our very Yeomen commonly leave their Lands to the eldest Son, and to the others nothing but a Flail or Plough? Did not every one, that had any Thing like an Estate, pinch himself in his Condition, to purchase a Knighthood or small Patent? What need further Proof? Our late Experience of that Glimpse and Shadow of Monarchy (though in Persons hated and scorned, and upon a most scandalous Account) yet (for mere Resemblance) admitted as tolerable, and, in Respect of a Commonwealth, courted, clearly evinces, how grateful the Substance would be to Englishmen.

For our Interest briefly (we wave tedious and politic Discourses) certain it is, that our Republic (were it like to settle) would alarm all our Neighbours, would make our best Allies, our bitterest Enemies, and (upon several Accounts) probably draw upon us the united Forces of Christendom to crush the Embryo. Which (the Nation being so weakened, and divided, as it is) must evidently endanger our total Oppression, or, at least, to bring in the King by Conquest. Besides, by what Title shall we pretend to hold Scotland and Ireland, since that of Descent is now avoided, and Consent we know there is none; nor, indeed, can any be expected?

THE SCOTS HOLDING THEIR YOVNG KINGES NOSE TO Y^e GRINSTO$^\text{NE}$
Come to the Grinſtone Charles tis now to late.
To Recolect his presbiterian Fate.

Thou Couenant pretenders muſt Ʒbee
The Subiect of your Tradgic Comedies

George Charles

Jockie

The Scots holding their Young Kinges Nose to y$^\text{e}$ Grinstone

I come now to assert, that our former Government eminently included all the Perfections of a free State, and was the Kernel, as it were, of a Commonwealth, in the Shell of Monarchy: First, I will begin with the essential Parts of a Commonwealth, which are three, viz. The Senate proposing, the People resolving, the Magistrate executing: For the Senate or Parliament, if ever there were a free and honourable one, it was here; where the Deputies of the whole Nation, most freely chosen, did, with like Freedom, meet, propound, debate and vote all Matters of common Interest: No Danger escaped their Representing; no Grievance, their Complaint; no public Right, their Claim; or Good, their Demand; in all which, the least Breach of Privilege was branded as a civil Sacrilege; and though there lay no Appeal to the dispersed Body of the People (a Decision manifestly impracticable in Government, and fitter indeed for Tribunes to move, than Nations to admit) yet (Elections being so popular, and Assemblies frequent) the same End was attained with much more Safety and Convenience. The Prince had, likewise (in Effect) but an executive Power, which he exercised by Ministers and Officers, not only sworn, but severely accountable: For, though both he and the Lords had their Negatives in making Laws, yet (no Tax being impossible,* but by Consent of the Commons, nor any Law (without it) of such Validity, that the Ministers of Justice durst enforce it) there was a wise and sweet Necessity for the King, and likewise for the Lords (who were but as a Grain in the Royal Scale) to confirm all such Bills, as were convenient for the People, and not greatly hurtful to the Prince; and so this Bug-bear Negative was resolved into a meer Target, to shelter and preserve the Government from being altered, at the Will of the Commons, if, at any Time, they should prove factious: Which (being in reason manifest) hath been also confirmed by great Experience: Our Kings having, rarely, obstructed any Bill, which they might safely grant; but, on the other Side, passed many high Acts of meer Grace, circumscribing their Prerogative, and clipping its Wings; nay, I could wish they had not pierced its Bowels. This was that triple Cord, which, one would think, could not be broken; nor, indeed, was it broken, but cut asunder: This was our Gold, seven Times refined; for every Bill, being thrice read, debated, and agreed, in either House, was, at last, brought to the King, for his Royal Assent, the Mint of our Laws: A Trial so exact, that, surely, no Dross could escape it; since all Interests must thereto concur (as truly, it was but fit they should, in the Establishment of that, which must bind them all). This was that Temperament, which poised our Humours, and, at once,

* Clearly a misprint for 'possible'.

endued us with Health, Vigour, and Beauty: No Vote was precipitated, no Act was huddled up; as by sad Events, we have since seen, that, Power being ingrossed by one of the Estates, purged and modeled to the Interests of a Faction; a Consequence natural to such Premises: (As in a Balance consisting but of one Scale) nothing hath been weighed, our Laws have been Mandrakes of a Night's Growth, and our Times as fickle as the Weather, or Multitude.

The King, indeed, had the Power of making War, but he had not the Means; and then, it signified no more, than giving him Leave to fly, if he could get Wings; or to go beyond Sea, so he went without Shipping: He had a Sword, but he alone could never draw it; for the Trained-bands were a Weapon, which he (decently) wore, but the Nation, only, could use: He chose his Ministers (as who doth not his Servants?) But alas, he was accountable for them, to the Triennial Parliament, which none but the soundest Integrity could abide: He could hinder the Stroke of Justice with his Pardon (though still, the Jaws not being muzzled, it would bite terribly) but certainly, it was great Wisdom, rather, to give Way; since (with his own Scandal) he could afford Offenders but a lame and scurvy Protection; and since the Power of relieving his Wants rested in the Commons, to balance his Will, and oblige him to a Correspondence with Parliaments.

That his Person should be most sacred, it was but needful; to avoid Circulation of Account; reasonable, since it carries with it the Consent of Nations; just, that he should not be the meer Butt of Faction and Malice, in worse Condition, than the basest of Vassals; honourable, that the Nakedness of Government might not be daily uncovered; wise, in the Constitution, not, at once, to trust and provoke, by forcing him to shift for his own Indemnity, no Danger to the Public seeming so extreme, as the Outlawry of a Prince; no Task, by daily Experience, so difficult, as the arraigning of any Power, whether Regal or Popular; and since we make golden Bridges, for flying Enemies, much more may we afford them to relenting Sovereigns; (upon which Account, in our neighbour Kingdom of France, even Princes of the Blood are not subjected to capital Punishments;) finally, very safe, in the Consequent, for (being, by the Danger, threatening his corrupt Ministers, in all Probability, stripped of Agents) his personal Impunity might well signify somewhat to himself, but nothing to the People.

A Revenue he had, for the Support of his State and Family, ample; for the ordinary Protection of his People, sufficient; but for any Undertaking, defective; and for public Oppression, so inconsiderable, that when Prerogative was most rampant, our greatest Princes (and some, doubtless, we have had, the most renowned Warriors of their Ages) could never prudently aspire to make themselves sole Legislators, nor presumed to maintain Red-coats in Times of Peace. If any object (as some, concerned, are ready enough) That kingly Power could, here, no longer subsist, for Want of Revenue; it is easily answered, That a King of France, indeed, could not, and God forbid he should; but a King of England might, and (for aught I see) still may (the Sale of Crown-Lands, which exceeded not the Value of 100000 *l.* per Annum, being, methinks, no Matter of utter Ruin, but rather of easy Compensation). For the public Revenue was proportioned to the Maintenance of Courts, not Camps and Fleets: A Gentleman of reasonable Estate may live well on his Rents; but then, it is not convenient, he should keep Wenches, or Hangers-on, nor build, nor study Chymistry. In fine, the Revenue was very competent for ordinary Disbursements; as for extraordinary, if he resorted to Parliaments, the wiser he, the safer and happier we.

I Desire all our Projectors of Commonwealths, to contrive greater Freedom for their Citizens, than is provided by Magna Charta, and the Petition of Right; or shew us, that it is not much easier to violate, than to mend them: For, thereby our Lives, Liberties, and Estates were, under Monarchy secured, and established, I think, as well as any Thing, on this Side Heaven: It were no Solecism to say, the Subject had his Prerogative, as well as the King; and, sure I am, he was in as good (if not better) Condition to maintain it, the Dependence being less on his Side: Liberty was no less sacred than Majesty: *Noli me tangere* was likewise its Motto; and, in Case of any, the least Infringment (as Escapes in Government may happen even in the most perfect) it was resented, as if the Nation had received a Box on the Ear: If it be, as they say, the Glory of a free State, to exalt; the Scandal of Tyranny, to embase our Spirits; doubtless, this was our only Commonwealth: For, ever since, methinks, we have learned quietly to take the Bastonade.

I wish we now could, or could ever hope, under our Commonwealth (whatever Promises may be made us) so perfectly to distinguish the Legislative from the Ministerial Authority, as once we did; when the House of Commons had not the Power of a Court-Leet, to give an Oath, nor of a Justice of the Peace, to make a *Mittimus*: Which Distinction, doubtless, is the most vital Part of Freedom, and far more considerable to poor Subjects, than the pretended Rotation; as, on the contrary, the Confusion of them is an Accomplishment of Servitude; for which the best Republicks, I fear, have more to answer, than any limited Prince can have. Certain it is, that as our King, in his personal

Capacity, made no Laws, so neither did he, by himself, execute or interpret any. No Judge took Notice of his single Command, to justify any Trespass; no, not so much, as the Breaking of an Hedge; his Power limited by his Justice, he was (equally with the meanest of his Subjects) concerned in that honest Maxim, We may do just so much and no more, than we have Right to do. And it was most properly said, He could do no Wrong; because, if it were wrong, he did it not, he could not do it; it was void in the Act, punishable in his Agent. His Officers, as they were alike liable, so, perhaps, they were more obnoxious to Indictments and Suits, than any other, by how much their Trespass seemed to be of a higher Nature, and gave greater Alarm: His private Will could not countermand his public; his Privy-seal, ever buckled to the great Seal, as being the Nation's, more than his; his Order superseded no Process, and his Displeasure threatened no Man with an Hour's Imprisonment, after the Return of Habeas Corpus. An Under-Sheriff was more terrible, a Constable more saucy, a Bailiff more troublesome, than he: And yet, by his gentle Authority, this Scabbard of Prerogative (as some, in Derision, have called it) which (if it would) could scarce oppress an Orphan; Tumult was curbed, Faction moderated, Usurpation forestalled, Intervals prevented, Perpetuities obviated, Equity administered, Clemency exalted, and the People made only nice and wanton with their Happiness, as appears by their (now so impatient) Calling for that Manna, which they so (causelesly) loathed.

To conclude, what shall I add? The Act, enjoining the Keepers of the Great Seal, under Pain of High-Treason, to summon a Triennial Parliament, or course, by Virtue of the Act, without further Warrant; the Act, forbidding the Privy-Councel, under like Penalty, to intermeddle with *Meum & Tuum*; the Laws, abolishing the Star-chamber, High-commission, &c. branding all past, and bridling all future Enormities; the Statutes, limiting the King's Claims, and relieving his Tenants from Exaction of Forfeitures; besides many other principal Immunities, wherewith (by the special Favour of God, and Bounty of our Princes) we were blessed, far beyond any of our Neighbours; above all, our Assurance, that we might readily have obtained such farther Addition and Perfection of Liberty (if, yet, any such, there were) as would consist with Modesty, or Liberty itself, to ask: Do they not, aloud, proclaim, that we were, then, the Mirror of Governments, Envy of Monarchies, and Shame of Commonwealths; who could not but blush, to see themselves so eclipsed and silenced, in all their Pretences to Freedom? Do they not more than justify my Assertion, That, with all the Ornaments of the noblest Kingdom, we had, likewise, all the Enjoyments of the freest State?

THE PEOPLES ANCIENT
AND JUST LIBERTIES ASSERTED

*T*HE *later Stuarts, unlike James I and Charles I, had no interest in religious persecution. On the contrary, Charles II as a secret Papist, and James II as an open one, had a direct interest in toleration—partly to be attributed to their hope of including the Catholics in such a policy, but partly (in the case of Charles) out of a naturally easy-going disposition and even from some personal respect and affection for individual non-conformists, other than Catholics. A notable example of this was the friendly relationship between Charles II and William Penn—the Quaker founder of Pennsylvania, whose trial in 1670 is the subject of our next pamphlet.*

But Restoration parliaments were of another opinion; and Charles (unlike the Bourbons when placed in a similar situation) had both learnt and forgotten a good deal. He had forgotten the Divine Right of Kings, which proved so disastrous to his father, and remembered that a head-on collision with Parliament was inadvisable. So it came about that Parliament, which had fought (among other things) for freedom of worship against Anglican persecution, now used its established authority to maintain a persecution of the Presbyterians and independent sects in the same interest which it had formerly opposed—that of the Church of England. The Crown, on the other hand, having lost a war in which it had been identified with High Church bigotry and oppression, was restored on sufferance, and could only maintain its prestige by acquiescing in the very policy which had previously proved so suicidal—a situation the more remarkable because the Stuarts were now anxious to provide that very toleration which they had so bitterly opposed. The two sides had exchanged policies, but Parliament was still the stronger. Hence, in spite of the Stuart efforts (partially successful) to grant freedom of worship, and in defiance of the Declaration from Breda (in which Charles had promised religious toleration when restored to the throne) the reigns of Charles II and James II were marked by a great deal of persecution, sponsored by the dominant Anglican faction.

An example is the trial of William Penn and William Mead in 1670, on a charge of conspiracy to address (and addressing) a tumultuous assembly. The case needs no comment, other than those provided in the preface and the 'observations' which were interwoven with the report when published as a pamphlet. Certainly it was one of the most disgraceful exhibitions of injustice ever known in an English court; and there is some satisfaction in the fact that the case was reviewed, on a writ of Habeas Corpus, *by Chief Justice Vaughan, and the rights of juries established by his ruling.*

The case was immediately capitalised, in the interest of the victims, by the issue of this pamphlet in the year of the trial. It ran through several editions and was evidently something of a best-seller. The authorship (i.e. of the preface and comments) is attributed to William Penn himself in all catalogues and in all biographies of Penn which we have consulted; but we can find no justification for this assumption. In the course of our enquiry into this matter we received valuable help from the Librarians at Friends House, Euston, and from Mr. D. R. Lacey, whose researches overlapped our own at this point. We inclined to the view, shared by Mr. Lacey, that Thomas Rudyard (author of the second part of this tract, not included here) was as likely as any man to have written the account of the trial, but we took the precaution of consulting Mr. C. L. Boltz, who has made a close study of Penn's life and works. Mr. Boltz assures us that he knows of no proof of Penn's authorship, but that he considers there is indirect evidence of Penn having 'had a hand in it', probably in collaboration with Rudyard and spectators supplying notes.

It may be worth noting that this fining of a jury for not bringing in the verdict desired by the judge was by no means unique. Serjeant Keeling, who introduced the Act of Uniformity in 1662, had, as a judge, fined a jury 100 marks each for acquitting certain persons who had assembled for worship with bibles but without prayer books. The Recorder who made the classic remark about the desirability of the Inquisition was Sir John Howell.

A list of errata is given at the end of this pamphlet; but as the errors in no way invalidate the sense, except in one instance, we have merely given this in a footnote to page 150. The names of John Robinson, Alderman, and Richard Brown are also to be added to the list of those present, on page 143. The missing first name of the admirable Mr. Bushel, as later appears, was Edward.

We have enclosed the 'Observations' in square brackets to avoid unnecessary confusion in following the drama of the trial. The technique anticipates that of the radio, with drama interspersed by narrative.

THE PEOPLES ANCIENT AND JUST LIBERTIES ASSERTED

Anon.

To the English Reader

IF ever it were time to speak, or write, tis now, so many strange Occurrances, requiring both.

How much thou art concerned in this ensuing Tryal (where not only the Prisoners, but the Fundamental Laws of England) have been most Arbitrarily Arraigned, Read, and thou mayst plainly judge.

Liberty of Conscience, is counted a Pretence for Rebellion, and Religious Assemblies, Routs, and Riots; and the Defenders of both, are by them, reputed Factious and dis-affected.

Magna Charta, is Magnaf—— with the Recorder of London; and to demand Right an Affront to the Court.

Will and Power are their great Charter, but to call for Englands, is a Crime, incurring the penalty of their Bale-Dock, and Nasty-hole, nay, the menace of a Gag, and Iron Shackles too.

The Jury (though proper Judges of Law and Fact) they would have over-ruled in both, as if their Verdict signified no more, then to eccho back the illegal charge of the Bench; and because their courage, and honesty did more than hold pace, with the threat and abuse of those, who sate as Judges, (after two dayes and two nights restraint for a Verdict) in the end were fined and imprisoned, for giving it.

O! what monstrous, and illegal proceedings are these? Who reasonably can call his Coat his own? When Property, is made subservient to the Will and Interest of his Judges; or, who can truly esteem himself a Free man? When all Pleas for liberty are esteemed Sedition, and the Laws, that give, and maintain them, so many insignificant pieces of formality.

And What do they less then plainly tell us so, who at will and plea-sure break open our Locks, rob our Houses, raze their Foundations, imprison our Persons, and finally deny us Justice, to our relief; as if they then acted most like Christian men, when they were most barbar-ous, in ruining such, as really are so; and that no Sacrifice could be so acceptable to God, as the destruction of those, that most fear him.

In short, That the Conscientious should only be obnoxious, and the just demand of our Religious Liberty, the reason, why we should be denyed our civil freedom (as if to be a Christian and an English-man were inconsistant) and that so much solicitude and deep contrivance, should be imployed only, to ensnare, and ruin, so many ten thousand conscientious Families) so eminently, industrous, serviceable, and exemplary; whilst Murders can so easily obtain pardons, Rapes be re-mitted, publique Uncleanness pass unpunisht, and all manner of Levity, Prodigallity, Excess, Prophaneness, and Atheism, universally con-nived at; if not in some respect manifestly encouraged) cannot but be detestably abhorrent, to every serious and honest mind.

Yet that this lamentable state is true, and the present Project in hand, let London's Recorder, and Canterburies Chaplain be heard.

The first in his publique Panegerick, upon the Spanish inquisition, highly admiring the Prudence of the Romish Church, in the erection of it, as an excellent way, to prevent Schism, which unhappy expression, at once passeth sentence, both against our fundamental Laws, and Protestant Reformation.

The second, In his printed Mercenary discourse against Toleration, asserting for a main Principle, That it would be less injurious, to the Government, to dispence with prophane and loose Persons, then to allow a toleration to religious Dissenters: It were to over-do the business, to say any more, where there is so much said already.

And therefore to conclude, we cannot choose but admonish all, as well Persecutors, to relinquish their Heady, Partial and Inhuman Pro-secutions (as what will certainly issue in disgrace here, and inevitable condign punishment hereafter) as those who yet dare express their moderation (however out of fashion, or made the brand of Phanati-schism) [*sic*] not to be huf'd or menaced, out of that excellent temper, to make their parts, and persons subservient, to the base humors, and sinister designs of the bigest mortal upon Earth: But to reverence and obey, the Eternal just God, before whose great Tribunal, all must render their accounts, and where he will recompence to every Person according to his works.

THE TRYAL OF WILLIAM PENN AND
WILLIAM MEAD

As there can be no Observation, where there is no Action; so its impossible, there should be a juditious Intelligence, without due Observation.

And since there can be nothing more seasonable then a right Information, especially of Publick Acts; and well knowing, how industrious some will be, to mis-represent, this Tryal to the disadvantage of the Cause and Prisoners, it was thought requisite, in defence of both, and for the satisfaction of the People, to make it more publick; nor can there be any business wherein the people of England are more concerned, then in that which relates to their civil and Religious Liberties, questioned in the Persons above-named, at the Old-Baily, the first, third, fourth and fifth of Sept. 1670.

There being present,

SAM. STARLING, *Mayor*,	RICHARD FORD, *Alderman.*	
THO. HOWEL, *Recorder.*	JOSEPH SHELDEN, *Alderman.*	
THO. BLUDWORTH, *Alder.*	JOHN SMITH,	*Sheriffs.*
WILLIAM PEAK, *Alderm.*	JAMES EDWARDS,	

CRYER. O Yes, Thomas Veer, —— Bushel, John Hammond, Charles Milson, Gregory Walklet, John Brightman, Wil. Plumsted, Henry Henley, Thomas Damask, Henry Michel, William Lever, John Baily.

The Form of the Oath.

You shall well and truely try, and true Deliverance make betwixt our Soveraign Lord the King, and the Prisoners at the Bar, according to your Evidence; So help you God.

That, William Penn Gent. and William Mead late of London, Linnen Draper, with divers other Persons to the Jurors unknown, to the number of three hundred, the 14th day August, in the 22nd year of the King, about eleaven of the clock in the forenoon, the same day, with force and arms, &c. in the Parish of St. Bent Grace-Church in Bridge-ward, London, in the Street called Gratious-Church-Street, unlawfully and tumultuously did assemble and congregate themselves together, to the disturbance of the Peace of the said Lord the King: and the aforesaid William Penn, and William Mead, together with other Persons, to the Jurors aforesaid unknown, then and there so assemble and congregate together; the aforesaid William Penn, by agreement between him and William Mead, before made; and by abetment of the aforesaid William Mead then and there, in the open Street, did take upon himself to preach and speak, and then, and there, did preach and speak unto the aforesaid William Mead, and other Persons there, in the Street aforesaid, being assembled and congregated together, by reason whereof a great concourse and tumult of People in the Street aforesaid, then, and there, along time did remain and continue, in contempt of the said Lord the King, and of his Law, to the great disturbance of his peace, to the great terror and disturbance of many of his Leige people and Subjects, to the ill example of all others, in the like case Offenders, and against the peace of the said Lord the King, his Crown, and dignity.

What say you, William Penn and William Mead, are you guilty, as you stand indicted, in manner and form, as aforesaid, or not guilty.

PENN. It is impossible, that we should be able to remember the indictment verbatim, and therefore we desire a Copy of it, as is customary in the like occasions.

REC. You must first plead to the indictment, before you can have a Copy of it.

PEN. I am unacquainted with the formality of the Law, and therefore, before I shall answer directly, I request two things of the Court. First, that no advantage may be taken against me, nor I deprived of any benefit, which I might otherwise have received. Secondly, that you will promise me a fair hearing, and liberty of making my defence.

COURT. No advantage shall be taken against you; you shall have liberty, you shall be heard.

PEN. Then I plead not guilty in manner and form.

CLA. What sayest thou William Mead, art thou guilty in manner and form, as thou standest indicted, or not guilty?

MEAD. I shall desire the same liberty as is promised William Penn.

COURT. You shall have it.

MEAD. Then I plead not guity in manner and form.

The Court adjourned until the afternoon.

CRYER. O yes, &c.

CLA. Bring William Penn and William Mead to the Bar.

[OBSER. The said Prisoners were brought, but were set aside, and other business prosecuted. Where we cannot choose but observe, that it was the constant and unkind practices of the Court, to the

Prisoners, to make them wait upon the Tryals of Fellons and Murderers, thereby designing in all probabillity, both to affront and tire them.

After five hours attendance, the Court broke up and adjourned to the third instant.]

The third of September, 1670. the Court sate.

CRY. O yes, &c.

CLA. Bring William Penn and William Mead before the Bar.

MAYOR. Sirrah, who bid you put off their Hats? put on their Hats again.

[OBSER. Whereupon one of the Officers putting the Prisoners Hats upon their Heads (pursuant to the Order of the Court) brought them to the Bar.]

RECORD. Do you know where you are?

PEN. Yes.

RECORD. Do not you know it is the Kings Court?

PEN. I know it to be a Court, and I suppose it to be the Kings Court.

RECORD. Do you not know there is respect due to the Court?

PEN. Yes.

RECORD. Why do you not pay it then?

PEN. I do so.

RECORD. Why do you not pull off your Hat then?

PEN. Because I do not believe, that to be any respect.

RECORD. Well, the Court sets forty Marks a piece upon your Heads, as a Fine for your contempt of the Court.

PEN. I desire it might be observed, that we came into the Court with our Hats off, (that is, taken off) and if they have been put on since, it was by order from the Bench; and therefore not we, but the Bench should be fined.

MEAD. I have a question to ask the Recorder, Am I fined also?

RECOR. Yes.

MEAD. I desire the Jury, and all people to take notice of this injustice of the Recorder; who spake to me to pull off my Hat. and yet hath he put a fine upon my head. O fear the Lord, and dread his Power, and yeild to the guidance of his holy Spirit, for he is not far from every one of you.

The Jury Sworn again.

[OBSER. J. Robinson Lieutenant of the Tower, disingeniously objected against —— Bushell, as if he had not kist the Book, and therefore would have him sworn again; though indeed, it was on purpose, to have made use of his tenderness of Conscience in avoiding reiterated Oaths, to have put him by his being a Jury-man, apprehending him to be a person, not fit to Answer their arbitrary ends.]

The Clark read the indictment, as aforesaid.

CLAR. Cryer, Call James Cook into the Court, give him his Oath.

CLA. James Cook lay your hand upon the book, the evidence you shall give to the Court, betwixt our Soveraign the King, and the Prisoners at the Bar, shall be the Truth, and the whole Truth, and nothing but the Truth; so help you God, &c.

COOK. I was sent for, from the Exchange, to go and disperse a Meeting in Gratious-street, where I saw Mr. Penn speaking to the people, but I could not hear what he said, because of the noise; I endeavoured to make way to take him, but I could not get to him for the crowd of people; upon which Captain Mead came to me, about the Kennel of the Street, and desired me to let him go on; for when he had done. he would bring Mr. Penn to me.

COUR. What number do you think might be there?

COOK. About three or four hundred People.

COUR. Call Richard Read, Give him his Oath.

READ being sworn was askt, what do you know concerning the Prisoners at the Bar.

READ. My Lord, I went to Gratious-street, where I found a great croud of People, and I heard Mr. Pen preach to them; and I saw Captain Mead speaking to Leiutenant Cook, but what he said, I could not tell.

MEAD. What did William Penn say?

READ. There was such a great noise, that I could not tell what he said.

MEAD. Jury observe this Evidence, He saith he heard him preach, and yet saith, he doth not know what he said.

Jury take notice, he swears now a clean contrary thing, to what he swore before the Mayor, when we were committed: For now he swears that he saw me in Gratious-street, and yet swore before the Mayor, when I was committed, that he did not see me there. I appeal to the Mayor himself, if this be not true; but no answer was given.

COUR. What number do you think might be there?

READ. About four or five hundred.

PEN. I desire to know of him what day it was?

READ. Answ. the 14th day of August.

PEN. Did he speak to me, or let me know he was there; for I am very sure I never saw him?

CLA. Cryer call————————into the Court.

COUR. Give him his Oath.

My Lord, I saw a great number of People, and Mr Penn I suppose was speaking; I see him make a motion with his hands, and heard some noise, but could not understand what he said; but for Captain Mead I did not see him there.

REC. What say you Mr. Mead? were you there?

MEAD. It is a Maxim in your own Law, *Nemo tenetur accusare seipsum*, which if it be not true Latine, I am sure it is true English, That no man is bound to accuse himself: And why dost thou offer to ensnare me, with such a question? Doth not this shew thy malice? Is this like unto a Judge, that ought to be Counsel for the Prisoner at the Bar?

RECORD. Sir, Hold your Tongue, I did not go about to insnare you.

PEN. I desire we may come more close to the point, and that silence be commanded in the Court.

CRY. O yes, All manner of Persons keep silence upon pain of imprisonment——silence in the Court.

PEN. We confess our selves to be so far from recanting, or declining to vindicate the assembling of our selves, to Preach, Pray, or Worship the Eternal, Holy, Just God, that we declare to all the World, that we do believe it to be our indispensable duty, to meet incessantly upon so good an account; nor shall all the powers upon Earth, be able to divert us from reverencing and adoring our God, who made us.

BROWN. You are not here for worshipping God, but for breaking the Law; you do your selves a great deal of wrong in going on in that discourse.

PEN. I affirm I have broken no Law, nor am I guilty of the Indictment, that is laid to my charge, and to the end, the Bench, the Jury, and my self, with these that hear us, may have a more direct understanding of this procedure I desire you would let me to know by what Law it is you prosecute me, and upon what Law you ground my indictment.

REC. Upon the common Law.

PEN. Where is that common Law?

REC. You must not think that I am able to run up so many years, and over so many adjudged Cases, which we call Common Law, to answer your curiosity.

Pen. This Answer I am sure is very short of my Question, for if it be Common, it should not be so hard to produce.

Rec. Sir, will you plead to your Indictment?

Pen. Shall I plead to an Indictment, that hath no Foundation in Law, if it contain that Law you say I have broken, why should you decline to produce that Law, since it will be impossible for the Jury to determine, or agree to bring in their Verdict, who have not the Law produced, by which they should measure the truth of this Indictment, and the guilt, or contrary of my Fact?

Rec. You are a sawcy Fellow, speak to the Indictment.

Pen. I say, it is my place to speak to matter of Law; I am arraigned a Prisoner, my liberty, which is next to life it self, is now concerned; you are many Mouths and Ears against me, and if I must not be allowed to make the best of my Case, it is hard: I say again, unless you shew me, and the People, the Law you ground your Indictment upon; I shall take it for granted, your proceedings are meerly Arbitrary.

[Obser. At this time several upon the Bench urged hard upon the Prisoner to bear him down.]

Rec. The Question is whether you are guilty of this Indictment?

Pen. The Question is not whether I am guilty of this Indictment, but whether this Indictment be legal, it is too general and imperfect an Answer, to say it is the Common Law, unless we knew both where, and what it is; For where there is no Law, there is no Transgression; and that Law which is not in being, is so far from being Common, that it is no Law at all.

Rec. You are an impertinent Fellow, will you teach the Court what Law is? Its *Lex non scripta*, that which many have studied thirty or forty years to know, and would you have me to tell you in a moment?

Pen. Certainly, if the Common Law be so hard to be understood, its far from being very Common; but if the Lord Cook, in his Institutes, be of any consideration, he tells us, That Common Law is Common Right, and that Common Right is the great Charter-Priviledges: Confirmed 9 Hen. 3. 29. 25 Edw. 1. 1. 2 Edw. 3. 8. Cook Instit. 2. p. 56.

Rec. Sir, you are a troublesom Fellow, and it is not for the honour of the Court to suffer you to go on.

Pen. I have asked but one Question, and you have not answered me; though the Rights and Priviledges of every English man be concerned in it.

Rec. If I should suffer you to ask Questions till to morrow morning you would be never the wiser.

Pen. That is according as the Answers are.

Rec. Sir, We must not stand to hear you talk all night.

Pen. I design no affront to the Court, but to be heard in my just Plea, and I must plainly tell you, that if you will deny me Oyer of that Law, which you suggest I have broken, you do at once deny me an acknowledged right, and evidence to the whole World your resolution to sacrifice the Priviledges of English men to your Sinister and Arbitrary designs.

Rec. Take him away: my Lord, if you take not some course with this pestilent Fellow, to stop his mouth, we shall not be able to do any thing to Night.

May. Take him away, Take him away, turn him into the Baledock.

Pen. These are but so many vain exclamations; Is this Justice or true Judgment? Must I therefore be taken away because I plead for the fundamental Laws of England? However, this I leave upon your Consciences, who are of the Jury (and my sole Judges) that if these Antient Fundamental Laws, which relate to liberty and property, and (are not limited to particular perswasions in matters of Religion) must not be indispensibly maintained and observed; Who can say he hath right to the Coat upon his back? Certainly our liberties are openly to be invaded, our Wives to be ravished, our Children slaved, our Families ruined, and our Estates led away in Triumph, by every sturdy Begger and malitious Informer, as their Trophies, but our (pretended) Forfeits for Conscience sake; the Lord of Heaven and Earth will be Judge between us in this matter.

Rec. Be silent there.

Pen. I am not to be silent in a Case wherein I am so much concerned, and not only myself, but many ten thousand Families besides.

[Obser. They having rudely haled him into the Bale-dock, William Mead they left in Court, who spake as followeth.]

Mead. You men of the Jury, here I do now stand, to answer to an Indictment against me, which is a bundle of Stuff, full of Lyes and Falshoods; for therein I am accused, that I met *vi et armis, illicite et tumultuose*: time was, when I had freedom to use a carnal Weapon, and then I thought I feared no man; but now I fear the Living God, and dare not make use thereof, nor hurt any man; nor do I know I demeaned my self as a tumultuous person: I say, I am a peaceable man, therefore it is a very proper question what William Penn demanded in this Case, An Oyer of the Law, on which our Indictment is grounded.

RECOR. I have made answer to that already.

MEAD. Turning his face to the Jury, saith, You men of the Jury, who are my Judges, if the Recorder will not tell you what makes a Riot, a Rout, or an unlawfull Assembly, Cook, he that once they called the Lord Cook, tells us what makes a Riot, a Rout, and an unlawfull Assembly—A Riot is when three, or more, are met together to beat a man, or to enter forcibly into another mans Land, to cut down his Grass, his Wood, or break down his Pales.

[OBSER. Here the Recorder interrupted him, and said, I thank you Sir, that you will tell me what the Law is, scornfully pulling off his Hat.]

MEAD. Thou mayst put on thy Hat, I have never a Free* for thee now.

BROWN. He talkes at random, one while an Independent, another while some other Religion, and now a Quaker, and next a Papist.

MEAD. *Turpe est doctori cum culpa redarguit ad ipsum.*

MAY. You deserve to have your Tongue cut out.

REC. If you discourse on this manner, I shall take occasion against you.

MEAD. Thou didst promise me, I should have fair liberty to be heard; Why may I not have the priviledge of an English man? I am an English man, and you might be ashamed of this dealing.

REC. I look upon you to be an Enemy to the Laws of England, which ought to be observed and kept, nor are you worthy of such priviledges, as others have.

MEAD. The Lord is Judge between me and thee in this matter.

[OBSER. Upon which they took him away into the Bale-dock, and the Recorder proceeded to give the Jury their charge, as followeth.]

REC. You have heard what the indictment is, It is for preaching to the People, and drawing a tumultuous Company after them, and Mr. Pen was speaking; if they should not be disturbed, you see they will go on; there are three or four Witnesses, that have proved this, that he did preach there, that Mr. Mead did allow of it; after this, you have heard by substantial Witnesses what is said against them: Now we are upon the Matter of fact, which you are to keep to, and observe, as what hath been fully sworn at your peril.

[OBSER. The Prisoners were put out of the Court, into the Bale-doke, and the charge given to the Jury in their absence at which W. P. with a very raised voyce, it being a considerable distance from the Bench, spake.]

PEN. I appeal to the Jury, who are my Judges, and this great Assembly,

* Misprint for 'Fee'.

whether the proceedings of the Court are not most arbitrary, and void of all Law, in offering to give the Jury their Charge in the absence of the Prisoners; I say, it is directly opposit to, and destructive of the undoubted right of every English Prisoner, as Cook in the 2 Instit. 29. on the Chap. of Magna Charta speaks.

[OBSER. The Recorder being thus unexpectedly lasht for his extrajuditial procedure, said with an inraged smile.]

REC. Why, ye are present, you do hear, do you not?

PEN. No thanks to the Court, that commanded me into the Bale-dock; and you of the Jury take notice, that I have not been heard, neither can you legally depart the Court, before I have been fully heard, having at least ten or twelve Material points to offer, in order to invallid their Indictment.

REC. Pull that Fellow down, pull him down.

MEAD. Are these according to the rights and priviledges of English men, that we should not be heard, but turned into the Bale-dock, for making our defence, and the Jury to have their Charge given them in our absence; I say these are Barbarous and Unjust proceedings.

REC. Take them away into the Hole; to hear them talk all night, as they would, that I think doth not become the honour of the Court, and I think you (i.e.) the Jury your selves would be tired out, and not have patience to hear them.

[OBSER. The Jury were commanded up to agree upon their verdict, the Prisoners remaining in the stinking Hole; after an hour and halfs time eight came down agreed, but four remained above, the Court sent an Officer for them, and they accordingly came down: The Bench used many unworthy threats to the four that discented; and the Recorder, addressing himself to Bushell, said, 'Sir, You are the cause of this disturbance, and manifestly shew your self an abettor of faction, I shall set a Mark upon you Sir.]

J. ROBINSON. 'Mr. Bushel, I have known you near this fourteen years; you have thrust your self upon this Jury, because you think there is some service for you; I tell you, you deserve to be indicted more then any man that hath been brought to the Bar this day.

BUSH. No Sir John, There were threescore before me, and I would willingly have got off, but could not.

BLOODW. I said when I saw M. Bushel, what I see is come to pass, for I knew he would never yield. Mr. Bushel, we know what you are.

MAY. Sirrah, you are an impudent Fellow, I will put a mark upon you.

[OBSER. They used much menacing Language, and behaved themselves very imperiously to the Jury, as persons not more void of Justice then sober Education: After this Barbarous Usage, they sent them to consider of bringing in their Verdict, and after some considerable time they returned to the Court. Silence was called for, and the Jury called by their names.]

CLA. Are you agreed upon your Verdict?

JURY. Yes.

CLA. Who shall speak for you?

JURY. Our Fore-man.

CLA. Look upon the Prisoners at the Bar; How say you? Is William Penn guilty of the matter wherefore he stands indicted in manner and form, or not guilty?

FORE-M. Guilty of speaking in Gracious-Street.

COURT. Is that all?

FORE-M. That is all I have in commission.

RECOR. You had as good say nothing.

MAY. Was it not an unlawful Assembly? you mean he was speaking to a Tumult of People there?

FORE-M. My Lord, This was all I had in Commission.

[OBSER. Here some of the Jury seemed to buckle to the questions of the Court, upon which Bushel, Hammond, and some others opposed themselves, and said, they allowed of no such word, as an unlawful Assembly in their Verdict; at which the Recorder, Mayor, Robinson and Bloodworth took great occasion to villifie them with most opprobious language; and this Verdict not serving their turns, the Recorder expressed himself thus.]

RECOR. The Law of England will not allow you to part till you have given in your Verdict.

JURY. We have given in our Verdict, and we can give in no other.

RECOR. Gentlemen, you have not given in your Verdict, and you had as good say nothing; therefore go and consider it once more, that we may make an end of this troublesome business.

JURY. We desire we may have Pen, Ink and Paper.

[OBSER. The Court adjourned for half an hour; which being expired, the Court returns, and the Jury not long after.

    The Prisoners were brought to the Bar, and the Juries names called over.]

CLAR. Are you agreed of your verdict.

JURY. Yes.

CLAR. Who shall speak for you?

JUR. Our Fore-man.

CLAR. What say you, look upon the Prisoners; Is William Penn guilty in manner and form, as he stands indicted, or not guilty.

FORE-M. Here is our Verdict, holding forth a piece of Paper to the Clark of the Peace, which follows.

We the Jurors, hereafter named, do find William Pen to be guilty of Speaking or Preaching to an Assembly, met together in Gratious Street, the 14th of August last 1670. And that William Mead not guilty of the said indictment.

Fore-m.

Thomas Veer,	Charles Milson,
Edward Bushel,	Gregory Walklet,
John Hammond,	John Baily,
Henry Henley,	William Lever,
Henry Michel,	James Damask,
John Brightman,	Wil. Plumsted.

[OBSER. This both Mayor and Recorder resented at so high a rate, that they exceeded the bounds of all reason and civility.]

MAY. What will you be lead by such a silly Fellow as Bushel? an impudent canting Fellow; I warrant you, you shall come no more upon Juries in haste: You are a Fore-man indeed, addressing himself to the Fore-man, I thought you had understood your place better.

REC. Gentlemen, You shall not be dismist till we have a Verdict, that the Court will accept; and you shall be lockt up, without Meat, Drink, Fire, and Tobacco; you shall not think thus to abuse the Court; we will have a Verdict, by the help of God, or you shall starve for it.

PEN. My Jury, who are my Judges, ought not to be thus menaced; their Verdict should be free, and not compelled; the Bench ought to wait upon them, but not forestaul them; I do desire that Justice may be done me, and that the arbitrary resolves of the Bench may not be made the measure of my Juries verdict.

REC. Stop that prateing Fellows mouth, or put him out of the Court.

MAY. You have heard that he preacht, that he gathered a company of tumultuous people, and that they do not only disobey the martial Power, but civil also.

PEN. It is a great mistake, we did not make the tumult, but they that interrupted us; the Jury cannot be so ignorant as to think, that we met there, with a design to disturb the civil Peace, since (1st.) we were by force of Arms kept out of our Lawful House, and met as near it in the street, as their Souldiers would give us leave; and (2d). because it was no new thing, (nor with the circumstances exprest in the indictment) but what was usual and customary with us; tis very well known that we are a peaceable People, and cannot offer violence to any man.

[OBSER. The Court being ready to break up, and willing to huddle the Prisoners to their Goal, and the Jury to their chamber, Penn spoke as follows.]

PEN. The agreement of twelve men is a Verdict in Law, and such a one being given by the Jury, I require the Clark of the Peace to record it, as he will answer it, at his peril. And if the Jury bring in another Verdict, contradictory to this, I affirm they are perjured men in Law. (and looking upon the Jury said) You are English men, mind your Priviledge, give not away your Right.

BUSH. &c. Nor will we ever do it.

[OBSER. One of the Jury men, pleaded indisposition of body, and therefore desired to be dismist.]

MAY. You are as strong as any of them; starve them; and hold your Principles.

REC. Gentlemen, You must be contented with your hard fate, let your patience overcome it; for the Court is resolved to have a verdict, and that before you can be dismist.

JURY. We are agreed, we are agreed, we are agreed.

[OBSER. The Court swore several persons, to keep the Jury all night without Meat, Drink, Fire, or any other accommodation; they had not so much as a Chamber-pot, though desired.]

CRY. O yes, &c.

[OBSER. The Court adjourns till seven of the Clock next morning (being the fourth instant, vulgarly called Sunday) at which time the Prisoners were brought to the Bar; the Court sate, and the Jury called to bring in their Verdict.]

CRY. O yes, &c.—Silence in the Court, upon pain of imprisonment. The Juries names called over.

CLA. Are you agreed upon your verdict?

JUR. Yes.

CLA. Who shall speak for you?

JUR. Our Fore-man.

CLA. What say you? Look upon the Prisoners at the Bar; Is he guilty of the matter whereof he stands indicted, in manner and form as aforesaid, or not guilty?

FORE-MAN. William Penn is guilty of Speaking in Gratious-street.

MAY. To an unlawful Assembly?

BUSH. No my Lord, We give no other verdict, then what we gave last night, we have no other verdict to give.

MAY. You are a factious Fellow, ile take a course with you.

BLOOD. I knew Mr. Bushel would not yield.

BUSH. Sir Tho. I have done according to my Conscience.

MAY. That Conscience of yours would cut my throat.

BUSH. No my Lord, it never shall.

MAY. But I will cut yours so soon as I can.

REC. He has inspired the Jury, he has the spirit of Divination, methinks I feel him; I will have a positive Verdict, or you shall starve for it.

PEN. I desire to ask the Recorder one Question; Do you allow of the Verdict given of William Mead?

REC. It cannot be a verdict, because you were indicted for a Conspiracy, and one being found not guilty, and not the other, it could not be a verdict.

PEN. If Not guilty be not a verdict, then you make of the Jury and Magna Charta but a meer nose of Wax.

MEAD. How! is Not guilty no verdict?

REC. No, tis no verdict.

PEN. I affirm that the consent of a Jury, is a verdict in Law; and if W. M. be not guilty, it consequently follows, that I am clear, since you have indicted us of a conspiracy, and I could not possibly conspire alone.

[OBSER. There were many passages, that could not be taken, which past between the Jury and the Court. The Jury went up again, having received a fresh charge from the Bench, if possible to extort an unjust verdict.]

CRY. O yes, &c. Silence in the Court.

COUR. Call over the Jury. Which was done.

CLA. What say you? is William Penn guilty of the matter whereof he stands indicted, in manner and form aforesaid, or not guilty?

FORE-MAN. Guilty of speaking in Gratious-Street.

REC. What is this to the purpose? I say, I will have a verdict. And speaking to Edw. Bushel said, You are a factious Fellow; I will set a Mark upon you; and whilst I have any thing to do in the City, I will have an eye upon you.

MAY. Have you no more wit then to be led by such a pittiful Fellow? I will cut his Nose.

PEN. It is intolerable that my Jury should be thus menaced; Is this according to the fundamental Laws? Are not they my proper Judges by the great Charter of England? What hope is there of ever having justice done, when Juries are threatned, and their Verdicts rejected? I am concerned to speak and grieved to see such arbitrary proceedings. Did not the Lieutenant of the Tower render one of them worse than a Fellon? And do you not plainly seem to condemn such for factious Fellows, who answer not your ends? Unhappy are those Juries, who are threatned to be fined, and starved, and ruined, if they give not in Verdicts contrary to their Consciences.

REC. My Lord, you must take a course with that same Fellow.

MAY. Stop his Mouth; Jaylor bring Fetters, and stake him to the ground.

PEN. Do your pleasure, I matter not your Fetters.

REC. Till now I never understood the reason of the policy and prudence of the Spaniards, in suffering the Inquisition among them: And certainly it will never be well with us, till something like unto the Spanish-Inquisition be in England.

[OBSER. The Jury being required to go together to find another Verdict, and steadfastly refusing it (saying they could give no other Verdict, then what was already given) the Recorder in great passion was running off the Bench, with these words in his mouth, I protest I will sit here no longer to hear these things; at which the Mayor calling, Stay, stay, he returned, and directed himself unto the Jury, and spoke as followeth:]

REC. Gentlemen, we shall not be at this Trade alwayes with you; you will find the next Sessions of Parliament, there will be a Law made, that those that will not conform shall not have the protection of the Law. Mr. Lee, draw up another Verdict, that they may bring it in special.

LEE. I cannot tell how to do it.

JUR. We ought not to be returned, having all agreed, and set our hands to the Verdict.

REC. Your Verdict is nothing, you play upon the Court; I say you shall go together, and bring in another Verdict, or you shall starve; and I will have you charted about the City, as in Edward the thirds time.

FORE-M. We have given in our verdict, and all agreed to it, and if we give in another, it will be a force upon us to save our lives.

MAY. Take them up.

OFFIC. My Lord, they will not go up.

[OBSER. The Mayor spoke to the Sheriff, and he came off of his seat, and said.]

SHER. Come, Gentlemen, you must go up; you see I am commanded to make you go.

[OBSER. Upon which the Jury went up; and several sworn, to keep them without any accomodation as aforesaid, till they brought in their verdict.]

CRY. O yes, &c. The Court adjourns till to morrow morning, at seven of the clock.

[OBSER. The Prisoners were remanded to New-Gate, where they remained till next morning, and then were brought unto the Court, which being sate, they proceeded as followeth.]

CRY. O yes, &c. Silence in the Court upon pain of imprisonment.

CLA. Set William Pen and William Mead to the Bar. Gentle- of the Jury, answer to your Names, Tho. Veer, Edw. Bushel, John Hammond, Henry Henly, Henry Michell, John Brightman, Charles Milson, Gregory Walklet, John Baily, William Leaver, James Damask, William Plumstead. Are you all agreed of your Verdict?

JUR. Yes.

CLA. Who shall speak for you?

JUR. Our Foreman.

CLA. Look upon the Prisoners. What say you? is William Penn guilty of the matter whereof he stands indicted, in manner and form &c. or not guilty?

FORE-MAN. Here is our verdict in writing, and our hands subscribed.

[OBSER. The Clark took the Paper, but was stopt by the Recorder from reading of it; and he commanded to ask for a posstive verdict.]

FORE-MAN. That is our verdict, we have subscribed to it.

CLA. How say you is William Penn guilty, &c. or not guilty?

FORE-MAN. Not guilty.

CLA. How say you? is William Mead guilty, &c. or not guilty?

FORE-MAN. Not guilty.

CLA. Then hearken to your verdict, you say that William Penn is not guilty in manner and form as he stands indicted; you say that William Mead is not guilty in manner and form as he stands indicted, and so you say all,

JUR. Yes, we do so.

[OBSER. The Bench being unsatisfied with the verdict, commanded that every person should distinctly answer to their names, and give in their verdict, which they unanimously did, in saying, Not guilty, to the great satisfaction of the Assembly.]

REC. I am sorry, Gentlemen, you have follollowed [*sic*] your own judgments and Opinions, rather then the good and wholsom advice, which was given you; God keep my life out of your hands; but for this the Court fines you forty Mark a man; and imprisonment, till paid. At which Penn stept up towards the Bench, and said.

PEN. I demand my liberty, being freed by the Jury.

MAY. No, you are in for your Fines.

PEN. Fines, for what?

MAY. For contempt of the Court.

PEN. I ask, if it be according to the fundamental Laws of England, that any English-man should be fined or amerced, but by the judgment of his Peers or Jury; since it expresly contradicts the fourteenth and twenty ninth Chap. of the great Charter of England, which say, No Free-man ought to be amerced, but by the Oath of good and Lawful men of the Vicinage.

REC. Take him away, Take him away, take him out of the Court.

PEN. I can never urge the fundamental Laws of England, but you cry, Take him away, take him away. But it is no wonder. Since the Spanish Inquisition hath so great a place in the Recorders heart. God Almighty, who is just, will judge you all for these things.

[OBSER. They haled the Prisoners into the Bale-dock, and from thence sent them to New-Gate, for non payment of their Fines; and so were their Jury.]

THE VERY COPY OF A PAPER

*W*E *have already noticed the use of the published sermon as a vehicle of propaganda, and (in our last item) the report of a trial used—very appropriately—to discredit a corrupt court of law. Our next is an example of the scaffold speech, which became very popular in the late seventeenth century. The morbid interest that surrounded a public figure, condemned to death on a political charge, could always be used by the victim in a last bid to make party capital, even out of his own death. The public character of these executions, and the greater fervour with which opinions were held in the seventeenth century, provided favourable circumstances for such political apologies. But one can still wonder at the sporting spirit, as demonstrated by the authorities who allowed their victims such scope in their curtain speeches, for it has no contemporary parallel.*

Algernon Sidney, who wrote this speech before his execution on Tower Hill, was at that time an old man who had a long and distinguished record as a republican. He had fought against Charles I, opposed Cromwell, showed his ability as a diplomatist, and (during many years of exile at the beginning of the Stuart Restoration) was regarded by Charles II as the most dangerous of the many republicans then living abroad. His enemies, in fact, were agreed as to his great courage and ability.

He was at last allowed to return to England, where the Government of the time no doubt felt he was less dangerous than he could be abroad, and he might have died in peace if he had not joined with a mixed group of discontented politicians, who formed a 'Council of Six' to organise political resistance to the growing power of the Crown.

The political situation was certainly serious. By 1682 Charles II had freed himself from the necessity of asking Parliament for money, by accepting substantial subsidies from France—the effect of which policy was to restore absolute monarchy in England, with a king who was himself entirely dependent on the French court. British courts of law were meanwhile made subservient to the royal will by the appointment of judges from among those whom Algernon Sidney rightly described in this paper as 'Blemishes to the Bar'. Sidney also complained with good reason about the packing of juries.

The trial of Sidney and other members of the 'Council of Six', in connection with the 'Rye House Plot', was itself to show dramatically what good reason had the 'Whigs' (as the anti-Court party came to be called) to fear the results of this tinkering with justice. Sidney and his colleagues—except Monmouth, who escaped overseas—were arrested as conspirators in a plot which was real enough. The flaw in the trial was that no evidence was ever advanced of their complicity in this plot, except the solitary testimony of Lord Howard of Escrick, one of the Six, who was terrified into swearing away the lives of his associates. But the case was heard before Judge Jeffries, of infamous memory, and was something of a foretaste of Jeffries' 'Bloody Assizes', two years later, following the unsuccessful revolt led by Monmouth.

The unpublished manuscript found among Sidney's papers (and mentioned in his statement) was undoubtedly his own work—though even this, as he points out, was never proved before the court. It was a treatise on political theory and a reply to a book by Sir Robert Filmer, a deceased Royalist, whose Patriarcha (a defence of absolute monarchy) had been posthumously published, with reprints of his lesser writings, since the Restoration. Judge Jeffries ruled that a treatise favouring constitutional government proved participation in a plot to kill the king; and the bullied, bewildered jury (itself selected with an eye to politics) brought in a verdict of guilty against Sidney on the strength of this ruling and the perjured accusations of Howard. Such was history's indiscriminate revenge for the equally unjust sentences, based on the perjured evidence of Oates and Bedloe, whereby so many Catholics had been judicially murdered a few years previously, as supposed conspirators in the 'Popish Plot'. The party which had applauded this outrage most heartily was now to taste its own medicine.

During his last years, after his return to England, Sidney had made various unsuccessful efforts to obtain election to Parliament; and it is of interest that William Penn (himself, as we have seen, a victim of legal injustice) had assisted him in this, in spite of Penn's good personal relationship with Charles II. The 'Old Cause' to which Sidney refers in this paper was that of the Protestants and Constitutionalists, and it is a term which links up the Parliamentarians of the early seventeenth century with the Whig Party and its 'Protestant Succession' policy which was to emerge triumphant in the succeeding reigns. The situation at the end of Charles II's reign makes an interesting comment on the Plea for Limited Monarchy. Not only was the Parliamentary control of the purse subverted by French subsidies (as Charles I had attempted to circumvent it by 'Ship Money'), but the claim of independent courts of justice had also proved false.

This paper was published immediately after Sidney's execution in 1683, and several editions followed. In modern times we do not think it has been reprinted in full until now.

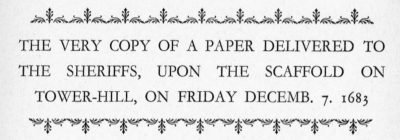

THE VERY COPY OF A PAPER DELIVERED TO THE SHERIFFS, UPON THE SCAFFOLD ON TOWER-HILL, ON FRIDAY DECEMB. 7. 1683

By Algernon Sidney, Esq;

Before his Execution there

Men, Brethren, and Fathers; Friends, Countrymen, and Strangers;

It May be expected that I should now say some Great matters unto you, but the Rigour of the Season, and the Infirmities of my Age, encreased by a close Imprisonment of above Five months, doth not permit me.

Moreover, we live in an Age that maketh Truth pass for Treason: I dare not say any thing contrary unto it, and the Ears of those that are about me will probably be found too tender to hear it. My Tryal and Condemnation doth sufficiently evidence this.

West, Rumsey, and Keyling, who were brought to prove the Plot, said no more of me, than that they knew me not; and some others equally unknown unto me, had used my Name, and that of some others, to give a little Reputation unto their Designs. The Lord Howard is too infamous by his Life, and the many Perjuries not to be denied, or rather sworn by himself, to deserve mention; and being a single Witness would be of no value, though he had been of unblemished Credit, or had not seen and confessed that the Crimes committed by him would be pardoned only for committing more; and even the Pardon promised could not be obtained till the Drudgery of Swearing was over.

This being laid aside, the whole matter is reduced to the Papers said to be found in my Closet by the Kings Officers, without any other Proof of their being written by me, than what is taken from suppositions upon the similitude of an Hand that is easily counterfeited, and which hath been lately declared in the Lady Car's Case to be no Lawful Evidence in Criminal Causes.

But if I had been seen to write them, the matter would not be much altered. They plainly appear to relate unto a large Treatise written long since in answer to Filmer's Book, which by all Intelligent Men is thought to be grounded upon wicked Principles, equally pernicious unto Magistrates and People.

If he might publish unto the World his Opinion, That all Men are born under a necessity derived from the Laws of God and Nature, to submit unto an Absolute Kingly Government, which could be restrained by no Law, or Oath; and that he that hath the Power, whether he came unto it by Creation, Election, Inheritance, Usurpation, or any other way had the Right; and none must Oppose his Will, but the Persons and Estates of his Subjects must be indispensably subject unto it; I know not why I might not have published my Opinion to the contrary, without the breach of any Law I have yet known.

I might as freely as he, publickly have declared my Thoughts, and the reasons upon which they were grounded, and I persuaded to believe, That God had left Nations unto the Liberty of setting up such Governments as best pleased themselves.

That Magistrates were set up for the good of Nations, not Nations for the honour or glory of Magistrates.

That the Right and Power of Magistrates in every Country, was that which the Laws of that Country made it to be.

That those Laws were to be observed, and the Oaths taken by them, having the force of a Contract between Magistrate and People, could not be Violated without danger of dissolving the whole Fabrick.

That Usurpation could give no Right, and the most dangerous of all Enemies unto Kings were they, who raising their Power to an Exorbitant Height, allowed unto Usurpers all the Rights belonging unto it.

That such Usurpations being seldom Compassed without the Slaughter of the Reigning Person, or Family, the worst of all Villanies was thereby rewarded with the most Glorious Privileges.

That if such Doctrines were received, they would stir up men to the Destruction of Princes with more Violence than all the Passions that have hitherto raged in the Hearts of the most Unruly.

That none could be Safe, if such a Reward were proposed unto any that could destroy them.

That few would be so gentle as to spare even the Best, if by their destruction of [*sic*] a Wild Usurper could become God's Anointed; and by the most execrable Wickedness invest himself with that Divine Character.

This is the Scope of the whole Treatise; the Writer gives such Reasons as at present did occur unto him, to prove it. This seems to agree with the Doctrines of the most Reverenced Authors of all Times, Nations and Religions. The best and wisest of Kings have ever acknowledged it. The present King of France hath declared that Kings have that happy want of Power, that they can do nothing contrary unto the Laws of their Country, and grounds his Quarrel with the King of Spain, *Anno.* 1667. upon that Principle. King James in his Speech to the Parliament *Anno.* 1603. doth in the highest degree assert it: The Scripture seems to declare it. If nevertheless the Writer was mistaken, he might have been refuted by Law, Reason and Scripture; and no Man for such matters was ever otherwise punished, than by being made to see his Errour, and it hath not (as I think) been ever known that they had been referred to the Judgment of a Jury, composed of Men utterly unable to comprehend them.

But there was little of this in my Case; the extravagance of my Prosecutors goes higher: the above-mentioned Treatise was never finished, nor could be in many years, and most probably would never have been. So much as is of it was Written long since, never reviewed nor shewn unto any Man; and the fiftieth part of it was produced, and not the tenth of that afford [*sic*] to be read. That which was never known unto those who are said to have Conspired with me, was said to be intended to stir up the People in Prosecution of the Designs of those Conspirators.

When nothing of particular Application unto Time, Place, or Person could be found in it, (as hath ever been done by those who endeavour'd to raise Insurrections) all was supplied by Innuendo's.

Whatsoever is said of the Expulsion of Tarquin; the Insurrection against Nero; The Slaughter of Caligula, or Domitian; The Translation of the Crown of France from Meroveus his Race unto Pepin; and from his Descendants unto Hugh Capet, and the like applied by Innuendo unto the King.

They have not considered, that if such Acts of State be not good, there is not a King in the World that has any Title to the Crown he bears; nor can have any, unless he could deduce his Pedigree from the Eldest Son of Noah, and shew that the Succession had still continued in the Eldest of the Eldest Line, and been so deduced to him.

Every one may see what advantage this would be to all the Kings of

Collonel Sidney's Overthrow;

OR,

An account of his Execution upon *Tower-Hill*, on *Friday* the 7*th.* of *December*, 1683. who was Condemned for High Treason against His Sacred Majesty, for endeavouring the Subversion of the Government, *&c.*
To the Tune of, *Now, now the Fight's done.*

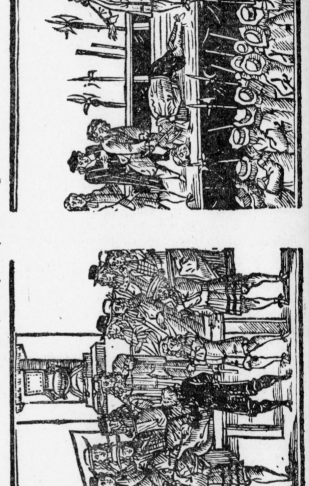

the World; and whether that failing, it were not beter for them to acknowledge they had received their Crowns by the Content of Willing Nations; or to have no better Title unto them than Usurpation and Violence, which by the same ways may be taken from them.

But I was long since told that I must Dye, or the Plot must Dye.

Least the means of destroying the best Protestants in England should fail, the Bench must be filled with such as had been Blemishes to the Bar.

None but such as these would have Advised with the King's Council, of the means of bringing a Man to death; Suffered a Jury to be packed by the King's Solicitors, and the Under-Sheriff; Admit of Jury-men who are not Freeholders; Receive such Evidence as is above mentioned; Refuse a Copy of an Indictment, or to Suffer the Statute of 46. Ed. 3. to be read, that doth expresly Enact, It should in no Case be denied unto any Man upon any occasion whatsoever; Over-rule the most important Points of Law without hearing. And whereas the Stat. 25 Ed. 3. upon which they said I should be Tried, doth Reserve unto the Parliament all Constructions to be made in Points of Treason, They could assume unto themselves not only a Power to make Constructions, but such Constructions as neither agree with Law, Reason, or Common Sence.

By these means I am brought to this Place. The Lord forgive these Practices, and avert the Evils that threaten the Nation from them. The Lord Sanctifie these my Sufferings unto me; and though I fall as a Sacrifice unto Idols, suffer not Idolatry to be Established in this Land. Bless thy People, and Save them. Defend thy own Cause, and Defend those that Defend it. Stir up such as are Faint; Direct those that are Willing; Confirm those that Waver; Give Wisdom and Integrity unto All. Order all things so as may most redound unto thine own Glory. Grant that I may Dye glorifying Thee for all thy Mercies; and that at the last Thou hast permitted me to be Singled out as a Witness of thy Truth; and even by the Confession of my Opposers, for that OLD CAUSE in which I was from my Youth engaged, and for which Thou hast Often and Wonderfully declared thy Self.

WE DO APPOINT ROBERT HORN, JOHN BAKER, AND JOHN REDMAYNE, TO PRINT THIS PAPER, AND THAT NONE OTHER DO PRESUME TO PRINT THE SAME.

PETER DANIEL
SAM. DASHWOOD

SOME CAUTIONS FOR CHOICE
OF MEMBERS IN PARLIAMENT

*G*EORGE *Savile, Marquis of Halifax, played a very important part in the political history of the late seventeenth century. Living at the very inception of party politics, he saw with almost prophetic clarity the evils that arose from loyalty to (and dependence upon) a political party. His own political career was pursued with such independence of these ties that he earned the name of 'The Trimmer'—a label which he wore with pride, and even wrote with his usual wit and good sense in defence of changing sides as a necessary activity of honest men if the vessel of state was to keep an even keel. This he achieved so effectively that Dryden said he*

> '. . . turned the balance too,
> So much the weight of one brave man can do.'

In the extracts which follow we are given a glimpse of political foibles which are even more pronounced in our own days than they were when Halifax recorded his views—the unnatural eagerness of men, not distinguished as saints, to serve their countrymen without self-interest; the gentlemen who would 'think it a disparagement to their understandings' to miss an opportunity for dishonesty; the lawyers who, being in 'the habit of taking money for their opinion', are so absent-minded as to take it for a vote. There is also a brief discussion of the evils attending the party system, a theme which the writer had discussed at greater length in his Character of a Trimmer.

In a world that has since been dominated by party men it is not remarkable that a statesman who held this system in contempt should have failed to receive the full recognition of his talents. Halifax was actually a far greater man than any of the party leaders of his time or since. He was also considered remarkable for his incorruptibility, which earned him many enemies. But in his time he was feared universally as the most brilliant satirical writer then living, whose mastery of irony has, indeed, never since been excelled. The dearth of biographical material relating to Halifax, who influenced English history more than any other single individual of any period, is a curious thing in an age when so many mediocrities have been disinterred by the zeal of English biographers.

The 'Cautions' were published in 1695, the year of the author's death, having been written in anticipation of the General Election, which took place in October. Halifax died six months before this event; but his caustic comments, written with his usual wit and composure from his death-bed, served the purpose for which they had been intended.

As the pamphlet which follows is more directly concerned with issues specific to the period, we shall deal with the historical background of England under William III in the note which precedes it. Halifax needs no historial introduction: he writes for all time.

SOME CAUTIONS FOR CHOICE OF MEMBERS IN PARLIAMENT

By George Savile, Marquis of Halifax

A VERY extraordinary earnestness to be chosen, is no very good Symptom: A desire to serve the Nation in Parliament, is an English Man's Ambition: Always to be Encouraged, and never to be disapproved.

A Man may not only be willing to stand, but he may declare that willingness to his Friends, that they may assist him, and by all the means becoming a modest and prudent Man, he may endeavour to succeed, and prevent the being disappointed in it.

But there is a wide difference between this and the raising a kind of petty War in the County or Corporation; entring the Lists rather for a Combat than an Election; throwing Fire-balls to put Men into heat, and omitting to spread no Reports, whether true or false, which may give an advantage by laying a Blemish upon a Competitor.

These Methods will ever be suspicious; it will never be thought a Natural thing for Men to take such extravagant pains for the meer sake of doing good to others.

To be content to suffer something for a good end, is that which many would do without any great repugnance: but where a Man can honestly propose nothing to himself, except Troubles, Charge, and Loss, by absence from his own Affairs, to be so violent in the pursuit of so ill a Bargain, is not at all suited to the languishing Virtue of Mankind so corrupted.

Such a self-denying Zeal in such a self-seeking Age, is so little to be imagin'd, that it may without injury be suspected.

Therefore when these blustring Pretenders come upon the Stage, their natural Temper and other Circumstances ought to be very well consider'd, before Men trust them with the disposal of their Money, or their Liberty.

And I am apt to believe, there could hardly be found one single Man whose other Qualifications would over-balance the Objections that lie against such importunate Suitors.

Recommending Letters ought to have no effect upon Elections.

In this I must distinguish: for tho in strictness perhaps there should be no Exception; yet in compliance with long practice, and out of an Indulgence that is necessary in a time when Mankind is too much loosened from severe Rules, to be kept close up to them, Letters sent only from Equal Men, doing Good Men right by giving Evidence in their behalf, offering them as fitly qualified, when they really are so, and freeing them from unjust Aspersions, may be still allowed.

The Letters I mean, are from Men of Power, where it may be beneficial to comply, and inconvenient to oppose.

Choice must not only be free from Force, but from Influence, which is a degree of Force: There must be no difficulty, no apprehension that a Refusal will be ill taken, or resented.

The Freeholders must be Freemen too; they are to have no Shackles upon their Votes in an Election: and the Men who stand, should carry their own Letters of Recommendation about them, which are there good Character and Behaviour in the World, without borrowing Evidence, especially when it comes from suspected hands.

Those who make use of these Epistles, ought to have no more advantage from them, than the Muscovites have from the Letters put into their hands, when they are buried, to recommend them to St. Nicholas.

The first should as little get admittance for Men into the Parliament, as these Letters can introduce the Bearers into Heaven.

The Scandal of such Letters lieth first in the arrogant imposing of those that write them, and next in the wretched Meanness of those that need them.

Men must be fallen very low in their Credit, who upon such an occasion have a recourse to Power to support it: Their Enemies could not give stronger Evidence of their not being fit for that which they pretend to. And if the Electors judge otherwise, they will be pretty sure in a little time to see their Mistake, and to repent it.

Non-Attendance in former Parliaments ought to be a Bar against the Choice of Men who have been guilty of it.

It is one of the worst kinds of Non-Residence, and the least to be excused: It is very hard that Men should despise a Duty, which perhaps is the only ground of the respect that is paid to them.

It is such a piece of Sawciness for any one to press for the Honour of serving in Parliament, and then to be careless in Attending it, that in a House where there were so many Officers, the Penalty had not been improper to have Cashier'd them for not appearing at the General Muster.

If men forbear to come out of Laziness, let them be gratified by taking their ease at Home without Interruption; If out of small Cunning to avoid Difficulties, and to escape from the Inconvenience of Voting in Critical Cases, let them enjoy that despicable pitch of Wisdom, and never pretend to make a Figure where the Publick is to be served.

If it would not be thought advisable to trust a Man immediately after he hath been drawn out of a Gaol, it may be as reasonable to look upon one who for his Non-attendance in the House hath been sent for in Custody, as a kind of Bankrupt, which putteth him upon unequal terms with those who have been assiduous in the discharge of their Duty.

They who thought fit in one Session to neglect the Publick Business, may be justly suspected, by their standing, in the next to intend their own.

Besides these more deliberate Offenders, there are some who do not Attend even when they are in the House; absent in their Thoughts for want of Comprehending the Business that is doing, and therefore diverted from it by any thing that is Trivial.

Such men are Nusances to a serious Assembly; and when they are Numerous, it amounteth almost to a Dissolution; it being scarce possible for good sense to be heard, whilst a noise is made by the buzzing of these Horse flies.

The Roman Censors who degraded a Senator for yawning whilst there was a Debate, would have much more abundant matter here upon which they might exercise their Jurisdiction.

To conclude this Head, There are so few that ever mended in these Cases, that after the first Experiment it is not at all reasonable to take them upon a new Tryal.

Men who are unquiet and busy in their Natures, are to give more than ordinary proofs of their Integrity, before the Electing them into a Publick Trust can be justified. As a hot Summer breedeth greater swarms of Flies, so an active time breedeth a greater number of these shining Gentlemen.

It is pretty sure, That men who cannot allow themselves to be at rest, will let no body else be at quiet. Such a perpetual Activity is apt by degrees to be applied to the pursuit of their private interest. And their thoughts being in a continual motion, they have not time to dwell long enough upon any thing to entertain a scruple.

So that they are generally at full liberty to do what is most convenient for them, without being fettered by any Restraints.

Nay further; Whenever it hapneth that there is an Impunity for Cheating, these nimble Gentlemen are apt to think it a disparagement to their Understandings not to go into it.

I doubt it is not a wrong to the present Age, to say, that a Knave is a less unpopular Calling than it hath been in former times. And to say truth, it would be ingratitude in some Men to turn Honest, when they owe all they have to their Knavery.

The People are in this respect unhappy; they are too many to do their own business; their numbers, which make their strength, are at the same time the cause of their weakness; they are too unweildy to move; and for this Reason nothing can ever redeem them from this incurable Impotency: So that they must have Solicitors to pursue and look after their Interests; who are too often disposed to dispense with the Fidelity they owe to those that trust them; especially if the Government will pay their Bills without Abatement.

It is better these Gentlemen's dexterity should be employed any where than in Parliament, where the ill consequence of their being Members is too much diffused, and not restrained to the County or Borough who shall be so unwary as to Chuse them.

Great Drinkers are less fit to Serve in Parliament than is apprehended.

Men's Virtue, as well as their Understanding, is apt to be tainted by it.

The appearance of it is Sociable and well-natur'd, but it is by no means to be rely'd upon.

Nothing is more frail than a Man too far engaged in wet Popularity.

The habit of it maketh Men careless of their business, and that naturally leadeth them into Circumstances, that make them liable to Temptation.

It is seldom seen, That any Principles have such a root, as that they can be proof against the continual droppings of a Bottle.

As to the Faculties of the Mind, there is not less Objection; the vapours of Wine may sometimes throw out sparks of Wit, but they are like scattered pieces of Ore, there is no Vein to work upon.

Such Wit, even the best of it, is like paying great Fines; in which case there must of necessity be an abatement of the constant Rent.

Nothing sure is a greater Enemy to the Brain, than too much

moisture; it can the least of any thing bear the being continually steeped: And it may be said, that Thought may be resembled to some Creatures which can live only in a dry Country.

Yet so arrogant are some men, as to think they are so much Masters of Business, as that they can play with it; they imagine they can drown their Reason once a day, and that it shall not be the worse for it; forgetting, that by too often diving the Understanding at last groweth too weak to rise up again.

I will suppose this fault was less frequent when Solon made it one of his Laws, That it was Lawful to Kill a Magistrate if he was found Drunk. Such a Liberty taken in this Age, either in the Parliament or out of it, would do terrible Execution.

I cannot but mention a Petition in the year 1647, from the County of Devon, to the House of Commons, against the undue Election of Burgesses, who are strong in Wine and weak in Wisdom.

The cause of such Petitions is to be prevented by Chusing such as shall not give handle for them.

Wanting-Men give such cause of suspicion where ever they deal, that surely the Chusers will be upon their guard, as often as such dangerous pretenders make their application to them.

Let the behaviour of such Men be never so plausible and untainted, yet they who are to pitch upon those they are to trust with all they have, may be excused, if they do not only consider what they are but what they may be.

As we Pray our selves we may not be led, into Temptation, we ought not by any means to thrust others into it; even though our own Interest was not concerned; And sure when it is, the Argument hath not less force.

If a Man hath a small Estate, and a numerous Family; where it happeneth that a Man hath as many Children as he hath Tenants, It is not a Recommending Circumstance for his Election.

When it cometh to be the Question with such a Man, Whether he shall be Just to the Publick, or Cruel to his Family? It is very possible the decision may be on the side of Corrupted Nature.

It is a Complement to this Age, which it doth not deserve, to suppose Men are so ty'd up to Morality, as that they cannot be pinched out of it: especially now when it is called Starving not to be Embroidered, or served in Plate.

The Men Chosen to serve their Country, should not be loaden with Suits that may tempt them to assume Privileges; much less under such Necessities as may more immediately prepare them for Corruption.

Men who need a Parliament for their own particular Interest, have more reason to offer their Service than others have to accept of it. And though I do not doubt, but there may be some whose Virtue would triumph over their Wants, let them be never so pressing; yet to expose the Publick to the hazard of being deceived, is that which can never be justifi'd by those that Chuse. And tho it must be allow'd possible for a wanting-Man to be honest, yet it is impossible for a Man to be wise that will depend upon it.

There is a sort of Men that have a Tinsel-wit, which make them shine among those who cannot judge.

Club and Coffee-house Gentlemen, Petty Merchants of small Conceits, who have an Empty habit of prating without meaning; They always aim at Wit and generally make false Fire.

Their business is less to learn, than to set themselves out; which makes them chuse to be with such as can only be Witnesses of their small Ingenuity, rather than with such as might improve it.

There is a subordinate Wit, as much inferior to a Wit of business, as a Fidler at a Wake is to the lofty Sound of an Organ.

Men of this Size are in no degree suited to the business of redressing Grievances, and making Laws.

There is a Parliament Wit to be distinguish'd from all other kinds; those who have it, do not stuff their heads only with Cavils and Objections.

They have a deliberate and an observing Wit, a Head turned to Publick things; Men who place a greater pleasure in mending a Fault than in finding it out.

Their Understanding directeth them to object in the right place, and not like those who go by no other Rule, than to conclude, That must be the best Counsel which was not taken.

These Whole-sale Judges shew such a gross and peevish Ignorance that it appeareth so openly in all they say or do, That they give loud warning to all considering Men, not to chuse them.

The dislike of slight Airy Men must not go so far, as to recommend heaviness in opposition to it, especially where men are convicted of it by Experience in former Sessions.

As a lively Coxcomb will seldom fail to lay in his claim for Wit; so a Blockhead is apt to pretend, That his heaviness is a proof of his Judgment.

Some have an universal Lethargy spread upon their Understanding without exception; others have an Insufficiency *quoad hoc*, as in some Cases men have *quoad hanc*; These last can never so turn their thoughts to publick Business, as to give the attention that is necessary to Comprehend it.

There are those who have such a thick Shell upon their Brains, that their Ignorance is impenetrable, and maketh such a stout resistance against Common Sense, that it will never be subdued by it: True Heart of Oak, Ignorance that will never yield, let Reason beat never so hard upon it; and though their kind Neighbours have at several Elections sent them up to School again, they have still return'd the same incurable Dunces.

There is a false Gravity that is a very ill symptom; and it may be said, That as Rivers, which run very slowly, have always the most Mud at the bottom; so a solid stiffness in the constant course of a man's Life, is a sign of a thick bed of Mud at the bottom of his Brain.

A dull man is so near a dead Man, that he is hardly to be ranked in the List of the Living; and as he is not to be buri'd whilst he is half alive, so he is as little to be imploy'd whilst he is half dead.

Parliaments are now grown to be quite other things than they were formerly.

In Ancient Times they were little more than Great Assizes; A Roll of Grievances; Magna Charta confirmed; Privileges of Holy Church preserved; so many Sacks of Wool given, and away.

Now there are Traps and Gins laid for the well-meaning Country-Gentleman; he is to grapple with the Cunning of Men in Town, which is not a little improv'd by being rewarded and encourag'd.

So that men whose good Intentions are not seconded and supported by some degree of Ability, are as much the more dangerous, as they are less criminal than Cunning Knaves. Their honest Mistakes, for want of distinguishing, either give a Countenance to, or at least lessen the Scandal of the injurious things that are done to the Publick: and with leave ask'd for so odd an expression, Their Innocent Guilt is as mischievous to the Laws and Liberties, as the most deliberate Malice of those that would destroy them.

There is an Abuse which daily increaseth, of sending such to Parliament, as are scarce old enough to be sent to the University.

I would not in this restrain the Definition of these Boys to the Age of Twenty One: If my Opinion might take place, I should wish that none might be chosen into the House of Commons under Thirty. . . .

* * * *

. . . But to come to the point in question; It is not without Precedent, that Practising-Lawyers have been excluded from serving in Parliament; and, without following those Patterns strictly, I cannot but think it reasonable, that whilst a Parliament sitteth, no Member of Parliament should plead at any Bar.

The reason of it is in many respects strong in it self, and is grown much stronger by the long sitting of Parliaments of late; but I will not dwell upon this: The matter now in question being concerning Lawyers being Elected, which I conceive should be done with so much circumspection, that probably it would not often happen.

If Lawyers have great Practice, that ought to take them up; if not, it is no great sign of their Ability; and at the same time giveth a suspicion, that they may be more liable to be tempted.

If it should be so in Fact, That no King ever wanted Judges to soften the stiffness of the Laws that were made, so as to make them suit better with the Reason of State; and the Convenience of the Government; it is no Injury now to suppose it possible for Lawyers in the House of Commons, so to behave themselves in the making of New Laws, as the better to make way for the having their Robes lined with Fur.

They are Men used to argue on both sides of a Question; And if ordinary Fees can inspire them with very good Reasons in a very ill Cause, that Faculty exercised in Parliaments, where it may be better encouraged, may prove very inconvenient to those that chuse them.

And therefore, without arraigning a Profession, that it would be scandalous for a man not to honour; one may, by a Suspicion, which is the more excusable when it is in the behalf of the People, imagine that the habit of taking Money for their Opinion, may create in some such a forgetfulness to distinguish, that they may take it for their Vote.

They are generally Men who by a laborious study hope to be advanced: They have it in their Eye as a Reward for the Toil they undergo.

This maketh them generally very slow, and ill disposed (let the Occasion never so much require it) to wrestle with that Soil where Preferment groweth.

Now if the Supposition be in its self not unreasonable, and that it should happen to be strengthened and confirm'd by Experience, it will be very unnecessary to say any more upon this Article, but leave it to the Electors to consider of it.

I cannot forbear to put in a Caveat against Men ty'd to a Party.

There must in every body be a Leaning to that sort of Men who profess some Principles, more than to others who go upon a different Foundation; but when a man is drowned in a Party, plunged in it beyond his depth, he runneth a great hazard of being upon ill terms with good Sense, or Morality, if not with both of them.

Such a man can hardly be called a Free-Agent, and for that reason is very unfit to be trusted with the Peoples Liberty, after he hath given up his own.

It is said, That in some part of the Indies they do so affect little Feet, that they keep them squeezed while they are Children, so that they stay at that small size after they are grown Men.

One may say something like this of Men lock'd up in a Party; They put their Thoughts into such a Narrow Mould, that they can never be enlarged nor released from their first Confinements.

Men in a Party have Liberty only for their Motto; in reality they are greater Slaves than any body else would care to make them.

A Party, even in times of Peace, (tho against the Original Contract, and the Bill of Rights) sets up and continues the exercise of Martial Law: Once inrolled, the Man that quitteth, if they had their will, would be hanged for a Deserter.

They communicate Anger to one another by Contagion: And it may be said, that if too much Light dazzleth the Eyesight, too much Heat doth not less weaken the Judgment.

Heat reigneth in the Fancy; and Reason, which is a colder Faculty of the Brain, taketh more time to be heard, than the other will allow.

The Heat of a Party is like the Burning of a Fever; and not a Natural Warmth, evenly distributed to give Life and Vigor.

There was a time indeed when Anger shew'd a good sign of Honesty; but that Evidence is very much weakned by Instances we have seen since the Days of Yore: And the Publick spirited Choler hath been thrown off within time of Memory, and lost almost all its Credit with some People, since they found what Governments thought fit to make their so doing a step to their preferment.

A strong blustring Wind seldom continues long in one Corner.

Some men knock loud only to be let in; the Bustle they make is animated by their private Interest. The outward Blaze only is for Religion and Liberty: The true lasting Fire, like that of the Vestals which never went out, is an eagerness to get somewhat for themselves.

A House of Commons composed of such Men, would be more properly so many Merchants incorporated in a Regular Company, to make their particular Adventures, than Men sent from the People to serve and represent them.

There are some Splenetick Gentlemen who confine their favourable Opinion within so narrow a compass, that they will not allow it to any man that was not hanged in the late Reigns.

Now by that rule one might expect they should rescue themselves from the disadvantage of being now alive; and by abdicating a World so little worthy of them, get a great Name to themselves, with the general satisfaction of all those they would leave behind them.

Amongst the many other ill consequences of a stated Party, it is none of the least, that it tempteth low and insignificant men to come upon the Stage, to expose themselves, and to spoil Business.

It turneth a Cypher into a Figure, such a one as it is: A man in a Party is able to make a noise, let it be never so empty a sound.

A weak man is easily blown out of his small senses, by being muster'd into a Party; he is flatter'd till he liketh himself so well, that he taketh it extremely ill if he hath not an Employment.

Nothing is more in fashion, than for men to desire good Places, and I doubt nothing is less so than to deserve them.

From Nobody to somebody is such a violent stride, that Nature, which hath the Negative Voice, will not give its Royal Assent to it: So that when insufficient Men aim at being in business, the worst of their Enemies might out of malice to them, pray for their Preferment.

There could be no end, if one did not stop till this Theme had no more matter to furnish. I will only say, Nothing is more evident, than that the Good of the Nation hath been sacrificed to the Animosities of the several Contending Parties; and without entring into the dispute which of them are more or less in the right, it is pretty sure, that whilst these Opposite Sets of Angry Men are playing at Foot-ball, they will break all the Windows, and do more hurt than their pretended Zeal for the Nation will ever make amends for.

In short, a man so engaged is retained before the people take him for their Council; he hath such a Reverse for his Party, that it is not adviseable for those who would chuse him, to depend upon his Professions. All Parties assuming such a Dispensing Power, that by their Sovereign Authority they cancel and dissolve any Act or Promise that they do not afterwards approve.

These things considered, those who will chuse such men deserve whatever followeth.

Pretenders to Exorbitant Merit in the late Revolution, are not without Objections against them, when they stand to serve in Parliament. It would not only be a low, but a Criminal kind of Envy, to deny a distinguishing Justice to Men who have been instrumental and active, when the Service of their Countrey requir'd it. But there ought to be Moderation in men's Claims, or else it is out of the Power of our poor Island to satisfy them. It is true, Service of all kinds is grown much dearer, like Labourer's Wages, which formerly occasioned several Statutes to regulate them.

But now the men who only carried Mortar to the Building, when it is finished, think they are ill dealt with if they are not made Master-Workmen.

They presently cry out, The Original Contract is broken, if their Merit is not rewarded, at their own Rate too.

Some will think there never ought to be an end of their Rewards; when indifferent Judges would perhaps be puzzled to find out the beginning of their Merit.

They bring in such large Bills, that they must be examin'd: Some bounds must be put to men's Pretensions; else the Nation, which is to pay the Reckoning, will every way think it a scurvy thing to be undone, whether it be by being over-run by our Enemies, or by the being exhausted by our Friends.

[*Extracts*]

A LETTER TO A MEMBER OF PARLIAMENT, SHEWING THAT A RESTRAINT ON THE PRESS IS INCONSISTENT WITH THE PROTESTANT RELIGION, AND DANGEROUS TO THE LIBERTIES OF THE NATION

THE Revolution of 1688 was the result of a temporary agreement between the leading Whigs and Tories, as the two major parties came to be called. Alone, the Whigs could not have brought about such a revolution. They had been divided between adherents of the Duke of Monmouth and those who supported William of Orange, with a fair number of republicans who would have preferred to revert to the Commonwealth—still a live (and, to some, inspiring) memory of a great opportunity that had been lost or thrown away.

After Monmouth's defeat and execution the hopes of the King's enemies centred mainly in William of Orange, son-in-law to James II, whose wife was a Protestant like himself, and next heir to the throne. The Tories found themselves unwillingly thrown into alliance with the Whigs when James revived the 'Declaration of Indulgence' by which his brother had twice attempted to override the religious persecution which was an article of faith with Tories and the Church of England. Charles II had withdrawn under pressure, but James, more stupid and stubborn than his brother, proceeded to prosecute seven Anglican bishops who refused to read the Declaration and signed a protest against it. In spite of the usual picked judge and packed jury, the Bishops were acquitted by a court that had more reason to fear the anger of the country than the threats of the king and his adviser—Judge Jeffries, who was now Lord Chancellor.

We have already noticed the paradox of the Stuarts, who first lost a throne partly on account of the religious intolerance embodied in their rule, and after the Restoration tried in vain to introduce toleration. When one considers the many misdeeds of the later Stuarts, it is certainly odd that nothing made them more unpopular than the little good they attempted to do. Their policy, extended to Ireland, re-established for awhile the position of the Catholic majority, and so endeared these later Stuarts to the Irish people that for years the Jacobite cause was to be the rallying point of Irish nationalism. But in England seven men who stood by persecution, and refused to implement a policy of religious toleration, became the heroes of the country. The trial of the seven bishops was the most important of the events which caused the Tories, solidly High-Anglican, to drop their policy of 'passive obedience' and intrigue with the Whigs against the King.

The position of the Whig leaders was clear. Historically they were the enemies of Stuart despotism and of the Catholic Church, in whose interest the Declaration of Indulgence had been issued. They had suffered considerably under the increasingly lawless reigns of Charles II and his brother. But the Declaration of Indulgence, like those of the previous reign, was artfully devised to include all Dissenters and win their support for the king in a measure so beneficial to themselves. As the Dissenting interest stood behind these Whig leaders, and the Dissenters were a large body numerically (though unrepresented in Parliament, owing to the intolerant laws) there appeared to be some danger of a split between the Dissenters and the 'moderate' Churchmen. It was at this time that Lord Halifax, whose work we have already considered, addressed one of his most famous pamphlets to the Dissenters, arguing that the Declaration was made in the interests of Popery, and that with patience the Dissenters would obtain redress from their grievances in the next reign—a curiously insubstantial offer, for which Halifax was quite unable to give the slightest security except that the heir apparent was a Protestant.

The Dissenters, however, being even more intent on persecuting Catholics than on obtaining freedom from persecution themselves, held with the Whigs. Temporary union between Whigs and Tories secured an overwhelming majority against the king; and when a son was born to the Queen a united nation was ready to act. A male heir to James meant that the claim of his daughter Mary was no longer valid. She and her Dutch husband therefore became the focus of a revolutionary movement, into which the Tories were drawn; for the alternatives were either to accept the leadership of William and Mary, or to allow James to consolidate his position and leave behind him a successor brought up as a Catholic. The Tories in 1688 were perhaps the most unwilling revolutionaries the world has ever known; but fate pushed them into that position, and the result was the flight of James II (interpreted as an 'abdication' to satisfy royalist consciences) followed by the joint enthronement of William III and Mary. Even the story that the child—the 'Old Pretender' of later years—was smuggled in a warming pan into the Queen's bed-chamber had to be exploited in order to satisfy Tory consistency.

Such was the background to the position when the anonymous pamphlet, extracts from which follow, came to be written in 1698. Ten years had passed since the Revolution. Protestantism had been 'secured' according to the politico-religious theories of the time. The prospects offered by Halifax to the Dissenters *had proved to be partially justified, for a very limited toleration was granted them; but—what was equally, or more, important in their eyes—the Catholics were not included in this toleration policy. The Dissenters, however, were still officially excluded from all public offices and from Parliament.*

Ten years after the Revolution the party system in politics, as we know it to-day, had begun to 'crystallize', with responsible governments (dependent upon Parliamentary majorities) and with all the abuses already noted by Halifax. In 1696 a Whig majority had refused to sanction William's efforts to censor the press, and it was the revival of this controversy, which had once evoked Milton's powerful plea, that occasioned the Letter to a Member of Parliament.

Backing the demand for censorship was the Church of England, still attempting to secure its position and increase its power by persecuting its opponents. But the attack on this policy is made here from a standpoint of which there had been little evidence in the past. The writer does not state his case as a sectarian, concerned with furthering a particular religious cause, but rationally, as a believer in liberty. We have already seen hints of such a view, though sometimes of doubtful sincerity. In this pamphlet of 1698 it rings out clearly again with the confidence that the future is on the side of the writer. He lashes the Anglicans with the taunt of being no better than the Papists whom they condemn, and using the very methods employed by the Catholic Church to secure conformity. He belongs in spirit to the later eighteenth century—rational and cultured, the type of man to whom Voltaire and Rousseau were to make so much appeal in the days before the French Revolution. But he is concerned with an issue which had ceased to worry the writers of that later period—the last efforts of the Anglican Church to control the press. The persecution of writers continued in England, but in political interests which were only incidentally 'religious' in certain instances.

No modern edition exists of this interesting pamphlet.

A LETTER TO A MEMBER OF PARLIAMENT, SHEWING THAT A RESTRAINT ON THE PRESS IS INCONSISTENT WITH THE PROTESTANT RELIGION, AND DANGEROUS TO THE LIBERTIES OF THE NATION

Anon.

. . . . There's no medium between Mens judging for themselves, and giving up their Judgments to others. If the first be their Duty, the Press ought not to be restrained, because it debars them from seeing those Allegations by which they are to inform their Judgments. All the Arguments that are or can be urged for the regulating the Press, have no other Foundation than that of People's being liable to mistake, and subject to be imposed on by fallacious Arguments and specious Pretences: which instead of proving what they design, only shows the greatest Necessity for the freedom of the Press; for the more apt Men are to mistake and to be deceiv'd, the less reason there is for their relying on any one Party, but the more to examine with all care and diligence the Reasons on all sides, and consequently for the Press being open to all Parties, one as well as the other. So that those that are for allowing Men the liberty of judging for themselves (if any such can be for regulating the Press) are very unhappy in their Arguments, because they all make against themselves, and out of their own Mouths they are condemned.

But if Men are to give up their Reason to the Clergy, of whatsoever Denomination, there's nothing, I confess, more inconsistent with that blind Obedience than the Liberty of the Press, because it gives them an opportunity to see what can be said against that or any other Darling

Notion of the Priests; and then it's a great odds but that rational Creatures will be governed by their own Reason, and no longer endure the Clergy to be Lords of their Faith.

In fine, if it be unlawful to let the Press continue free, lest it furnish Men with the Reasons of one Party as well as the other, it must be as unlawful to examine those Reasons: for if the last be a Duty, the first cannot be unlawful, because it's only a Means to the last in providing those Reasons which Men are bound to try and examine; except an implicit Belief be a Duty, which must necessarily bring Men back again to Popery. For if it be now unlawful to examine the Reasons on all sides, for fear of having other Sentiments than those the Clergy approves, it was no less unlawful at the time of the Reformation, which was wholly built upon this freedom of examining the Opinions of the Priests, and rejecting them if they judged them false. This the brave Luther did singly and by himself in defiance of the whole Church, and this any Man now hath the same right to do: So that it's evident the Freedom or Restraint of the Press depends on this single Question, Whether we ought to be free, or Slaves in our Understandings? or, in other words, Protestants or Papists? If the first, there cannot be the least colour for leaving the Conduct of Religion so wholly to a few Priests, that nothing shall be published about it but what they think fit, than which nothing can favour more of a Popish, slavish, and prostitute Compliance.

What, Sir, could be more surprizing to that Honourable House, whereof you are a most worthy Member, than a Motion to this purpose; That because making of Laws is a thing of great Consequence, and Country Gentlemen are subject to mistake, that therefore the House ought to be regulated, by appointing a Licenser to judg what should be spoke in it? As ridiculous as such a Motion would be, I would willingly know why 'tis not as unaccountable to hinder a whole Nation the freedom of debating Matters of Religion, which (since they are not able, like their Representatives, to assemble in one Room) cannot well be done but by letting the Press be open to every one to publish his Reasons; which ought not to be denied, as long as every one in the Nation has as much a right, not only to judg for himself in religious, as any Legislators can have to judg for him in Civil Matters, but is as much obliged to use all possible means to inform his Judgment; and consequently there is as little reason to deny Liberty of debating in one Case as the other.

The Reformation is wholly owing to the Press: For tho there were several able Men who, before Printing was known, most vigorously opposed the growing Errors of the Western Church; yet all they could do was to little or no purpose, because they had no easy and ready way to communicate their thoughts to any great number: but no sooner was the Invention of Printing made useful, but a poor Monk who discovered at least the grosser Cheats of the Priesthood, was made capable of imparting those Notions, which drew almost a Moiety from the Romish Superstition, which lost ground every where, as the Press was either more or less free. Therefore it was not strange that the Popish Clergy, since they could not confound the Art of Printing, should endeavour to turn it to their own Advantage, not only by hindring any new Book from being printed, but by expunging out of old ones whatever did not serve their turn: and herein they acted consistent with their Principles, which allows no Liberty of examining, and consequently denies all Freedom of the Press, which of all things does engage Men the most to do it. But what Pretence can the Protestants have for restraining it, who as they owe their Religion to its Liberty, so they cannot hinder it without destroying that Religion which has no other Foundation than that of every ones having a Right to examine those Reasons that are for or against any Opinion, in order to make a true and impartial Judgment? which can never be justified, if it be unlawful to permit the Press to be open for all Men to propose their Reasons to one another in order to their examining them.

And it cannot be denied, but that the Protestant Clergy, who are as ambitious for the most part as the Papists themselves to impose on the Consciences of the People, have by Persecution, Restraint of the Press, and other such methods, given the Papists (who have scarce any thing to plead for themselves but the Practice of their Adversaries) too just an occasion to insult them, who are (they say) no other than a pack of Hypocrites, in doing the very same things they so loudly condemn, and that it's little less than a Demonstration, that the Principles by which they pretend to justify their Separation, are very absurd, since they are forced to act contrary to them in every point. And what was it in truth but these shameful Practices, that put a stop to the Reformation, which at first, like a mighty Torrent, overwhelmed all that oppos'd it, but has ever since gone back both in esteem and interest, and at last, if Men do not change their conduct, will be quite lost? For how can it be otherwise, since that method (Protestantism and Popery being so opposite) that preserves the one, must necessarily destroy the other?

The taking a contrary method not only hinder'd the farther spreading of the Reformation, but was the cause that where it did prevail it was no more perfect: for tho the Reformers deserve just Commendation for what they did, yet being bred up in so much Ignorance and

FACTION DISPLAY'D

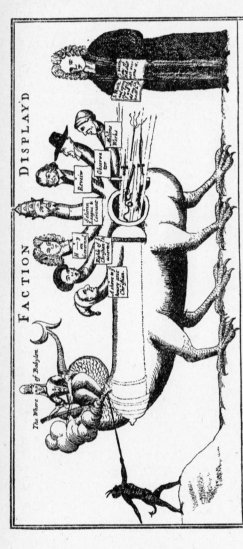

The Whore of Babylon

If e'er I did project a useful print, —
I've hit it now, or els the Deel is in't: —
Was e'er a fouer peice brought from the mint. —
Here's Pop'ry plac'd Infalibly ith' middle. —
And Six Scismaticks Dancing to the Fiddle: —
But who they represent, You'l say's, a Riddle: —
Yet view them near, and You, without a glass, —
May by the ears of me, see he's an Ass; —
And, by the others Fizz, 'tappears as plain, —
What they intend, and that they've all one aim: —

But truth's its own best Shield, and Innocence, —
Without a Barrier, is its own Defence; —
Nor can Fanatick Cannon drive it hence; —
Tho Pr——s Load it deep with powder, —
And In——s Ram on, to Bounce the Louder —
Nay, tho' the An——s, with chain-Shot, —
Do over load it, while the Cole's kept hot, —
By the Fanatick Champion at Its tayle, —
Not they, nor all their Black-guard, shall prevail.
But if they'll Try th' experiment e'en let 'em, —
The Cannon fir'd, will Burst, and so o'erset 'em. —

Faction Display'd

Superstition, they could not remove those vast loads of Corruptions which had been so long a gathering. But if those that succeeded them had taken the same liberty in examining theirs as they did their Predecessors Opinions, it's impossible but that time must have discover'd the Truth, and made them agree at least in all matters of moment. But instead of this, they became as guilty of a blind Obedience as the Papists; and it was a sufficient proof of any thing amongst the different Sects, if Luther, Calvin, Church of England, said so: nothing more common than that I submit all to Mother Church, and such like Phrases; which that Men should effectually do, there were Penal Laws enacted to force them, and no Printing or Preaching allow'd to those that durst see farther than the first Reformers (whose Eyes at the best were but half open, tho they saw very well for those times of Darkness, and in respect of the Papists who may justly be reckoned to be quite blind) the consequence of which was, that the Differences between the several Sects were widened, and they all run daily farther and farther into Uncharitableness, Ignorance, Superstition, and Fanaticism.

Whosoever observes with what Zeal our Divines condemn the Popish Clergy for not suffering their Laity to read Protestant Authors, would hardly think it possible for them to be so disingenuous as to appoint some spritual Dragons to watch the Press, lest any thing should steal from thence that's not for their turn. . . .

. . . And have not the Protestant Clergy (from whom one ought to expect better things) taken the same method to make People blindly submit to their Determinations? Nay, have they not outdone the Popish Clergy, in wresting the Holy Writ to destroy the English Constitution, and enslave the Nation, and in preaching up the Doctrine of Absolute Obedience, than which nothing can be more inconsistent with the goodness of God, and the happiness of Humane Societies, as knowing the only way to secure Tyranny in the Church was to get it establish'd in the State? So that if the Protestant Clergy do not keep the People in as vile a Subjection as the Popish do, tis not owing to their good will; and therefore none that have any value for Religion, or any kindness for their Liberties, will trust those that lie under such Temptation to pervert the Scripture, with the sole licensing Books of Religion. As we pray not to be led into Temptation, so we should avoid leading others into it, especially such as in all probability they cannot withstand.

The Discovery of Printing seems to have been design'd by Providence to free Men from that Tyranny of the Clergy they then groan'd under. And shall that which was intended by divine Goodness to deliver all from Sacerdotal Slavery, be made the means of bringing it on again? And if our Ancestors could not defend themselves from more than Egyptian Bondage, which the Pulpits brought on them, without the assistance of the Press, it's scarce possible that we should be able to secure our Liberties against both, when by the help of the latter the Clergy have got better Abilities, as well as Opportunities, to impose on the Understandings of the People: and when Men are once enslaved in their Understandings (which of all things ought to be most free) it's scarce possible to preserve any other Liberty.

The trusting not only the Pulpits but the Press in the hands of the Clergy, is causing the Blind to lead the Blind, because the generality of them are more likely to be guilty of a blind Obedience than the Laity, since they are obliged, as they value their Subsistence, right or wrong, to affect those Religious Tenets they find establish'd by Law; the truth of which they cannot any more be presum'd to have impartially examin'd, than a mercenary Soldier the Justice of the Cause he is engag'd in; being sent by their Friends to the Universities not to try the establish'd Religion, whether 'tis right or wrong, but to profess it as a Trade they are to earn their bread by: and lest they should examine it, they are, even before they are capable, shackled with early Oaths and Subscriptions. Which is the reason that the Priests are wondrous hot in every Country for the Opinions to which their Preferments are annexed; in one place fierce Calvinists, in another violent Lutherans, in a third bigotted Papists; which could not so universally happen, did they in the least examine those Opinions they are engag'd to profess. And therefore there can be no reason to trust the Press in hands of men so biass'd and prejudic'd, who cannot but be highly affronted to see the Laity do, what they durst not, judg for themselves, and not be blindly guided by them, who (poor men) are not trusted to guide themselves. Yet for all this extraordinary precaution to keep the Clergy right and tight, and the great disproportion of numbers between the Laity and them, 'tis evident that almost all the Errors and wrong Notions in Religion have had their rise and chief Support from them. So that upon the whole, if the Press should be trusted with any, it ought to be with Lay-men, who have no Powers, Prerogatives, or Privileges to gain by perverting of Scripture, since they pretend to none but what they receive from the Society. Tho I cannot but presume that our Legislators, were there no other reason, yet out of respect to the Clergy, would not enact such a Law as supposeth the greatest and most learned of them not fit to be trusted with the printing but a Half-sheet in Religion without consent of a Lay Licenser, who is to have an arbitrary Power over their Works.

[*Extracts*]

A NEW TEST OF THE CHURCH
OF ENGLAND'S HONESTY
A SERIOUS ENQUIRY
ROYAL RELIGION

(EXTRACTS FROM THREE PAMPHLETS BY DANIEL DEFOE)

IT is not for any literary merit that we include extracts from three pamphlets by Defoe. The author of Robinson Crusoe *could tell a good story, and he must have been one of the most prolific writers of all time; but he is singularly lacking in the brilliant qualities which made so many writers of his period perennially famous. The polished style which we have seen in Halifax, the wit which we shall notice again in Swift and Arbuthnot, were things unknown to Defoe. He 'bashed on regardless' of their contempt, which indeed he could well afford to do, for he was the first of a long line of best sellers. Defoe, in fact, marks the entry into politics and literature of the successful Low-Brow, an event claiming our closest attention.*

Scribblers itch (to paraphrase an old Latin tag) when the times are scabby. Defoe felt that itch. He had to be writing about everything that was topical— even his Crusoe was a quick exploitation of recent news. But above all he had to write about the grievances of the urban middle-class, which included everything from the 'servant problem' (on which he was quite incredibly reactionary) to the treatment of Dissenters. Since Dissent flourished among the middle-class trades- men, his views on this subject were 'ahead of the times', but popular among his own readers.

Most famous of Defoe's political pamphlets was his Shortest Way with Dissenters. *It owes its reputation really to its literary inferiority, for it was so crude and laboured that the Tories took it seriously, and hailed it at first as a literal expression of their own opinions. No one would ever have taken Swift's* Modest Proposal, *published later in this volume, as a serious advocacy of cannibalism. But Defoe's pedestrian style never hinted at satire; and so his* Shortest Way *had the distinction of first deceiving his enemies and then arousing their anger when the mistake was discovered. It landed the author in jail, from which he only emerged by leaving behind most of the principles he may once have* had and becoming the pensioner of Robert Harley, the great leader of the moderate Tories. In an age of transition, when the Tory party was slowly reconciling itself to Whig theories of the monarchy, Harley represented that section which already inclined rather to the House of Hanover than to the Pretender. It appeared to be the lesser evil, though it meant a further step (beyond the Revolution of 1688) from hereditary right in the monarchy. Defoe, who was a Dissenter, and therefore a Whig in so far as he was anything, could find some comfort in his new spiritual home, as a defender of the moderate Tories and still at liberty to attack the Jacobites.

The first two pamphlets with which we are here concerned deal with the 'Occasional Conformity' Bills, passed by the Commons in 1703 and 1704, but rejected by the Whig majority in the House of Lords. For some years past those Dissenters whose consciences were sufficiently malleable had been in the habit of 'conforming' with the practices of the Church of England once annually—a practice known as 'occasional conformity', which enabled such Dissenters to qualify for public offices, whilst it did not prevent them from being good Dissenters for the remaining 51 weeks in the year. The Occasional Conformity Bills were devised in order to prevent such chicanery, and eventually (in 1711) an Occasional Conformity Act was passed—an agreement being struck in the House of Lords that certain Whig peers would support an Occasional Conformity Bill if certain Tories would agree to oppose the peace policy at that time demanded by the Tory majority in the Commons. In this peace controversy Defoe also played a part, writing as industriously in favour of a Tory peace as he had once written in defence of a Whig war.

In these two pamphlets of 1704, opposing the Occasional Conformity Bill, Defoe was writing as a Whig and on good ground. He turned the tables effectively on the High Churchmen, who claimed (quite rightly) that occasional conformity was dishonest, and showed how dishonest was their own attitude. His personal target was Dr. Sacheverell, to whose 'Bloody flag and banner of defiance' the reader will find allusion. Sacheverell, by the sheer power of noise, became the popular hero of the High Church party, and was as appropriate an opponent for Defoe as Steele and Addison were for Swift and Arbuthnot.

These three pamphlets are selected from Defoe's work as some of his best written, though not his best known, political writings. In his discussions of occasional conformity the reader may notice Defoe's view that the Dissenting interest was adequately protected by a government of 'moderate men' (Whig Low Churchmen) and his apparently strange disclaimer of any desire that political rights should be granted to the Dissenters themselves. This shows indeed a great descent from the days when Presbyterians and Independents had fought for the control of the country. But in a later note we shall examine more fully the decline of the Dissenters as a political force, and observe how the settlement of 1714 did, *in fact, give the Dissenters exactly what Defoe was asking—50 years of Whig supremacy, government by Low Churchmen, and permanent freedom of worship without, for many years to come, those political rights which Defoe regarded as beyond his demand.*

Royal Religion *(1710) is more lively than most of Defoe's work—as far as this extract takes us. The full title, however, continues with the words: 'Being Some Enquiry after the Piety of Princes, with Remarks on a Book entitled, A Form of Prayers us'd by King William'. The latter part of the tract, indicated in this sub-title, is concerned with the piety of William III, in which Defoe professed to believe. He may have been sincere, and so (even more probably) may King William; but Defoe's defence of the royal hero of 1688 relapses into the usual dead level of platitude common to such apologies, and even more common to Defoe's writings, from which the first part of the pamphlet (reproduced here) is remarkably free. The reference to 'D——' is puzzling, as it clearly signifies England, and the remarks which follow have to do with Charles I. The initial is beyond our powers to explain.*

All three of these Defoe pamphlets have been out of print since the eighteenth century. They were all published anonymously, and it is amusing to observe the way in which Defoe refers to his own acknowledged writings as though they were by another person (e.g. The Shortest Way*). For nonsense on royal religion the reader is referred to the note preceding* An Harborowe *(ref. to the astonishing 'Protestantism' of a Moslem Emir) on page 28. In the reference to Charles I 'A.B.L.' is, of course, Archibshop Laud. The* Eikon Basilike *(once believed to have been a forgery—as Defoe evidently assumes) is now accepted as an authentic work by Charles, the prayer to which Defoe alludes (lifted from Sidney's* Arcadia*) having been inserted after the original edition. An attempt was even made to prove that this was done at the instigation of Milton and Bradshaw, to discredit the book; but this is without a shadow of reliable evidence.*

A NEW TEST
OF THE CHURCH OF ENGLAND'S HONESTY

By Daniel Defoe

. . . I have the just Satyr on the Modesty and Good Manners of those Clergy-Men, who have both Preach'd and Printed against the Morality of what the Parliament thought reasonable to pass into a Law, and the Queen has thought fit to give her Word to continue.

The scandalous Terms they have been pleased to bestow upon the Act of Toleration, have been just so many Satyrs upon the Queen's promise to Maintain it; And the same Breath that has shewn their Want of Charity to the Act of Toleration, has shewn their want of Manners to their Sovereign.

This the famous Mr. Sa—rel calls, Complimenting a People into our Church and Government, who are sworn Enemies to Both; and at no less an Expence, than the hazarding our Eternal Safety and Preservation, our Ancient Faith, Constitution and Form of Worship. Political Union, Page 59. If the Reverend Author would have us think he means any thing but a Reproaching the Government with Tolerating the Dissenters, and the Queen with promising to continue it, let him further Explain it: For, as it stands, 'tis too plain to bear any other Comment.

When he tells us, Every Man that wishes the Welfare of the Church, ought to hang out a Bloody Flag, and Banner of Defiance against the Dissenters, as open and avow'd Enemies to its Communion, Page 59. What can any Man suppose he means, but the Shortest Way? What's the difference between Mr. Sa—rel's Bloody Flag, and de Foe's Gallows and Galleys? Only, that one is an Oxford Modern Dialect, and the other put into downright plain English: One is a Church Phrase, and the other a City Comment.

Now, pray, Gentlemen, where's the Incendiary all this while? Who is the Honest Party ? How can the Church answer this Language to the Great Judge of the World, who Commanded, that our Moderation should be known unto All?

'Tis most plain, That the Act of Toleration is a just Debt to the Capitulations of the late Revolution, due to the present Settlement and Peace of the Nation, claim'd of Right by the Dissenters, as the Conditions upon which they Embark'd in the Common Cause of Liberty with the Church, when both were Invaded in the former Reigns: And as the Queen's Majesty, and the Government, have thought fit to confirm this Truth, by adding the Royal Word to the Sanction of the Law; tho' it does not make it more a Law, yet 'tis an abundant Satisfaction to us, that Her Majesty is so fully convinc'd of its being the proper Right of her Subjects to Enjoy the Freedom of their Consciences, that she has taken all Opportunities to Assure them She will Preserve them in that Right.

Now, as this Toleration stands upon the Foundation of an Act of Parliament, and that Act of Parliament was the effect of the Agreement between the Church and the Dissenters, in their Memorial to the Prince of Orange, and produc'd as an Effect of his Declaration; It remains to enter a little into the History of the late Revolution, and examine how it came to be Express'd, either in the first Memorial to the Prince, or afterward in his Declaration.

The Depredations made upon the People's Liberties in the Reign of the late King James, were carried on with more Assurance than Ordinary, upon two Dependencies which the King's Party had flatter'd themselves into: Both which fail'd them, and the Consequence was their Ruine.

First, They had Cajol'd the Dissenters into an Acceptance of Liberty of Conscience, by the Dispensing Power of the King, without an Act of Parliament.

Secondly, They depended upon the Church-Doctrine of Passive Obedience and Non-Resistance, which had been push'd on to such a Height, and made so much the Distinguishing Mark of the Church, that the Clergy had interwoven it with her Essentials, and boasted of it in an Innumerable croud of Sermons and Pamphlets. This the Government thought had prepar'd the Church for all manner of Submissions.

Both these Pillars of Smoak vanishing, the Precipice of Destruction appear'd so near, that the King saw it Unavoidable, and therefore thought fit to take Sanctuary Abroad.

The Dissenters, tho' at first deceiv'd by the Blessing of Liberty, soon began to see they were upon a wrong Bottom, and began first to hesitate at the taking off the Penal Laws; not but that they would gladly have had them remov'd from themselves, but they were loth to lay open the Field to the Papists, against whom those Laws were made.

The Church, who by this time began to feel the Weight of the King's Hand, had been Dispossess'd of Magdalen College in Oxford, and saw an Ecclesiastical Commission erected, to which all the Clergy in the Nation were like to submit, their Glebes and Perquisites all in danger. At this they all took Fire; away fled the Chimerick Notion of Passive Obedience. Natural Right began to take place, and their Eyes to be open'd to their own Safety.

But least the Dissenters, who enjoy'd their Liberty under King James, and had never, or but very little, enjoy'd it from the Church, should refuse to Join with them; and least they should close with the King, and his Roman Catholick Friends, from whom they were sure of Liberty of Conscience; they attack them two Ways:

First, To possess them with a Belief, that the Liberty given them by King James was a Trojan Horse, a Snare to draw them in; and that the design was first to destroy the Church, and with Polyphemus's courtesie, reserve them to the last.

The Second Artifice was to tell them, That if they would open their Eyes, and shake Hands with their Protestant Brethren, they would unanimously join to Suppress Popery; and they should be assured of the same Liberty of Conscience from their Protestant Brethren, and with an Honester Design.

And 'tis here to be noted, That as now, in their Prosperity, their Pulpits are sounding with nothing but Cruisado's and Bloody Flags against the Dissenters, so then we were always wheel'd with Charity and Tenderness for one another: Generous Principles forgetting and forgiving former Grudges, laying aside Ancient Quarrels, and the like.

The Dissenters, willing to embrace any Opportunity to weaken the Power of Popery, and more willing to enjoy even their Liberty, on a Treaty with their Friends, than as the Gift of their Enemies, fall in with the Church-men upon their own Terms; and Unanimously concur in the Memorial presented to the Prince of Orange, Inviting him to come and Rescue them from Popery and Arbitrary Power. In this Memorial, 'tis particularly and expresly stipulated, That a due Liberty of Conscience be granted to Protestant Dissenters: And accordingly the Prince of Orange, at his coming over, Engages to settle this Liberty by Parliament; and on the Success of the Affair, and his coming to the Crown, he very honestly Perform'd it.

THE ARTICLE OF THE DECLARATION RUNS
IN THESE WORDS:

'*This Our Expedition is intended for no other Design, but—— And that so the Two Houses may Concur in the preparing such Laws as may Establish a good Agreement between the Church of England, and all Protestant Dissenters; as also for the Covering and Securing of all such who live Peaceably under the Government, as becomes good Subjects, from all Persecution upon the Account of their Religion.*

The Preamble also of the First Occasional Bill, tho' for private Reasons left out in the Second, Confirms the Divinity of the Thing:

'*Whereas Persecution of Tender Consciences is contrary to the Principles of the Christian Religion, and the Doctrine of the Church of England, &c.*

If then this Toleration be a League with the Dissenters; if it be the Contract between them and the Church of England; if it be the effect of a formal Treaty, and executed as a Branch of the late King William's Declaration; it ought to be kept Sacred. The Church-men can never break it without the blackest Mark of Dishonesty in the World; and as Intentional Guilt, in the Eyes of the Scripture, is the same with Actual, all those People who would willingly break such a League, are as Guilty of the Act, as if it were brought to pass.

Such are Knaves in the most Intense Degrees of Knavery. Never let such brand the French King with Breach of Honour, Disregard to his Word, with Infractions of Leagues and Treaties: For as no Treaty can be plainer than this, so no People ever did less to Forfeit the thing they enjoy'd.

Where then can the Church find room for her Honesty, while she shews her self desirous to break down the Contract and Capitulations of so famous a Treaty, and to Rob the Dissenters of their Native as well as Purchased Right.

Besides, there are unhappy Circumstances in this Case, which very much aggravate the Dishonesty of it: As, First, The Dissenters were sure of their Liberty under King James; they had not only the security of his Word, but it was really his Interest to continue it to them. And in the Sense of this, the Church-Party cajoles and wheedles them to quit the faith of the King, though back'd with his own Interest, and to join with them, on the Promise of making an equal or a more large Concession of Liberty, and to confirm it by Law. Now, to bring them off from a Privilege they were sure of, and to bring them to Join with what they were not sure of, any farther than by the Word of the Party, to execute the Conditions of the Bargain or League; and after this, without any Provocation, or any thing done to Forfeit the Privilege, to attempt to take it away again: This is the Vilest, the most Dishonest, Unjust, Knavish Thing can possibly be! And no Church in the World can be Guilty of a worse. They who can do this, ought never to make any further Pretence to Honesty, or to Principle; nor never to blame their Neighbours with Breach of Faith.

No wonder Men of so little Honesty as this, can Preach up a Doctrine to Day, and Preach it down to Morrow. No wonder such Men can be for Passive Obedience one day, and Abjure their Prince the next. I am free to say, That the Premises consider'd, and no Man can prove them Untrue, there is not a Man in the Church of England, who can so much as wish the Toleration to be Repeal'd, but ought to blush at his own Knavery, and make no more Pretences to the Title of an Honest Man.

The Second Article of the Church's Honesty respects the Matter of their Reproaching the Dissenters about Schism, Separation, Occasional Communion, and the like.

In this, 'tis plain to me, they act a Part, a meer Farce, and only carry on the [sic] the Politick Jest, for the Interest of the Party; to run down the Dissenters with a Full Cry, for being Dissenters, and yet, at the same time, would not have them Conform.

I think a few Arguments may suffice to prove, that this Exalted Church, this High-flying Party, as they are fond of being call'd, cannot be chargeable with any Symptoms of a desire to Convert the Dissenters, to bring them over, or draw them to the Church. My Reasons are these:

First, They either Industriously avoid, or very Weakly manage all Argument, Conference, or Dispute; in order either to Defend the Causes in Controversie, or Convince the Gain-saying Dissenter. But all the Essays of this Nature, which the World has lately seen, amount to nothing but Raillery and Billinsgate, and that without Reason or Justice; Charging all the Crimes of the Ages past, to the Accompt of the Present Dissenters, and Loading them with the Iniquity of their Forefathers, as if 'twas a Crime to be born of a Soldier, because that Soldier fought against the King: Nor considering, that the Sons of those Soldiers, who then fought for their King, have since that fought against the Son of that King, and Treated him as bad if not worse than they did his Father.

This is the Dishonestest Thing in the World, and I wonder with what Face, and how free from Blushes, Dr. S—— could in a Railing Sermon say, 'the Dissenters were not fit to be suffer'd in Church or State, because they were the Spawn of Rebels, and a Viprous Brood of King-killers and Commonwealthsmen; when the Doctor's own Father was both a Round-head in the Army, and an Independant in the Pulpit.

If 'tis a Crime in the Dissenters, that their Fathers were Rebels; why then, Gentlemen, all those Sons of Rebels, who degenerating from their Fathers have since come into your Church, ought to be turn'd out again, and cast off as the Spawn of King-killers and Commonwealths men: For their own Merit cannot alter the Taint of Blood, which is charg'd upon them from their Fathers.

And if we deserve to be thus treated, because our Fathers took up Arms against their King; of how much Sorer Punishment should they be thought worthy, whose Fathers, being Men of Loyalty and Zeal, Died Fighting for their King, and Defending him against his People? And these their Degenerate Children. have follow'd the very Steps of our Rebellious Ancestors; and, in Spite of the Loyal Blood, which 'twas hop'd might be Infus'd into their Veins by Generation, have taken up Arms against their Lawful Sovereign, and Abjur'd his Posterity.

Not that I am of the Opinion what was done was Unlawful in it self, because the Invasion of Right, Law, and Liberty, by the Unhappy Councils of the late betray'd King went before: But where was the Honesty of the Church of England? Either 'twas a baseness that can never be Justify'd, to Reproach Dissenters with it, or a double Crime in them to put it in Practice themselves.

Where now is your Honesty, Gentlemen? The World would be glad to see you defend it in this Article: And if you can't, 'tis hop'd, since we are no more rebels than your selves, you will forbear giving us any farther Occasion to Recriminate.

As now the Church has left off Argument, and fallen to Raillery, how can any Man say they desire the Conversion of the Dissenters? And if they neither Endeavour nor Desire the Conversion of the Dissenters, how can they Reproach them with their Dissent, and blame them for what they neither wish nor desire them to alter? Where's the Honesty of Reproaching a Dissenter with making a Breach in the Church, and yet neither Wishing, nor Endeavouring, nor, indeed, being Willing, he should return, and make it up?

Secondly, Your not desiring the Return of the Dissenters to the Church, appears in the Publick Aversion you have declar'd on all Occasions to the Men of Temper and Moderation, who are in the Church already: These are represented to be worse than Phanaticks, Secret Enemies Nurs'd in the Bowels of their Mother which they betray, Dissenters in Masquerade. Now 'tis plain you cannot desire the Dissenters should all Conform to the Church, unless you are all beside your Selves, and have, together with your Honesty, lost your Understanding, unless you have forgot your own Names, are fitter for Bedlam than the Pulpit, and to be taken from the Altar, and sent to an Hospital. For,

1. If all the Dissenters in England should, by some special and miraculous Work of Providence, Conform to the Church, and all this Schism, as you call it, should cease at once; I would be glad to have an Answer from any, or all the Divines of our Church Rampart, What sort of Church-men would they be? Would they Join with you, the Men of the Steeple, or with the Moderate Party? In short, Would they be High Church-men, or Low Church-men?

I believe all Men will answer Negatively, Not of the last? If so, then let any Man but Examine your Character of a Low Church-man, the general Opinion all your Party has, of what we call a Moderate Church-man, and judge whether you would be one Jot the better pleas'd with them. 'Twould be endless to name the Numerous Authors, the Pamphlets, the Sermons, the Discourses of the present Ruling Party of the Church of England; and to set down the Reasons given to prove these Low Moderate Church-men to be worse than Presbyterians, to be Traitors to their Friends, Betrayers of the Church, and Enemies to her Peace.

No Man then can believe the Church-men so mad as to wish to have Us Conform, and so become worse Enemies to them than we were before. 'Tis plain, they covet not our Conversion as Christians, our Conforming as Members of the Church, unless we would Conform too, as Members of a Party. A politick Conversion they might possibly wish for; expecting, that as a Renegado is a worse Patron than a Turk; so if we espous'd their Quarrel as a Party, they might the easier run down the Moderate Church-men. But as to a Religious Conversion, it is impossible they should desire it, without concurring in the destruction of themselves, as a Party, and consequently be forsaken of their Senses.

2. If all the Dissenters in England should Conform to the Church, and as 'tis most certain they would in such a Case Join with the Moderate Church Party, the High Church-party would be immediately supprest, blown up, and disperst; the Ministers of the Church would have no more room to call upon us in the Language of Honest Jehu, and say, Come see our Zeal for the Lord: Sa———ell's Bloody Flag and Banner of Defiance would be taken down; Peace, Charity, and Christian Moderation, Things which these Gentlemen fear and hate, would flourish and spread through the whole Nation.

'Tis impossible the present Church of England, Distinguish'd as before, can without Suspicion of Lunacy, wish or desire the Annexing all the Dissenters to the Church; for it would certainly be their Ruine.

What then is the Meaning of all this Clamour at the Dissenters? What is to be done with us, Gentlemen, if we must neither Conform nor Dissent, and your Bloody Flag and Banner of Defiance is spread against us? What is to be done? Truly, there is nothing we can see before us but the Shortest Way. Alas, Poor De Foe! what hast thou been doing, and for what hast thou suffer'd? When all things are Examin'd. either these Gentlemen are guilty of the Vilest Dishonesty, are all Cheats and Hpyocrites [*sic,*] or else the Shortest Way is at the Bottom, and Mr. De Foe has done them no Wrong; and if he has done them none, some body has done him a great deal.

But how will our Church of England come off with the Honesty of these Proceedings? How will they defend their Morals, to fix their Arguments of Schism upon a Party of Men they would not have comply?

And why is this Great Out-cry rais'd against the Dissenters for their Occasional Communion? 'Tis indeed a most evident Proof of what has been said. These Gentlemen are Exasperated at it, as it lets the Dissenters into the Publick Exercise of the Government, and joins them to the Low Church-men; and what a late Reverend Clergy-man, and no less a State-sman [*sic,*] said of this Case: 'The Sacramental Test was not Contriv'd in order to Rejoin the Whigs to the Church, but to keep them out of the State; like the Gallows, (a blessed Comparison!) which was not Erected, in the Sense of the Law, to Hang Men, but really to keep them from being Hang'd.

'Tis a Thing needs no Demonstration: The Laws against the Dissenters were not properly made Laws against them, but against the Roman Catholicks. They who found it convenient to turn the Edge of them their way, did not do it with a supposed Prospect, that those Laws would bring the Dissenters to the Church; but in Hopes, that they, being resolved not to comply, would be thereby kept out of the State.

That this is a known Truth, I appeal to a known Speech of the late Famous Member of Parliament for the City of London, who most vigorously oppos'd this Sacramental Test: For what, says he, is this Test made? To Convert us you cannot pretend, the Papists are the Pretence: But that is Expos'd, by refusing to Confine it to such; and if it be against the Dissenters, 'tis to Exclude them from their Birth-right, and Rob the Government of their Service.

Now that the Dissenters, by complying with this Test, have both defeated the End and Design of it, and also discover'd it, is plain from the Exceeding Clamour rais'd at them about it: For to what End do the Gentlemen of the Church of England clamour at our Occasional Conformity? They cannot allow, 'tis unlawful for us to conform, that would be to condemn themselves; as to our Dissenting again, that can be of no Damage to them: But the Business is, by thus conforming to the Communion of the Church, the Trick of this State Ceremony is defeated, the Trap is discover'd, the Snare is broken, and the Bird is escaped; the Dissenter lets himself into publick Employments, in the Cities and Corporations where he lives, from which they had Hopes, his Scruple of Conformity would have kept him out.

Upon the Discovery, the Church clamours and cries out Hypocrites! Pretenders to Religion! For God, or for Baal, and the like. No, Gentlemen, 'tis you are the Hypocrites, who make a Law with a Face of Religion; a Law which in its own Nature enjoins us to conform to the Church on such and such Occasions: And now you see we are willing to do it, cry out upon us for doing it. Is this your Honesty? If we Dissent, we are Schismaticks; if we conform, we are Hypocrites: Is this your Sincerity?

Let me say, Gentlemen, whether those who Occasionally conform are Hypocrites or no, is a dispute by it self; but you cannot but own your selves to be Hypocrites to the last Degree, who having made a Law, pretending to bring us to the Church, plainly now discover, 'twas only a Flam, to keep us out of the Service of our Country, on a Supposition that we would not comply.

If this be the Church of England's Honesty, for shame, Gentlemen, never charge the Dissenters with Hypocrisie in Occasional Conformity, 'till you reform this shameful Defection from your own Integrity, and only testifie your Repentance before God, and the World. And to me nothing seems plainer than the Dishonesty and unfair Dealings of those Gentlemen, who rail at the Dissenters for Occasional Conformity.

Sir H—— M—— in the Name of all the rest of our Church Authors, tell us, It cannot be safe to trust any Part of the publick Administration with Persons who do not conform to the National Church.

I cannot but wonder with what Face that Gentleman, who is a Member of Parliament, and an English Representative, could impose that upon the World, when he himself, and with him most of those furious Gentlemen, thought it safe to venture our whole Administration in the Hands of a Popish King.

Had those Gentlemen been honest, and us'd but the same Arguments with themselves they now use with us, they had never been against the Bill of Exclusion, which if they had pass'd, all this Revolution, this bloody and expensive War, and a thousand worse Mischiefs, had been prevented.

All the Blood of Essex, Russel, Sidney, and a Multitude more had been sav'd; and I wonder no Body ever put them in Mind of this before.

But what shall we now do for our Sister in the Day when she shall be spoken for? What shall we say for, and in behalf of, the Thousands of those honest Gentlemen, the Multitudes of Moderate Christians in the Church of England, whose Candor speaks them to be Gentlemen, and whose Charity speaks them to be Christians; who neither Envy, Despise, or Persecute their Dissenting Brethren, but receive them with Kindness, and judge them with Charity? This Charge must not, it cannot concern them.

These are the Genuine Church of England; These are the Foundation of her Character, and the Pillars of her very Being in these Nations, and are only blameable for the Easiness and Calmness with which they bear the Insolence of their Hair-brain'd Clergy. These are they who, however the Priests may fancy to impose upon them with Flourishes and Fictions when it comes to the Point, will hold fast both their Religion, and their Property, their Religious, and their civil Liberties; and suffer neither the Clergy to destroy one, nor their Kings to devour the other.

To these the Dissenters willingly give the Right-hand, and had rather the Government were in their Hands, than in their own. If we were to choose a King to govern us, all Parties would Vote for one of their Number.

These Gentlemen are the Nation's Security against Popery, Slavery, and all sorts of Tyranny, whether Ecclesiastick or Temporal: Of These, no part of this Book is to be understood; they are no Branch of the Family of the Furioso's, no kin to the Sons of Nimshi.

These are they who, when the hot Men, for want of Discretion at any time, put Governments into Confusion, and bring the Nation about their Ears, are fain to set all to rights again. To These we have all recourse in Time of Exigence; and These alone are the safety of all Governments in the World.

No wonder the High Church-men fly out at these Moderate Men; for Temper, Prudence and Moderation, are fatal to their Designs, and at last will most certainly ruin them; and the sense of this Truth, makes them hate a Moderate Conformist worse than a Dissenter.

How soon might we be all One Nation, One People; and if not all of One Mind in Religion, be united in Affection, in Interest, and in Government; were the spirit of Moderation, Charity and Peace in the Chair of the Church.

So far as the Authors of the present Discord widen the Breaches between the Church, and her Dissenting Brethren, so far they Embroil the Nation, Disturb the Peace, Encourage the Enemy, Dethrone the Queen, and Expose Religion.

But Blessed be God! Every step they take, they lessen themselves; they cannot set a Foot forward in this fatal Work, but it treads upon their Honesty: Their Morals sink, as their Malice rises; and while they throw Dirt at their Brethren, the Dissenters, it flies back in their own Faces, and reproaches them with the Hypocrisie they charge upon their Neighbours.

This Temper must be laid aside, if they will ever bring to pass the blessed Peace, Union and Harmony, which Her Majesty, and the late Glorious King William, has always prest us to.

How many Speeches has the Queen made, to Excite us all to Union and Love! And how little does all the Methods of this Party tend to it! What does Her Majesty mean by Peace and Union, but Peace and Union? The Words are not Equivocal, but Univocal: The Queen's Meaning, certainly gives the Lye to Sachevrel's Oxford Sermons, and let the World know, that Her Majesty can wish well to the Church, and yet not hang out the Bloody Flag of Defiance against the Dissenters.

No Man can say, that the People we have been talking of are Friends to this Peace and Union; nor can it ever be obtain'd, while Men of Moderation are branded with Principles of Fanaticism, and Betrayers of the Church.

When all is done, 'tis the Men of Moderation which are the Church of England, the Other are but Wolves in Sheeps Cloathing; they are but a Party of those who, having turn'd the World upside down, are come hither also, Acts 11. 'Tis the Men of Temper and Charity are the Church; and to convince the World, that when such have the Reigns of Government in their Hands, the Dissenters are always Quiet and Content. Let them tell us, for the last 60 Years, whenever the Dissenters disturb'd a Government that proceeded upon Legal and Moderate Principles; whenever they desir'd any thing Destructive to Government and Law; or whenever they discovered any Dislike, that the Power of Government should not be in the Church of England; or that they were Enemies to Monarchy.

If they will go back to 48, and provoke us to Recriminate, by telling us of Killing the Father; let us bring them back to 88, and tell them of

Deposing the Son, and sending him Abroad to beg his Bread, fighting against him at the Boyne, &c. Here's Rowland, there's Oliver: Let them come off of it if they can. The better way is to drop the Discourse of Both, and keep both their Loyalty, and their Temper within its Bounds, and forgetting Things past, join Hands in Obeying, Serving and Submitting to the present Power; where nothing is Imposed, nothing Extorted; but the Laws direct the Sovereign, and protect the Subject, being left by Both to their Free Course. Long may it so continue; and so long all wise Men, and all honest Men will be both Obedient and Satisfied, and longer they cannot.

And if the Peace and Union which the Queen has so graciously call'd upon the Nation to Practise, be not obtain'd; these are the Men that Obstruct it, as contrary to their Designs, and the constant Practise of their Lives.

[*Extract*]

A SERIOUS INQUIRY INTO THIS GRAND QUESTION; WHETHER A LAW TO PREVENT THE OCCASIONAL CONFORMITY OF DISSENTERS, WOULD NOT BE INCONSISTENT WITH THE ACT OF TOLERATION, AND A BREACH OF THE QUEEN'S PROMISE

By Daniel Defoe

THESE Sheets having been wrote during the late Agitation between the two Houses, relating to a Law against Occasional Conformity; upon the demise of that Law, had been buried in the Grave with it, had not the restless endeavours, both of the Press and the Pulpit, been set on foot to revive it.

The end of this Paper is not so much in hopes to reclaim a Party, whose Malice is a constant Spurr to their Heads against Dissenters; as to let the Ignorant, and Well-meaning among them, if any such are to be found, see a little what they are a doing.

As for the Dissenters, tho' perhaps they have not Power to prevent the Mischief, 'tis convenient to let the World know, upon what Foot their Enemies Act; and that tho' they may have the Misfortune to feel the Consequences, they may not pass for Fools too; but as their Enemies trample upon the Honour and Character of their Sovereign, they may let them see they know it.

A Worthy Author of a Penny-sheet, spread about very industriously, and Entitled, *Reasons for this Law*, would prove it ought to Pass, because of Her Majesty's Promises of Maintaining the Church, and Encouraging such as were most Zealous for Her Interest.

This I take to be a design of making Her Majesty's Promises clash one against another, which they may come off from, if they can.

It seems, That these Gentlemen mistook Her Majesty's Meaning, in the Promise she made of Encouraging the most Zealous Men of the Church of England; by supposing Her Majesty meant thereby, such whose Zeal run highest against the Dissenters: Whereas Her Majesty, by declaring Her self since, the great Promoter of Peace and Union among Her Subjects, and by Repeating to the Dissenters Her Resolution of Maintaining the Toleration, has told them plainly what she meant.

It looks a little strange, That the Gentlemen, who are so hot for this Law, should think the Dissenters so blind, as not to see the Toleration struck at, in its most Essential Parts; and, as if they would hoodwink them with the Vapour of the Ænigma, all the Pamphlets and Sermons at the same time, that they would stigmatize Occasional Conformity, as the Badge of a Hypocrite . . .

. . . If then the Fact be not sinful in it self (tho' I do not grant that neither) and if it be but a Very Few of the Dissenters practis'd it: Pray, Gentlemen of the Pulpit, Where is your Honesty, your Justice, your Charity, to punish a Party for the Misdoings of a Few?

The Dissenters in England are not a Body, neither in a Politick, or any other Capacity; if they were, the whole might be answerable for the Parts, as having Power to call them to Account. How then are the Innocent Many to be Censur'd for the Guilty Few? And why then should your Furious Champions condemn them all in Print, to lose their Birth-Right, as English Men; because some among them do what you say they shou'd not do?

And why, Gentlemen, all this stir about Places! When 'tis but a very short while since some of your most Eminent Friends branded all People in Places, as Enemies to the Liberties of England, and under Temptations to betray us; People not fit to be trusted in the Legislature, Bond slaves to Arbitrary Power, perfectly subjected to Court Practices, and Enemies to the Safety of a Free Nation, *Væ vobis Hypocritæ!* We Dissenting Hypocrites have liv'd to see you Church Hypocrites possessing the Places and Pensions of those you rail'd at, and the Discourses of a Self-denying Ordinance are quite Dropt and Forgotten: Nay, so eager to engross all to themselves, that now Court Party and Country Party are laid aside, the Matter is come about, and the True-Born English Man appears in the right.

> *That all the Strife is plainly to be seen,*
> *To get some Men put out, and some put in.*

This is very hard, the Church-men can preach up Passive Obedience one Year, and take up Arms against their Prince the next; swear an Absolute Allegiance to the King and his Heirs to Day, and swear to a New Government to Morrow; Preach and Print against Schismaticks and Dissenters, and* King James, and seperate from their own Church, and set up private Schismatical Conventicles under King William.

Their States-men cry down Courtiers, and Pensioners set up for Patriots, and scorn Places as things Fatal to Liberty under King William, and strive to engross all the Places they can get under Queen Ann, and cry up Laws to keep all but themselves out: They can pretend, that no Man having an Office under the King, shall sit in the House of Commons under King William, and yet are willing both to sit in the House, and enjoy the principal Offices in the Kingdom under Queen Ann; and yet these are the People who cry out upon Two Millions of their Brethren as Hypocrites, because less than a Thousandth part of them have been guilty of Occasional Conformity.

What Justice, what Equity, can there be in this way of Dealing with the Dissenters? Nothing can justifie it that I know, but their being a People fit to be extirpated from the Face of the Earth: And as some have very piously mov'd it, you have nothing more to do, but to set about it the shortest Way.

'Tis hardly worth while to mention the unusual Exorbitance of our Church Mob, against their Brethren the Dissenters. Some are so hot, they can't stay till this Bill may be past into a Law, and other Opportunities may happen further to suppress them. But they are for depriving them of their Right of Voting for Parliament Men as Freeholders; to which I wou'd add, Let them go on, and take away their Freeholds too, a thing every jot as just, and then the Business wou'd be over. . . .

[*Extracts*]

* Misprint for 'under'?

ROYAL RELIGION: BEING SOME ENQUIRY AFTER THE PIETY OF PRINCES

By Daniel Defoe

Royal-religion! says the First Man that looks on the Book, what d'ye mean by that? Did ever Man write a Book on so empty a Subject? This is like my Lord Rochester's Poem upon Nothing, or the Niceties of Entity and Non-Entity. Royal-Religion! A Demonstration of a Vacuum in Nature, a Salamander in the Fire, Lawyers Honesty, Jews Charity, Turkish Humanity, a Brute's Abstinence, a Priest's Continence, or a Whore's Maidenhead.

Well Gentlemen, ha' Patience, while we make a little search after this Novelty: And since the Religion of Princes is under a little Scandal, bear with us a while, and we'll make Enquiry about it, perhaps we may find some Religion among Crown'd Heads; where we miss it, we'll let you know; and if we find it, we'll not fail to give you notice.

But why should any Man busie himself to no purpose? Says another Learned Objector. Name me one King that ever had any Religion in him, I'll name you Forty that never troubl'd their Heads about God or Devil; never liv'd as if there was either, or thought it worth while to enquire whether there was or no.

It may be so, Gentlemen; but don't discourage a Body in the Enquiry. Neither is that an Argument; for, if there be one Good Man in forty Kings, there's as many in proportion as there is of any Class of Men in the World; besides, there is not above one King to Five Millions of Subjects all over Europe, one with another, and if there be one Religious King in an Age, 'tis above a Proportion in the Account of Good and Bad; therefore, pray let us go on with the Enquiry, and if we can find out this One in Forty, if we can show you his Star in the East, we hope you will join with us to go and worship him.

But where shall we look for him? In what Quarter of the World shall we hear of him? Is there no Old Prophecy, to guide us in the Enquiry, Merlin, Nostradamus, Mother Shipton, Lilly, Gadbury, Partridge, and all the Soothsayers of the Age? Can his Character be found in none of the Calendars, or among the Strange and Wonderfuls of the Times? Let us enquire nicely, and who knows what may be the Consequence of a diligent Search.

Really, Gentlemen, after having ransack'd Europe for pious Kings, Men of Honesty and Principles, Men of Religion, wearing the Badge of Sovereignty upon their Heads, and the Stamp of Christian in their Hearts, having rummag'd History, and singl'd out a very few, I cannot but inform you who they are.

But before I come to them, I think 'tis needful to let you see how much fruitless Pains has been taken this way, and how much Labour lost; in short, to give you the Negatives where we found it not.

And, First; we came to Rome; Any body would ha' thought to ha' found Religion there; and tho' a Man with one Crown upon his Head, might be a Sinner, he that had three Crowns, who claim'd the Divine Succession, and the Mission of the Infallible Spirit, must needs be the Man; here we began to sing *Nunc Dimitis* with old Simeon, and design'd to call the Place Bethel, and to write over it, Surely the Lord is in this Place, and I knew it not.

But when we search'd into the Holy Juggle, and saw clearly the Sacred Fraud; how Interest govern'd all their Pretences, and what prodigious Cheats were conceal'd under the Pontif of St. Peter; when, with the Prophet Ezekiel, we were carry'd into the Inner Rooms, and visited the Chambers of Abomination; when, by the unbiass'd Eye of Reason and Reflexion; we entred into the Apartments of Darkness, and saw the Arcana of the Sanctified See, a sudden Light shone into the Place, and discovered this Golden Inscription, written on the Inside of the Sancta Casa of the Vatican,

Heu quantum prosuit hæc Fabula Christi!

Away we came; we had enough of the Search.

From thence we considered the Imperial Court, his Imperial Majesty's Piety, his Zeal in Religion, his Holy Life, his Bare-footed Processions, his Religious Observation of Treaties and Confederates, and the like, we concluded,

Hic jacet in Tumulo Religio Religiose.

But searching a little farther into the Treaties of Caschaw, and the sundry Capitulations with the poor Protestants of Hungaria, and finding among some Old Records of Count Teckley's, which were taken in the Castle of Mongatz, a sad and melancholy account of Bloody Massacres and Cruel Devastations committed on the Protestants, under the solemnest Treaties and Engagements, and repeated Oaths of Parties: And a Protestation made by Count [*illegible*] before his Death, that they found it safer to trust the Faith of the Turk than the Emperor, and a great deal of such Black Stuff as this: We concluded in the Words of the Angel, *Resurrexit, non est hic*.

We pass'd from hence into Poland; never did poor Enquirers meet with such Disappointments; here we found a new King, and a new Convert, both in one; they said, he had lately chang'd his Religion; but upon Enquiry, we found that a Mistake, for it was plainly prov'd he had none before: So it was concluded, he had newly embrac'd Religion, as such, and as might reasonably be expected from a Man newly become a Christian; we made no question but we should find a warm Zeal, a hearty Profession, and a Red-hot Christian; we found he went constantly to Mass, and said over his Aves and Paternosters most Religiously; was constantly at Vespers, and rose before Day to his Matins; and now we thought we had found Religion out: But all of a sudden his Saxon Troops began to march, and without so much as declaring War, without Quarrel, without Pretence, without the least Shadow of Honesty, he invaded Livonia, depe[n]ding upon the Minority of the King of Swedeland, and his being at the same time embarrassed with a War in Denmark.

We were a going to quit Poland upon this, when on a sudden we were call'd to look back to the Cardinal Primate, who being in the Interregnum the Sovereign of Poland, deserves our Notice; and being a Prince and a Priest, both together, sanctified in Life, and Sacred in Person, we had a wonderful Opinion of him; but hearing that he being a Roman Catholick Prelate, had join'd with a Heretick Prince to depose his Roman Catholick Master; it appear'd his Politick Interest had got Possession of his Religious; and so we laid him by as an Hermaphrodite in Religion, and made a Trip to Moscovy.

The Czar of Moscovy, we were told, was a Furious Christian, and we did not know but he might have something of this Divine Quality in him; but when we examined things, and found him executing two or three thousand People in a Day, putting whole Families to Death for the Offences of one of the Blood; we knew Religion too well, to look any longer for her in Tyranny and Barbarity, and so we found our Labour in vain there too.

The late Duke of Holstein, had been so Rakish with the Swede, and made such loud Clamours at the Dane, that we Despair'd of finding this Royal Religion in those parts; it had been entertain'd a great while by the Young King of Sweden's Father, Charles the Eleventh; but he being Dead, it fled from the Clime, for fear of being frozen to Death, before this young Hero was at Leisure for it.

We considered, France is a Kingdom, in which much of this Matter had been talk'd of: We examin'd the Crown'd Legend back to Henry the Third; he was a most Zealous Prince, and exceeding Pious; but the barbarous Murther of the Duke of Guise, blotted him quite out of our Roll.

Henry the Fourth, encourag'd us to find it in his Story; he having been a Champion for his Religion, and maintained a Bloody War for Seventeen Years, against almost all the Power of France and Spain; but when at last he was put to the Tryal, he shew'd the World, he fought for the Crown, and not for the Religion, for he Denied the last, to enjoy the first.

Lewis the Thirteenth, Gave us to understand, he had more Zeal than Religion; and at first view of his History, bid us not trouble our heads with it, for he was not the Man.

The present King of France, bids exceeding Fair, for the most Religious Prince in the World: If innumerable Reliques, which hang about every part of his Body, if alighting out of his Coach and Kneeling down in the Dirt, in the very Highway, while the Blessed Host is carried by, with Infinite *Te Deums* at Nostre-Dame; and thanking God for more Victories than ever he gave him, will distinguish a Monarch to be a Man of Religion, this is He.

What, tho' the Blood of Thousands of Towns and Villages, whose Inhabitants have been murthered in his Sight, are a Pretence for some People to lessen his Immortal Character; these are the Effects of War, which his Enemies have forced him to, by presuming to check the Current of his Conquests, and his just pursuit of Glory.

What, tho' 'tis pretended he has Unjustly Dispossess'd the Princes of Lorrain, and the Spaniard in Burgogne; what, tho' he invaded the Dutch in Seventy two, and over-run their whole Country, without Declaring War; what, tho' he Bombarded Genoa, and laid the most Glorious Palaces of the Senators in Ashes; all these are but necessary Corrections of those petty Neighbouring Princes, who justly deserv'd it for Disobeying the Commands of the Greatest Prince in the World.

What, tho' he has Dissolv'd the Edict of Nants, and Banish'd Three Hundred Thousand of his Protestant Subjects; this is but a farther Confirmation of his Steadiness and Zeal for the Church, and consequently of his being Master of Religion; and since no Faith is to be kept with Hereticks, who shall blame him for using his Protestant Subjects as he did, Zeal for Religion might move him to that: Besides, being an Absolute Monarch, and having the same Right to his People, as a Farmer has to his Cattel, shall any one ask him what he does with his own; if any one ask such a Foolish Question, 'tis a Sign they do not know what belongs to Arbitrary Power.

All these Things had never Diverted us from our fixing this Royal Quality with this Heroick King, had he not lately Disoblig'd us in breaking the Treaty of Partition, solemnly Made, Ratified and Exchang'd, and in seizing the Monarchy of Spain, which we can no way Reconcile to the Test of his most Illustrious Character.

The Duke of Savoy came next in Vew, for though he is not a King, he wou'd be one; and rather than not be call'd a King, is content with the empty Title, without a Kingdom, and be call'd King of Jerusalem; which, as the French Man said, is to be his, when he can catch.

There's a Prodigious Face of Religion, on all this Prince's Behaviour; and take him as a Man, I hardly find such another in a Station so high; Virtue seems to be mixt with Galantry, throughout all the Concerns of his Court, and they are the best Regulated Houshold in Europe; Religion has a peculiar Interest in his Family; and in short, had we never seen him in the Field, he had past for a very Religious Prince.

But, when we came into his Cabinet, and found him Tracing the Steps of his Subtil Progenitor, Charles Emanuel; when we found he first broke his Faith with the Confederacy, afterwards with the French, married his Daughter to a King, and then refus'd her the Title of a Queen; when we found him to Day persecuting his Subjects of the Valleys, to Morrow haranguing them as his faithful Friends, and putting Arms into their Hands.

In short, when we found him False and Fickle, we concluded the Princes of Europe were to blame to be cheated twice, but they must be mad that venture him the third Time; in short, we found 'twas to no purpose, to continue the Search of Religion among Politicks and Intrigues; and that whatever that Prince may do in advancing his Royal Character, 'tis past doubt, that he'll never much improve his Religious ; he may make himself to be own'd for a King, sooner than he will ever pass with us for a Christian, and so we turn'd our Backs upon him.

We were at some loss now, where to carry on the Search; Europe was found so barren of this Royal Quality, that we had some thought of going over into Asia, and look for it among the Turks, but we altered that rash Resolution, and turn'd about to look into Spain.

Here we found two Kings, but both Young, and having shown very little of their Piety in the World, we left them to fight it out. Not doubting but he will be the most Religious King that keeps the Crown longest, because Success sanctifies all the Frauds of Life.

We only wish, neither the French on one Hand, nor the English or Dutch on the other Hand, would concern themselves in the Quarrel, but leave that War for the Diversion of Europe, to be carried on by those Two Warlike Nations, the Spaniards, and the Portuguese: Never such a Farce was Acted on the Stage of the World, as wou'd be there; as to Fighting, Swaggering, Running away, &c.

Portugal came next in our Thoughts, and a great deal of the show of Religion and Piety has been seen in the Palace of the Court at Lisbon; but when we come to Deposing of Brothers, and going to Bed to their Wives; taking the Crown from the King's Head, and then lying with his Wife, we never examined Circumstances; but as to Religion-Royal, we found it would never do.

At last, we came to D——, K—— C—— the First, presented himself the likeliest Object; for if a Man can give a greater Demonstration of his Love to Religion, than Dying for the Church, we are mistaken; and therefore we cannot forbear affirming, that certainly we have found the first of the sort at home.

An Ill Natur'd Calves Head Dissenter, stept in, and objected Three Things; the Book of Sports, Executing L. Strafford against his Conscience, and taking a Prayer out of the Romance call'd —— and putting it into his Book of *Eikon Basilikè*.

As to the first and the last, they appear to be none of his Actions, the One put out by A. B. L. and the other put in by   and as to the Case of the Lord Strafford, he publickly Repented of it.

Great Claim has been put in for this Matter, on behalf of the Two Crown'd Sons of the last Mention'd P——ce.

As to the first, If above Fifty B——ds with Innumerable Instances of Lewdness; if pretending all his Days to be a Protestant, and at the same time being a supposed P——; if these things will not bar him from the Claim to Religion, he shall have my Vote.

His Brother without doubt, has a much better Claim, and there is no question, but when the Hundred Years are Compleat, shall receive a Badge of Saintship from Rome; mean time, this must be own'd, let his real Religion be what it will, he Suffer'd as much for it as any Man of his Character in the World, but his Memory won't go down with the English; and if I shou'd say, he was the Man, no Body would believe me. . . .

[Extract]

THE ART OF POLITICAL LYING

*W*ITH Dr. *Arbuthnot's* Art of Political Lying (*1712*) *we reach the last flourish of triumphant Toryism before the accession of George I brought in the long ascendancy of the Whig Aristocracy which ruled England for half a century.*

A member of the 'Scriblerus Club' (a group of Tory writers which included Pope, Swift, Gay and Prior), Arbuthnot's chief mark on our history is that left by his History of John Bull, *which gave a new character to our national mythology. But his* Art of Political Lying *is easily the wittiest of his works and a very shrewd commentary on his own times.*

Halifax's criticisms of the two political parties in his time expressed the impartial contempt of a man attached to neither. Arbuthnot's are the criticisms of one who is frankly partisan, and sees more at which to rail in the record of the Whigs; but he is not so blind as to be unaware of Tory faults, or so impolitic as to overstate his case. And, like Halifax, Dr. Arbuthnot seems to have hit on the perennial vices of politicians; so that his words still have sharp relevance and topical application. Though time does not appear to have endorsed the judgment of his contemporaries, Arbuthnot was regarded by them as at least the equal of Swift, Pope and Addison. Swift considered the doctor had 'more wit than we all have, and his humanity is equal to his wit'—an opinion on which the Dictionary of National Biography *comments that it appears to have been universal.*

The reference to 'translatory lies', specially applied to misplaced credit for a military victory, was clearly intended for the Duke of Marlborough, who, as Captain-General of the Army, had the reputation of stealing glory from other men's actions with the same unscrupulous rapacity that he showed in his pursuit of wealth. Originally a Tory, but willing to play any rôle that suited his personal interests, John Churchill (later Baron Churchill and finally Duke of Marlborough) had been trusted by James II, had deserted to William, had plotted again with James against his new master, and had finally risen to enormous power with Queen Anne, through his wife's influence at court. The long 'Spanish Succession War' with Louis XIV gave this adventurer scope for his undoubted ability as a general, inducing him also to identify himself increasingly with the Whig party, as the war was more to the interest of the Whigs than the Tories.

(It was a war for trade and colonies, and the Whigs, with mercantile interests were much more concerned than the Tories, a party of country landowners and clergy, led by the older nobility and the bishops. It was also, indirectly, an anti-Jacobite war). As the war dragged on it became increasingly unpopular with the Tories, and its purpose and conduct were bitterly attacked by Swift, Arbuthnot and others.

Marlborough was naturally, and quite rightly, the principal target of the Tory 'peace offensive'. They accused him of prolonging the war, when honourable peace by negotiation had long been possible, out of selfish motives (personal ambition and private profit). The charge has its modern echoes, but not the dénouement, which was exceptional. Ferocious attacks, particularly those of Swift in the Examiner, *turned public opinion completely against this cold and calculating schemer; and the Tories (who were in power with a Parliamentary majority at the end of Anne's reign) were able to dismiss the Duke from his command. He left in good time for the Continent, apprehensive of further proceedings against him, as the Government had been collecting evidence of his financial corruption.*

It need hardly be added that the Government itself was as disingenuous as the Duke. The gay remarks of Dr. Arbuthnot, at the end of this pamphlet, concerning rumours of a secret treaty with France, were no doubt written in full belief that the rumours were Whig lies, spread merely to discredit the government. Nevertheless, it was known that the Tories intended to bring the war to an end—which they would have done earlier, but for French intransigence. It was also known that Marlborough had been replaced by a new commander-in-chief who was suspected (justly, in fact) of being a Jacobite and (which was also true enough) of being under orders to soft-pedal the war. What was merely suspected at the time was that secret peace negotiations were in progress, whereby the British Government proposed to sell out at the cost of its Allies, contrary to solemn engagements. After Arbuthnot had laughed away this story and Swift had mystified the country still further with a spoof account of the proceedings, it turned out that Matthew Prior had, in fact, been sent on just such a mission. The subsequent revelation of Tory intrigues with the Pretender at this time showed that, on the whole, rumour was less of a lying jade on this occasion than Dr. Arbuthnot believed, and would have inclined his readers to believe. The secret negotiations, if Bolingbroke had been able to accomplish his schemes, would actually have been the first step towards a Stuart Restoration.

THE ART OF POLITICAL LYING

By John Arbuthnot

THERE is now in the Press, a Curious Piece, intitled, Ψευδολογία Πολιτική; or, *A Treatise of the Art of Political Lying:* Consisting of Two Volumes in 4to.

THE PROPOSALS ARE

I. *That if the Author meets with suitable Encouragement, he intends to deliver the First Volume to the Subscribers by* Hilary-Term *next.*

II. *The Price of both Volumes will be, to the Subscribers, Fourteen Shillings; Seven whereof are to be paid down, and the other Seven at the Delivery of the Second Volume.*

III. *Those that Subscribe for Six shall have a Seventh* gratis; *which reduces the Price to less than Six Shillings a Volume.*

IV. *That the Subscribers shall have their Names and Places of Abode Printed at length.*

Subscriptions are taken in at St. James's Coffee-house, Young Man's at Charing-Cross, the Grecian, Brydges's by the Royal Exchange, and most other Coffee-houses in Town.

For the Encouragement of so useful a Work, it is thought fit the Publick should be inform'd of the Contents of the First Volume, by one who has with great Care perus'd the Manuscript.

The Author, in his Preface, makes some very judicious Reflexions upon the Original of Arts and Sciences; That at first they consist of scatter'd Theorems and Practices, which are handed about amongst the Masters, and only reveal'd to the *Filii Artis,* till such time as some great Genius appears, who Collects these disjointed Propositions, and reduces them into a regular System. That this is the Case of that Noble and Useful Art of Political Lying, which in this last Age having been enrich'd with several new Discoveries, ought not to lie any longer in Rubbish and Confusion, but may justly claim a Place in the Encyclopædia, especially such as serves for a Model of Education for an able Politcian [*sic*], that he proposes to himself no small Stock of Fame in future Ages, in being the first who has undertaken this Design; and for the same Reason he hopes the Imperfection of his Work will be excused. He invites all Persons who have any Talent that way, or any new Discovery, to communicate their Thoughts, assuring them that honourable mention shall be made of them in his Work.

The First Volume consists of Eleven Chapters.

In the first Chapter of his excellent Treatise, he reasons Philosophically concerning the Nature of the Soul of Man, and those Qualities which render it susceptible of Lyes. He supposes the Soul to be of the Nature of a Plano-Cylindrical Speculum, or Looking-glass; that the plain side was made by God Almighty, but that the Devil afterwards wrought the other side into a Cylindrical Figure. The plain side represents Objects just as they are, and the Cylindrical side, by the Rules of Catoptricks, must needs represent true Objects false, and false Objects true; but the Cylindrical side being much the larger Surface, takes in a greater Compass of visual Rays. That upon the Cylindrical side of the Soul of Man depends the whole Art and Success of Political Lying. The Author, in this Chapter, proceeds to reason upon the other Qualities of the Mind; As, great Fondness of the Malicious and the Miraculous: The Tendency of the Soul towards the Malicious, springs from Self-love, or a Pleasure to find Mankind more wicked, base, or unfortunate, than our selves. The Design of the Miraculous, proceeds from the Inactivity of the Soul, or its Incapacity to be moved or delighted with any thing that is vulgar or common. The Author having establish'd the Qualities of the Mind, upon which his Art is founded, he proceeds,

In his Second Chapter, to treat of the Nature of Political Lying; which he defines, to be, The Art of convincing the People of Salutary Falshoods, for some good End. He calls it an Art to distinguish it from that of telling Truth, which does not seem to want Art; but then he would have this understood only as to the Invention, because there is indeed more Art necessary to convince the People of a Salutary Truth, than a Salutary Falshood. Then he proceeds to prove, that there are Salutary Falshoods, of which he gives a great many Instances both before and after the Revolution; and demonstrates plainly, that we could not have carried on the War so long, without several of those Salutary Falshoods. He gives Rules to calculate the Value of a Political Lye, in Pounds, Shillings, and Pence. By Good, he does not mean that which is absolutely so, but what appears so to the Artist, which is a sufficient Ground for him to proceed upon; and he distinguishes the Good, as it commonly is, into *Bonum utile, dulce, & honestum*. He shews you, that there are Political Lyes of a mix'd Nature, which include all the Three in different respects: That the *Utile* reigns generally about the Exchange, the *Dulce* and *Honestum* at the Westminster End of the Town. One Man spreads a Lye to sell or Buy Stock to greater Advantage; a second, because it is honorable to serve his Party; and a third, because it is sweet to gratify his Revenge. Having explain'd the several Terms of his Definition, he proceeds,

In his Third Chapter, to treat of the Lawfulness of Political Lying; which he deduces from its true and genuine Principles, by enquiring into the several Rights that Mankind have to Truth. He shews, that the People have a Right to private Truth from their Neighbours, and œconomical Truth from their own Family; that they should not be abused by their Wives, Children, and Servants; that they have no Right at all to Political Truth: That the People may as well all pretend to be Lords of Mannors and possess great Estates, as to have Truth told them in Matters of Government. The Author, with great Judgment, states the several Shares of Mankind in this Matter of Truth, according to their several Capacities, Dignities, and Professions; and shews you, that Children have hardly any share at all; in consequence of which, they have very seldom any Truth told them. It must be own'd, that the Author, in this Chapter, has some seeming Difficulties to answer and explain Texts of Scripture, and a Sermon lately Preach'd before Her Majesty at Windsor.

The Fourth Chapter is wholly employed in this Question, Whether the Right of Coinage of Political Lyes be wholly in the Government? The Author, who is a true Friend to English Liberty, determines in the Negative, and answers all the Arguments of the opposite Party with great Acuteness; That as the Government of England has a Mixture of Democratical in it, so the Right of Inventing and Spreading Political Lyes, is partly in the People; and their obstinate Adherence to this just Privilege has been most conspicuous, and shin'd with great Lustre of late Years: That it happens very often, that there is no other Means left to the good People of England to pull down a Ministry and Government they are weary of, but by exercising this their undoubted Right:

PROPOSALS

For PRINTING

A very Curious Difcourſe, in Two Volumes in *Quarto*,

Intitled,

ΨΕΥΔΟΛΟΓΙ'Α ΠΟΛΙΤΙΚΗ;

O R, A

TREATISE of the ART

O F

Political Lying,

W I T H

An ABSTRACT of the Firſt Volume of the ſaid TREATISE.

L O N D O N:

Printed for *John Morphew*, near *Stationers-Hall*. 1712. Price 3 d.

Title page: A Treatise of the Art of Political Lying

That abundance of Political Lying is a sure sign of true English Liberty: That as Ministers do sometimes use Tools to support their Power, it is but reasonable that the People should employ the same Weapon to defend themselves, and pull them down.

In his Fifth Chapter, he divides Political Lyes into their several Species and Classes, and gives Precepts about the Inventing, Spreading, and Propagating the several sorts of them: He begins with the *Rumores*, and *Libelli famosi*, such as concern the Reputation of Men in Power; where he finds Fault with the common Mistake, that takes Notice only of one sort, viz. the Detractory or Defamatory, whereas in truth there are three sorts, the Detractory, the Additory, and the Translatory. The Additory gives to a Great Man a greater share of Reputation than belongs to him, to enable him to serve some good End or Purpose. The Detractory or Defamatory, is a Lye which takes from a Great Man the Reputation that justly belongs to him, for fear he should use it to the Detriment of the Publick. The Translatory, is a Lye that transfers the Merit of a Man's good Action to another who is in himself more deserving; or, transfers the Demerit of a bad Action from the true Author, to a Person who is in himself less deserving. He gives several Instances of very great Strokes in all the Three Kinds, especially in the last, when it was necessary for the Good of the Publick to bestow the Valour and Conduct of one Man upon another, and that of many to one Man; nay, even upon a good Occasion, a Man may be rob'd of his Victory by a Person that did not Command in the Action. The Restoring and the Destroying the Publick may be ascrib'd to Persons who had no hand in either. The Author exhorts all Gentlemen Practitioners to exercise themselves in the Translatory, because the Existence of the Things themselves being visible, and not demanding any Proof, there wants nothing to be put upon the Publick but a false Author or a false Cause, which is no great Presumption upon the Credulity of Mankind, to whom the secret Springs of things are for the most part unknown.

The Author proceeds to give some Precepts as to the Additory. That when one ascribes any thing to a Person which does not belong to him, the Lye ought to be calculated not quite contradictory to his known Qualities: *Ex. gr.* One would not make the French King present at a Protestant Conventicle; nor, like Queen Elizabeth, restore the Overplus of Taxes to her Subjects. One would not bring in the Emperor giving two Months Pay in Advance to his Troops; nor the Dutch paying more than their Quota. One would not make the same Person zealous for a Standing Army and Publick Liberty; nor an Atheist support the Church;

nor a lewd Fellow a Reformer of Manners; nor a hot-headed crackbrain'd Coxcomb forward for a Scheme of Moderation. But if it is absolutely necessary that a Person is to have some good adventitious Quality given him, the Author's Precept is, that it should not be done at first in *extremo gradu*. For Example: They should not make a Covetous Man give away all at once, Five thousand Pounds in a charitable generous way; Twenty or Thirty Pounds may suffice at first. They should not introduce a Person of remarkable Ingratitude to his Benefactors, rewarding a poor Man for some good Office that was done him thirty Years ago; but they may allow him to acknowledge a Service to a Person who is capable still to do him another. A Man whose personal Courage is suspected, is not at first to drive whole Squadrons before him; but he may be allow'd the Merit of some Squabble, or throwing a Bottle at his Adversary's Head.

It will not be allow'd, to make a Great Man, that is a known Despiser of Religion, spend whole Days in his Closet at his Devotion; but, you may with Safety make him sit out publick Prayers with Decency. A Great Man, who has never been known willingly to pay a just Debt, ought not all of a sudden to be introduc'd making Restitution of Thousands he has cheated; let it suffice at first, to pay Twenty Pounds to a Friend who has lost his Note.

He lays down the same Rules in the Detractory or Defamatory kind; that they should not be quite opposite to the Qualities the Persons are supposed to have. Thus it will not be sound, according to the sound Rules of Pseudology, to report of a pious and religious Prince, that he neglects his Devotion, and would introduce Heresy; but, you may report of a merciful Prince, that he has Pardon'd a Criminal who did not deserve it. You will be unsuccessful if you give out of a Great Man, who is remarkable for his Frugality for the Publick, that he squanders away the Nation's Money; but, you may safely relate that he hoards it: You must not affirm he took a Bribe; but, you may freely censure him for being tardy in his Payments; Because though neither may be true, yet the last is credible, the first not. Of an open-hearted generous Minister you are not to say, that he was in an Intrigue to Betray his Country; but, you may affirm with some Probability, that he was in an Intrigue with a Lady. He warns all Practitioners to take good heed to these Precepts, for want of which, many of their Lies, of late, have prov'd abortive or short-liv'd.

In his Sixth Chapter he treats of the Miraculous; by which he understands any thing that exceeds the common Degrees of Probability. In respect of the People, it is divided into two sorts, the τὸ φοβερὸν, or

the τὸ θυμοειδὲς, Terrifying Lyes, and Animating or Encouraging
Lyes, both being extremely useful on their proper Occasions. Concerning the τὸ φοβερὸν, he gives several Rules; one of which is, that
terrible Objects should not be too frequently shewn to the People, lest
they grow familiar. He says, it is absolutely necessary that the People
of England should be frighted with the French King and the Pretender
once a Year, but, that the Bears should be chain'd up again till that time
Twelve-month. The want of Observing this so necessary a Precept, in
bringing out the Raw-head and Bloody-bones upon every trifling Occasion, has produc'd great Indifference in the Vulgar of late Years. As
to the Animating or Encouraging Lyes, he gives the following Rules;
That they should not far exceed the common degrees of Probability,
and that there should be variety of them, and the same Lye not obstinately insisted upon; that the Promissory or Prognosticating Lyes should
not be upon short Days, for fear the Authors should have the Shame
and Confusion to see themselves speedily contradicted. He examines
by these Rules, that well-meant, but unfortunate Lye of the Conquest of
France, which continued near twenty Years together; but at last, by
being too obstinately insisted upon, it was worn threadbare, and
became unsuccessful.

As to the τὸ τερατῶδες, or the Prodigious, he has little to advise,
but that their Comets, Whales and Dragons, should be sizable; their
Storms, Tempests, and Earthquakes, without the reach of a Days
Journey of a Man and a Horse.

The Seventh Chapter is wholly taken up in an Enquiry, Which of the
two Parties are the greatest Artists in Political Lying. He owns the
Tories have been better believed of late; but, that the Whigs have much
the greater Genius's amongst them. He attributes the late ill Success
of the Whig-Party to their glutting the Market, and retailing too much
of a bad Commodity at once: When there is too great a Quantity of
Worms, it is hard to catch Gudgeons. He proposes a Scheme for the
Recovery of the Credit of the Whig-Party, which indeed seems to be
somewhat Chimerical, and does not savour of that sound Judgment the
Author has shown in the rest of the Work. It amounts to this, That the
Party should agree to vent nothing but Truth for three Months to-
gether, which will give them Credit for six Months Lying afterwards.
He owns, that he believes it almost impossible to find fit Persons to
execute this Scheme. Towards the end of the Chapter, he inveighs
severely against the Folly of Parties, in retaining such Scoundrels and
Men of Low Genius's to retail their Lyes; such as most of the present
News-Writers are, who besides a strong Bent and Inclination towards

the Profession, seem to be wholly ignorant in the Rules of Pseudology, and not at all qualified for so weighty a Trust.

In his Eighth Chapter he treats of some extraordinary Genius's who have appear'd of late Years, especially in their Disposition towards the Miraculous. He advises those hopeful Young-men to turn their Invention to the Service of their Country, it being inglorious, at this time, to employ their Talent in prodigious Fox-Chases, Horse-Courses, Feats of Activity in Driving of Coaches, Jumping, Running, Swallowing of Peaches, Pulling out whole Sets of Teeth to clean, &c. when their Country stands so much in need of their Assistance.

The Eighth Chapter is a Project for Uniting the several smaller Corporations of Lyars into one Society. It is too tedious to give a full Account of the whole Scheme; what is most remarkable is, That this Society ought to consist of the Heads of each Party: that no Lye is to pass current without their Approbation, they being the best Judges of the present Exigencies, and what sort of Lyes are demanded: That in such a Corporation there ought to be Men of all Professions, that the τὸ πρέπον, and the τὸ εὐλόγον, that is, Decency and Probability, may be observ'd as much as possible: That besides the Persons abovementioned, this Society ought to consist of the hopeful Genius's about the Town (of which there are great plenty to be pick'd up in the several Coffee-houses) Travellers, Virtuoso's, Fox-hunters, Jockeys, Attorneys Old Sea-men and Soldiers out of the Hospitals of Greenwich and Chelsea. To this Society, so Constituted, ought to be committed the sole Management of Lying. That in their outer Room there ought always to attend some Persons endow'd with a great Stock of Credulity, a Generation that thrives mightily in this Soil and Climate: He thinks a sufficient Number of them may be pick'd up any where about the Exchange: These are to Circulate what the other Coin; for no Man spreads a Lye with so good a Grace as he that believes it. That the Rule of the Society be to invent a Lye, and sometimes two, for every Day; in the Choice of which, great Regard ought to be had to the Weather, and the Season of the Year: Your φοβερὰ, or Terrifying Lyes, do mighty well in November and December, but not so well in May and June, unless the Easterly Winds reign. That it ought to be Penal, for any body to talk of any thing but the Lye of the Day. That the Society is to maintain a sufficient Number of Spies at Court, and other Places, to furnish Hints and Topicks for Invention; and a general Correspondence in all the Market-Towns, for Circulating their Lyes. That if any one of the Society were observ'd to blush, or look out of Countenance, or want a necessary Circumstance in telling the Lye, he ought to be expell'd, and declar'd incapable. Besides the Roaring Lies, there ought to be a private Committee for Whispers, constituted of the ablest Men of the Society. Here the Author makes a Digression in Praise of the Whig-Party, for the right Understanding and Use of Proof-Lyes. A Proof-Lye is like a Proof-Charge for a Piece of Ordnance, to try a Standard-Credulity. Of such a nature he takes Transubstantiation to be in the Church of Rome, a Proof-Article, which if any one swallows, they are sure he will digest every thing else. Therefore the Whig-Party do wisely, to try the Credulity of the People sometimes by Swingers, that they may be able to judge to what heighth they may Charge them afterwards. Towards the End of this Chapter, he warns the Heads of Parties against Believing their own Lyes; which has prov'd of pernicious Consequences of late, both a Wise Party and a Wise Nation having regulated their Affairs upon Lyes of their own Invention. The Causes of this he supposes to be too great a Zeal and Intenseness in the Practice of this Art, and a vehement Heat in mutual Conversation, whereby they perswade one another, that what they wish, and report to be true, is really so. That all Parties have been subject to this Misfortune: The Jacobites have been constantly infested with it, but, the Whigs of late seem ev'n to exceed them in this ill Habit and Weakness. To this Chapter, the Author subjoins a Calendar of Lyes proper for the several Months of the Year.

The Ninth Chapter treats of the Celerity and Duration of Lyes. As to the Celerity of their Motion, the Author says it is almost incredible: He gives several Instances of Lyes that have gone faster than a Man can ride Post: Your Terrifying Lyes travel at a prodigious rate, above ten Miles an hour; your Whispers move in a narrow Vortex, but very swiftly. The Author says it is impossible to explain several Phænomena in relation to the Celerity of Lyes, without the Supposition of Synchronism and Combination. As to the Duration of Lyes, he says they are of all sorts, from Hours and Days to Ages; that there are some which, like your Insects, die and revive again in a different Form; that good Artists, like People who build upon a short Lease, will calculate the Duration of a Lye surely to answer their purpose; to last just as long, and no longer, than the Turn is serv'd.

The Tenth Chapter treats of the Characteristicks of Lyes; how to know, when, where, and by whom invented: Your Dutch, English, and French Ware, are amply distinguish'd from one another; an Exchange-Lye from one Coin'd at the other End of the Town; Great Judgment is to be shewn as to the Place where the Species is intended to Circulate: Very low and base Coin will serve for Wapping: There are several Coffee-houses that have their particular Stamps, which a judicious Practitioner may easily know. All your Great Men have their proper Phantateusticks. The Author says he has attained, by Study and Application, to so great Skill in this Matter, that bring him any Lye, he can tell whose Image it bears so truly, as the Great Man himself shall not have the face to deny it. The Promissory Lyes of Great Men are known by Shouldering, Hugging, Squeezing, Smiling, Bowing; and Lyes in Matter of Fact, by immoderate Swearing.

He spends the whole Eleventh Chapter on one simple Question, Whether a Lye is best contradicted by Truth, or another Lye. The Author says, that considering the large Extent of the Cylindrical Surface of the Soul, and the great Propensity to believe Lyes in the generality of Mankind of late Years, he thinks the properest Contradiction to a Lye, is another Lye: For Example; If it should be reported that the Pretender was at London, one would not contradict it by saying he never was in England; but you must prove by Eye-witnesses that he came no farther than Greenwich, but then went back again. Thus if it be spread about that a great Person were dying of some Disease, you must not say the Truth, that they are in Health, and never had such a Disease; but, that they are slowly recovering of it. So there was, not long ago, a Gentleman who affirmed, That the Treaty with France for bringing in Popery and Slavery into England, was Sign'd the 15th of September; to which another answered very judiciously, not by opposing Truth to his Lye, That there was no such Treaty; but that, to his certain Knowledge, there were many things in that Treaty not yet adjusted.

The Account of the Second Volume of this Excellent Treatise is reserv'd for another time.

A MODEST PROPOSAL

*T*HE *years 1714 to 1789 are recognised by historians as a distinct period in our history. For half a century (1714 to 1763) there is an undisputed Whig supremacy, consisting of a long interval of peace, under Walpole (lasting nearly thirty years) followed by the ministry of the elder Pitt, when two major colonial wars were fought with France. But the peaceful ministry of Walpole and the bellicose activities of his successor had this in common, that throughout this time no major political issue divided the country. Two Jacobite rebellions took place (the '15 and the '45) but their failure demonstrated the weakness of the Jacobite cause. Essentially a Tory cause, it had been deserted by the Tories, who now had nothing to fight for. They were a royalist party in search of a king, having thrown over the Stuarts but without, as yet, adapting themselves to the Hanoverians.*

Up to the year 1714 parties had divided mainly on their attitude to the monarchy. Politicians were monarchists or republicans, favoured limited or unlimited monarchy, were for or against the Protestant Succession. With the accesssion of George I these controversies became remote and academic. For good or for ill a foreign dynasty was established, as dependent upon the Whig supremacy as the Whigs were dependent on their German mascots. The Protestant Succession was established securely, and its basis was limited monarchy. The Revolution of 1688 left this decision still uncertain, for if Queen Anne had lived another year Bolingbroke and the Tory faction in power could, and probably would, have come to terms with the Pretender and tried to establish the Stuarts once more. It is therefore not without reason that Queen Anne's death is still news: it happened just in time to give us the four Georges and their successors, so it is a perpetual reminder of the fortuitous element in history.

We have seen that politics, right through the seventeenth century, were intimately tied up with religious controversy. The overwhelming (and in many respects permanent) victory of the Whigs in 1714 put an end to these religio-politics. Freedom of worship was established; the Schism Act and the Occasional Conformity Act were repealed. Other laws remained, which theoretically (though not always in practice) hindered the non-conformists from participating in public life, some of these laws continuing on the statute book well into the nineteenth century; but there could be no return from this time onwards to the persecutions of Tudor and Stuart days.

The Whig triumph, however, is not sufficient to account for the decline of the vigorous spirit expressed by sectarian partisans in earlier pamphlets at which we have glanced. In the very year of victory (1714) there was published An Enquiry into the Causes of the Decay of the Dissenting Interest. The Presbyterian tide, that had once swept England from the north, had gone out, leaving but few pools of Calvinism, south of the Cheviots, to mark its course. Other sects continued to split and dwindle. Some, like the Quakers, maintained their numbers but turned their attention inwards, individually and collectively, aloof from politics and even (in many instances) from social problems outside their own ranks. In short, the policy advocated by Defoe had been both realised by the country and accepted by the Dissenters: England was governed now by the 'moderate men', the Low-Church Whigs, who allowed freedom of worship. And, content with this situation, the non-conformists were no longer loud in their demand for freedom from other disabilities as citizens.

Only in Ireland, where a Catholic (and therefore ' non-conformist ') majority was excluded from all participation in the political life of its own country, did religio-politics survive. Here the oppression of the Catholics, largely reduced to tenants or landless labourers under the Protestant Ascendancy, led to the close identification of the Catholic Church with nationalism and with tenant rights. Protestantism, on the other hand—in spite of the efforts of certain eminent Protestant nationalists—came to be regarded as the religion of the ruling class and the foreign conqueror, the people who had stolen the land and exacted rent for it from their Catholic victims.

In England, after 1714, there is nothing comparable to this. The smugness, generally speaking, of English political and religious literature from that time onwards may be traced to the fact that the literate classes were remarkably well united, not only in a general acceptance of Protestantism (firmly balanced at dead centre on the Low Church) but on the ancient and honourable Protestant pastime of making money. About the time that Walpole was thrown over by his party (the Whig revolt of 1742) there began a new tide of non-conformity—that of the Wesleyans and their various off-shoots. But, unlike the dissenting sects of the previous century, these 'Methodists' were not in the least inclined to subvert the social or political order. Their attitude to all such matters was (originally) impeccably correct and conservative. They did not even consider themselves non-conformists. Their attitude to the Church of England was roughly that of the C. of E. to Rome—'It's the regiment which is out of step'.

It was not until the French Revolution (a hundred years after our own 'Glorious Revolution' set the stage for the Whig supremacy) that new issues revitalised political life in England. The new social clash which was precipitated *everywhere by that major event in human history gave us modern socio-politics, in place of the religio-politics which ended with Queen Anne's death. The history of pamphleteering from that time onwards will be the subject of our second volume. We are here concerned with the long 'interval' in English history which preceded the year 1789; and it will be noticed that after our close representation of the British pamphleteers up to 1714, we have selected only four pamphlets to cover the period from the accession of George I to the French Revolution.*

The first is by Swift, his famous satirical Proposal of 1729. For him, as for most other Tories, the times were out of joint. He hated the new German court, but regarded 'the coming of the Pretender as a greater evil than we are like to suffer under the worst Whig Ministry that can be found.' Such a position suited his paradoxical genius. He hated mankind, but loved men and women; hated (as he told Pope) all professions, groups and nations, but loved individuals from each classification. And in this Modest Proposal the man who had written so much in scorn of the Irish and dislike of their religion expressed in bitter satire the compassion he felt for their sufferings—compassion which was to endear him to the Irish people in spite of many harsh things which he had said about them. It is fair enough to add that as, in 1729, Walpole and the Whigs had every appearance of being the permanent rulers of England, one way of attacking them was to expose their maladministration of Ireland; so it also served the Dean's political spleen.

But in the main Swift's latter phase, in the retirement of his Dublin Deanery, was a retreat from the political battlefield. Indeed, he seldom returned to it after 1714 except on an Irish issue and in the Irish interest. But it was during that long period of comparative retirement from the political arena that the Dean wrote Gulliver's Travels, a satire not merely on contemporary politicians, but on Man himself. Great as it was, it was in some sense a confession of failure: powerless any more to influence human affairs with his pen, Swift could only scoff now at humanity itself. He outlived by over thirty years the age for which his talents appeared to have been intended, dying in 1745. Throughout Walpole's long tenure of office he had been politically ineffective. He was perhaps the best of the Old Tories, and the year of his death saw the end of the Jacobite cause with which Toryism had been so fatally and uneasily associated.

The rise of a new Toryism and the events of the late eighteenth century, prior to the French Revolution, will be discussed briefly in our next note. But it is important to realise the changes which came with the Hanoverian succession and the great gap which separates this swan song of Stuart Toryism, concerned (not without historical precedent) with justice for the Irish people, and the first note of a new Liberalism, of which the pamphlet which follows will provide an example. Our last three entries will be seen, in fact, to belong to a totally different world, in which the ideas of the French Revolution are already dimly foreshadowed.

A MODEST PROPOSAL FOR PREVENTING THE CHILDREN OF POOR PEOPLE FROM BEING A BURTHEN TO THEIR PARENTS OR COUNTRY, AND FOR MAKING THEM BENEFICIAL TO THE PUBLICK

By Jonathan Swift

IT is a melancholly Object to those, who walk through this great Town or travel in the Country, when they see the Streets, the Roads and Cabbin-Doors crowded with Beggars of the Female Sex, followed by three, four, or six Children, all in Rags, and importuning every Passenger for an Alms. These Mothers instead of being able to work for their honest livelyhood, are forced to employ all their time in Stroling to beg Sustenance for their helpless Infants, who, as they grow up, either turn Thieves for want of work, or leave their dear Native Country, to fight for the Pretender in Spain, or sell themselves to the Barbadoes.

I think it is agreed by all Parties, that this prodigious number of Children in the Arms, or on the Backs, or at the heels of their Mothers, and frequently of their Fathers, is in the present deplorable state of the Kingdom, a very great additional grievance; and therefore whoever could find out a fair, cheap and easy method of making these Children sound and useful Members of the common-wealth would deserve so well of the publick, as to have his Statue set up for a preserver of the Nation.

But my Intention is very far from being confined to provide only for the Children of Professed Beggers, it is of a much greater Extent, and shall take in the whole Number of Infants at a certain Age, who are born of Parents in effect as little able to support them, as those who demand our Charity in the Streets.

As to my own part, having turned my Thoughts, for many Years, upon this important Subject, and maturely weighed the several Schemes of our Projectors, I have always found them grossly mistaken in their computation. It is true, a Child just dropt from it's Dam, may be supported by her Milk, for Solar a year [*sic*] with little other Nourishment, at most not above the Value of two Shillings, which the Mother may certainly get, or the Value in Scraps, by her lawful Occupation of begging; and it is exactly at one Year Old that I propose to provide for them in such a manner, as, instead of being a Charge upon their Parents, or the Parish, or wanting Food and Raiment for the rest of their Lives, they shall, on the Contrary, contribute to the Feeding and partly to the Cloathing of many Thousands.

There is likewise another great Advantage in my Scheme, that it will prevent those voluntary Abortions, and that horrid practice of Women murdering their Bastard Children, alas! too frequent among us, Sacrificing the poor innocent Babes, I doubt, more to avoid the Expence than the Shame, which would move Tears and Pity in the most Savage and inhuman breast.

The number of Souls in this Kingdom being usually reckoned one Million and a half, Of these I calculate there may be about two hundred thousand Couple whose Wives are Breeders; from which number I subtract thirty Thousand Couples, who are able to maintain their own Children, although I apprehend there cannot be so many, under the present Distresses of the Kingdom; but this being granted, there will remain an hundred and seventy thousand Breeders. I again Subtract fifty Thousand, for those Women who miscarry, or whose Children die by accident, or disease within the Year. There only remain an hundred and twenty thousand Children of poor Parents annually born: The question therefore is, How this number shall be reared, and provided for, which, as I have already said, under the present Situation of Affairs, is utterly impossible by all the Methods hitherto proposed; for we can neither employ them in Handicraft or Agriculture; we neither build Houses, (I mean in the Country) nor cultivate Land: They can very seldom pick up a Livelyhood by Stealing till they arrive at six years Old; except where they are of towardly parts; although, I confess, they learn the Rudiments much earlier; during which time they can however be properly looked upon only as Probationers, as I have been informed by a principal Gentleman in the County of Cavan, who protested to me, that he never knew above one or two Instances under the

Age of six, even in a part of the Kingdom so renowned for the quickest proficiency in that Art.

I am assured by our Merchants, that a Boy or a Girl before twelve years Old, is no saleable Commodity, and even when they come to this Age, they will not yield above three Pounds, or three Pounds and half a Crown at most on the Exchange, which cannot turn to Account either to the Parents or Kingdom, the Charge of Nutriment and Rags having been at least four times that Value.

I shall now therefore humbly propose my own Thoughts, which I hope will not be lyable to the least Objection.

I have been assured by a very knowing American of my acquaintance in London, that a young healthy Child well Nursed is at a year Old a most delicious nourishing and wholesome Food, whether Stewed, Roasted, Baked, or Boiled, and I make no doubt that it will equally serve in a Fricasie, or a Ragoust.

I do therefore humbly offer it to publick consideration, that of the Hundred and twenty thousand Children, already computed, twenty thousand may be reserved for Breed, whereof only one fourth part to be Males; which is more than we allow to Sheep, black Cattle, or Swine, and my Reason is, that these Children are seldom the Fruits of Marriage, a Circumstance not much regarded by our Savages, therefore, one Male will be sufficient to serve four Females. That the remaining Hundred thousand may at a year Old be offered in Sale to the Persons of Quality and Fortune, through the Kingdom, always advising the Mother to let them Suck plentifully in the last Month, so as to render them Plump, and Fat for a good Table. A Child will make two Dishes at an Entertainment for Friends, and when the Family dines alone, the fore or hind Quarter will make a reasonable Dish, and seasoned with a little Pepper or Salt will be very good Boiled on the fourth Day, especially in Winter.

I have reckoned upon a Medium, that a Child just born will weigh 12 pounds, and in a solar Year if tolerably nursed, encreaseth to 28 Pounds.

I grant this food will be somewhat dear, and therefore very proper for Landlords, who, as they have already devoured most of the Parents seem to have the best Title to the Children.

Infant's flesh will be in Season throughout the Year, but more plentiful in March, and a little before and after, for we are told by a grave Author an eminent French Physician, that Fish being a prolifick Dyet, there are more Children born in Roman Catholick Countries about nine Months after Lent, than at any other Season, therefore reckoning a Year after Lent, the Markets will be more glutted than usual, because the Number of Popish Infants, is at least three to one in this Kingdom, and therefore it will have one other Collateral advantage, by lessening the Number of Papists among us.

I have already computed the Charge of nursing a Begger's Child (in which list I reckon all Cottagers, Labourers, and four fifths of the Farmers) to be about two Shillings per Annum, Rags included, and I believe no Gentleman would repine to give Ten Shillings for the Carcass of a good fat Child, which, as I have said will make four Dishes of excellent Nutritive Meat, when he hath only some particular Friend, or his own Family to Dine with him. Thus the Squire will learn to be a good Landlord, and grow popular among his Tenants, the Mother will have Eight Shillings neat profit, and be fit for Work till she produces another Child.

Those who are more thrifty (as I must confess the Times require) may flea the Carcass; the Skin of which, Artificially dressed, will make admirable Gloves for Ladies, and Summer Boots for fine Gentlemen.

As to our City of Dublin, Shambles may be appointed for this purpose, in the most convenient parts of it, and Butchers we may be assured will not be wanting, although I rather recommend buying the Children alive, and dressing them hot from the Knife, as we do roasting Pigs.

A very worthy Person, a true Lover of his Country, and whose Virtues I highly esteem, was lately pleased, in discoursing on this matter, to offer a refinement upon my Scheme. He said, that many Gentlemen of this Kingdom, having of late destroyed their Deer, he conceived that the want of Venison might be well supplied by the Bodies of young Lads and Maidens, not exceeding fourteen Years of Age, nor under twelve, so great a Number of both Sexes in every Country being now ready to Starve, for want of Work and Service: And these to be disposed of by their Parents if alive, or otherwise by their nearest Relations. But with due deference to so excellent a friend, and so deserving a Patriot, I cannot be altogether in his Sentiments, for as to the Males, my American acquaintance assured me from frequent Experience, that their flesh was generally Tough and Lean, like that of our Schoolboys, by continual exercise, and their Taste disagreeable, and to Fatten them would not answer the Charge. Then as to the Females, it would, I think with humble Submission, be a loss to the Publick, because they soon would become Breeders themselves: And besides it is not improbable that some scrupulous People might be apt to Censure such a Practice, (although indeed very unjustly) as a little bordering upon Cruelty, which, I confess, hath always been with me the strongest objection against any Project, how well so ever intended.

But in order to justify my friend, he confessed, that this expedient was put into his Head by the famous Sallmanaazor, a Native of the Island Formosa, who came from thence to London, above twenty Years ago, and in Conversation told my Friend, that in his Country when any young Person happened to be put to Death, the Executioner sold the Carcass to Persons of Quality, as a prime Dainty, and that, in his Time, the Body of a plump Girl of fifteen, who was crucifyed for an attempt to Poison the Emperor, was sold to his Imperial Majesty's prime Minister of State, and other great Mandarins of the Court, in Joints from the Gibbet, at four hundred Crowns. Neither indeed can I deny, that if the same use were made of several plump young Girls in this Town, who, without one single Groat to their Fortunes, cannot stir abroad without a Chair, and appear at a Play-House, and Assemblies in Foreign fineries, which they never will pay for; the Kingdom would not be the worse.

Some Persons of a desponding Spirit are in great concern about that vast Number of poor People, who are Aged, Diseased, or Maimed, and I have been desired to imploy my Thoughts what Course may be taken, to ease the Nation of so grievous an Incumbrance. But I am not in the least pain upon that matter, because it is very well known, that they are every Day dying, and rotting, by cold and famine, and filth, and vermin, as fast as can be reasonably expected. And as to the younger Labourers, they are now in almost as hopeful a Condition. They cannot get Work, and consequently pine away for want of Nourishment, to a degree, that if at any Time they are accidently hired to common Labour, they have not strength to perform it, and thus the Country and themselves are happily delivered from the Evils to come.

I have too long digressed, and therefore shall return to my Subject, I think the Advantages by the Proposal which I have made are obvious and many, as well as of the highest Importance.

For First, as I have already observed, it would greatly lessen the Number of Papists, with whom we are Yearly over-run, being the principal Breeders of the Nation, as well as our most dangerous Enemies, and who stay at home on purpose with a Design to deliver the Kingdom to the Pretender, hoping to take their Advantage by the Absence of so many good Protestants, who have chosen rather to leave their Country, than stay at home, and pay Tithes against their Conscience, to an Episcopal Curate.

Secondly, the poorer Tenants will have something valuable of their own which by Law may be made lyable to Distress, and help to pay their Landlord's Rent, their Corn and Cattle being already seized, and Money a Thing unknown.

Thirdly, Whereas the Maintenance of an hundred thousand Children, from two Years old, and upwards, cannot be computed at less than Ten Shillings a piece per Annum, the Nation's Stock will be thereby encreased fifty thousand Pounds per Annum, besides the Profit of a new Dish, introduced to the Tables of all Gentlemen of Fortune in the Kingdom, who have any Refinement in Taste, and the Money will circulate among our Selves, the Goods being entirely of our own Growth and Manufacture.

Fourthly, The constant Breeders, besides the gain of eight Shillings Ster. per Annum, by the Sale of their Children, will be rid of the Charge of maintaining them after the first Year.

Fifthly, This Food would likewise bring great Custom to Taverns, where the Vintners will certainly be so prudent as to procure the best Receipts for dressing it to Perfection, and consequently have their Houses frequented by all the fine Gentlemen, who justly value themselves upon their Knowledge in good Eating, and a skillful Cook, who understands how to oblige his Guests, will contrive to make it as expensive as they please.

Sixthly, This would be a great Inducement to Marriage, which all wise Nations have either encouraged by Rewards, or enforced by Laws and Penalties. It would encrease the Care and Tenderness of Mothers towards their Children, when they were sure of a Settlement for Life, to the poor Babes, provided in some sort by the Publick, to their Annual Profit instead of Expence; we should soon see an honest Emulation among the married Women, which of them could bring the fattest Child to the Market. Men would become as fond of their Wives, during the Time of their Pregnancy, as they are now of their Mares in Foal, their Cows in Calf, or Sows when they are ready to farrow, nor offer to beat or kick them (as is too frequent a Practice) for fear of a Miscarriage.

Many other Advantages might be ennumerated. For instance, the Addition of some thousand Carcasses in our Exportation of Barrell'd Beef. The Propagation of Swines Flesh, and Improvement in the Art of making good Bacon, so much wanted among us by the great Destruction of Pigs, too frequent at our Tables, which are no way comparable in Taste, or Magnificence to a well grown, fat Yearly Child, which roasted whole will make a considerable Figure at a Lord Mayor's

THE FESTIVAL OF THE GOLDEN RUMP.

Rumpatur, quiquis Rumpitur invidia.

UNA EURUS
NOTUSQ: RUEN
CREBERQ: PROC
AFRICUS.

Designed by the Author of Common-sense.

Publish'd according to Act of Parliament 1737. Price 1.

The Festival of the Golden Rump

Feast, or any other Publick Entertainment. But this, and many others, I omit being studious of Brevity.

Supposing that one thousand Families in this City, would be constant Customers for Infants Flesh, besides others who might have it at merry Meetings, particularly at Weddings and Christenings, I compute that Dublin would take off Annually about twenty thousand Carcases, and the rest of the Kingdom (where probably they will be sold somewhat cheaper) the remaining eighty Thousand.

I can think of no one Objection, that will possibly be raised against this Proposal, unless it should be urged that the Number of People will be thereby much lessened in the Kingdom. This I freely own, and 'twas indeed one principal Design in offering it to the World. I desire the Reader will observe, that I calculate my Remedy for this one individual Kingdom of IRELAND, and for no other that ever was, is, or, I think, ever can be upon Earth. Therefore let no Man talk to me of other Expedients: Of taxing our Absentees at five Shillings a Pound: Of using neither Cloaths, nor Houshold Furniture, except what is of our own Growth and Manufacture: Of utterly rejecting the Materials and Instruments that promote Foreign Luxury: Of curing the Expensiveness of Pride, Vanity, Idleness, and Gaming in our Women: Of introducing a Vein of Parcimony, Prudence and Temperance: Of learning to love our Country, wherein we differ even from LAPLANDERS, and the Inhabitants of TOPINAMBOO: Of quitting our Animosities, and Factions, nor act [sic] any longer like the Jews, who were murdering one another at the very Moment their City was taken: Of being a little cautious not to sell our Country and Consciences for nothing: Of teaching Landlords to have at least one Degree of Mercy towards their Tenants. Lastly, Of putting a Spirit of Honesty, Industry, and Skill into our Shopkeepers, who, if a Resolution could now be taken to buy only our Native Goods, would immediately unite to cheat and exact upon us in the Price, the Measure, and the Goodness, nor could ever yet be brought to make one fair Proposal of just Dealing, though often and earnestly invited to it.

Therefore I repeat, let no Man talk to me of these and the like Expedients, till he hath at least some Glimpse of Hope, that there will ever be some hearty and sincere Attempt to put them in Practice.

But as to my self, having been wearied out for many Years with offering vain, idle, visionary Thoughts, and at length utterly despairing of Success, I fortunately fell upon this Proposal, which, as it is wholly new, so it hath something Solid and Real, of no Expence and little Trouble, full in our own Power, and whereby we can incur no Danger in disobliging ENGLAND. For this kind of Commodity will not bear Exportation, the Flesh being of too tender a Consistence, to admit a long Continuance in Salt, although perhaps I cou'd name a Country, which would be glad to eat up our whole Nation without it.

After all, I am not so violently bent upon my own Opinion, as to reject any Offer, proposed by wise Men, which shall be found equally Innocent, Cheap, Easy, and Effectual. But before something of that Kind shall be advanced in Contradiction to my Scheme, and offering a better, I desire the Author or Authors, will be pleased maturely to consider two Points. First, As Things now stand, how they will be able to find Food and Raiment for a hundred Thousand useless Mouths and Backs. And Secondly, There being a round Million of Creatures in Humane Figure, throughout this Kingdom, whose whole Subsistence put into a common Stock, would leave them in Debt two Millions of Pounds Ster. adding those, who are Beggers by Profession, to the Bulk of Farmers, Cottagers and Labourers, with their Wives and Children, who are Beggers in Effect; I desire those Politicians, who dislike my Overture, and may perhaps be so bold to attempt an Answer, that they will first ask the Parents of these Mortals, Whether they would not at this Day think it a great Happiness to have been sold for Food at a Year Old, in the manner I prescribe, and thereby have avoided such a perpetual Scene of Misfortunes, as they have since gone through, by the Oppression of Land-lords, the Impobssiility [*sic*] of paying Rent without Money or Trade, the Want of common Sustenance, with neither House nor Cloaths to cover them from these Inclemencies of Weather, and the most inevitable Prospect of intailing the like, or greater Miseries, upon their Breed for ever.

I profess in the Sincerity of my Heart, that I have not the least Personal Interest in endeavouring to promote this necessary Work, having no other Motive than the Publick Good of my Country, by advancing our Trade, providing for Infants, relieving the Poor, and giving some Pleasure to the Rich. I have no Children, by which I can propose to get a single Penny; the youngest being nine Years Old, and my Wife past Child-bearing.

A CAUTION AND WARNING

THE last pamphlet was one of the first efforts to arouse the conscience of England on the subject of English responsibility for Irish misery. It is a reminder to-day that the long failure of English people to respond to such appeals created, in the century which followed, a situation described in the words: 'English politics means the Irish question'.

To a great extent that aphorism described late nineteenth-century politics in the British Isles; and the evil effects of such a situation only ceased when it became so acute as to make amputation an imperative necessity. Similarly, in our own time, India threatened to absorb the attention of British politicians if action had not been taken in time to avert this by yielding to the Indian demand for independence. Palestine affords another parallel case.

But in the third quarter of the eighteenth century it was America which threatened to become 'English politics'; and for awhile, until a short struggle decided the issue once and for all in favour of American independence, the affairs of the American colonists did absorb attention in England to the exclusion of almost every other political question. In each case freedom for the colony or the subject people has brought England freedom from an obsession, allowing Englishmen to mind their own business for awhile with a little less distraction.

It was through her commerce and her colonies, with the economic interests of generations of emigrants from England, that this country was long concerned with slavery and the slave traffic. In a previous note we referred to the secret and discreditable negotiations of the Tory ministers at the end of Anne's reign, which resulted in a 'Munich' peace with France. The result was the Treaty of Utrecht (actually a series of treaties signed between 1713 and 1714) which included an agreement, known as the Asiento Treaty, whereby England obtained a 30 years monopoly of the slave trade to Spanish America. This treaty is an illuminating rubric among the many marginal comments which treaties afford to the ostensible causes of wars and the high-sounding declarations of politicians.

Such was the fortune of this country that it was not Britain which eventually paid most heavily for the slave traffic. Englishmen were not further concerned with what happened to slaves sold in South America; and the revolt of the North American colonists was to relieve us of the problem as it would have faced us on the North American mainland. It was for the Americans to discover, in time, that white American politics meant the slave question; and even *the end of slavery, after a bitter civil war, has not relieved white Americans of a colour problem which our forefathers and theirs created for their mutual profit. Few people in the middle of the eighteenth century could see that the trade in slaves and the status of slavery were anything but desirable, from every point of view. Even in the War of Independence the indignant colonists who invoked 'natural rights' to justify their struggle against Britain did not, save in a very few cases, apply such doctrines to the Negroes. In such a paradoxical situation we find strange reactions. Dr. Johnson, for example, detested slavery and was opposed to the idea of self-government for the American colonists. Boswell, on the other hand, supported the colonists and regarded slavery as not merely justifiable, but a pious and sacred institution. Tom Moore, writing a little later (Epistle to Viscount Forbes, 1806), stated dramatically the contrast between the principles and practice of the Americans in this matter. He wrote:*

> *Of whips and charters, manacles and rights,*
> *Of slaving blacks and democratic whites.*

And in a land 'where bastard freedom waves Her fustian flag in mockery over slaves' he saw 'The brute made ruler and the man made brute.'

At least such issues gave the pamphleteers something to write about. Since the decline of religio-politics, after 1714, the readiest political writers, such as Junius, could find nothing better to discuss than personalities, trivialities or charges of jobbery and corruption (there was plenty of ground for such charges, but they struck at no roots.) It is impossible to obtain any pleasure or interest from reading Junius without a profound and detailed knowledge of the 'who's who' among his political contemporaries, because his targets and missiles were all exclusively personal. Even when the Whig ascendancy ended, in 1763, the party differences were not of any importance. The Tories had at last reconciled themselves to the House of Hanover; but not until the French Revolution split the Whigs did the Tories absorb the Whig aristocracy and find a new raison d'être as the main bulwark against revolution at home and in Europe. In the last 25 years before 1789, however, two live issues seemed to call for more than personal comment, and both were essentially colonial: there was this growing spirit of revolt among the American colonists; and there was the beginning of the anti-slavery agitation, which cut right across the other controversy and posed very much deeper questions—questions that were not to be answered finally till the middle of the nineteenth century.

Anthony Benezet was not by any means the first to pose these questions. Indeed, his pamphlet (published in 1766) urges, quite rightly, that the iniquity of the Slave Trade had been obvious to some people since its inception. But it was to Anthony Benezet and John Woolman, both Quakers living in America, that the great movement for the abolition of slavery owed its principal impetus at the outset. These two friends, working together, did most to make the anti-slavery cause a practical challenge—first in the Society of Friends and later (as the Quakers took up the cause whole-heartedly) among English-speaking people on both sides of the Atlantic. It was mainly from the pioneer work of these two that the great army of 'abolitionists' came into being which was eventually to secure the abolition of slavery in the United States and in the British colonies.

Benezet was a Frenchman by birth, whose Huguenot parents had found refuge, first in Holland, then in London, and finally in Philadelphia. Here Anthony came in contact with the Quakers, who had made history by their peaceful penetration of the country, living on excellent terms with the Indians, with whom they had solemn treaties. Benezet joined the Society and became known for his active testimony to their principles in his personal relationships with Indians and in his illuminating writings on this subject, also on the Quaker attitude to war. But he was also regarded by Clarkson, the historian of the abolition of the slave trade, as 'one of the most zealous, vigilant and active advocates . . . the oppressed Africans ever had.'

As a schoolmaster by profession, Benezet soon found a practical way of assisting Negroes, by opening a free evening school for them. His conclusion that their natural intelligence and ability was as high as that of Europeans must have been a novelty, and one very shocking to the notions on which slave-owning morality rested. But while the leaders of the Anglican Church and most of the sects still approved of the system and actively defended it, little progress could be made outside the ranks of the Society of Friends.

The close collaboration between Benezet and John Woolman is illustrated by the fact that two of Benezet's quotations in this pamphlet (from Bosman and Adanson) are also to be found in Woolman's writings on this subject. All the quoted authorities were well known and widely read at the time, being themselves men of great experience and able to speak with intimate knowledge of the conditions which they described.

A CAUTION AND WARNING TO GREAT BRITAIN
AND HER COLONIES

IN A SHORT REPRESENTATION OF THE CALAMITOUS STATE OF THE
ENSLAVED NEGROES IN THE BRITISH DOMINIONS

By Anthony Benezet

AT a time when the general rights and liberties of mankind, and the preservation of those valuable privileges transmitted to us from our ancestors, are become so much the subjects of universal consideration; can it be an inquiry indifferent to any, how many of those who distinguish themselves as the Advocates of Liberty, remain insensible and inattentive to the treatment of thousands and tens of thousands of our fellow men, who, from motives of avarice, and the inexorable degree* of tyrant custom, are at this very time kept in the most deplorable state of slavery, in many parts of the British Dominions?

The intent of publishing the following sheets, is more fully to make known the aggravated iniquity attending the practice of the Slave-Trade; whereby many thousands of our fellow-creatures, as free as ourselves by nature, and equally with us the subjects of Christ's redeeming Grace, are yearly brought into inextricable and barbarous bondage; and many, very many, to miserable and untimely ends.

The Truth of this lamentable complaint is so obvious to persons of candour, under whose notice it hath fallen, that several have lately published their sentiments thereon, as a matter which calls for the most serious consideration of all who are concerned for the civil or religious welfare of their country. How an evil of so deep a dye, hath so long, not only passed uninterrupted by Those in Power, but hath even had

* Typ. error for 'decree'.

239

their countenance, is, indeed, surprising, and, charity would suppose, must, in a great measure, have arisen from this, that many persons in government, both of the Clergy and Laity, in whose power it hath been to put a stop to the Trade, have been unacquainted with the corrupt motives which give life to it, and the groans, the dying groans, which daily ascend to God, the common Father of mankind, from the broken hearts of those his deeply oppressed creatures; otherwise the powers of the earth would not, I think I may venture to say, could not, have so long authorized a practice so inconsistent with the very idea of liberty and justice. . . .

*　　　*　　　*　　　*

Much might justly be said of the temporal evils which attend this practice, as it is destructive of the welfare of human society, and of the peace and prosperity of every country, in proportion as it prevails. It might be also shewn, that it destroys the bonds of natural affection and interest, whereby mankind in general are united; that it introduces idleness, discourages marriage, corrupts the youth, ruins and debauches morals, excites continual apprehensions of dangers, and frequent alarms, to which the Whites are necessarily exposed from so great an increase of a People, that, by their bondage and oppressions, become natural enemies, yet, at the same time, are filling the places and eating the bread of those who would be the support and security of the Country. But as these and many more reflections of the same kind, may occur to a considerate mind, I shall only endeavour to shew, from the nature of the Trade, the plenty which Guinea affords to its inhabitants, the barbarous Treatment of the Negroes, and the observations made thereon by Authors of note, that it is inconsistent with the plainest precepts of the gospel, the dictates of reason, and every common sentiment of humanity.

*　　　*　　　*　　　*

Some who have only seen Negroes in an abject state of slavery, broken-spirited and dejected, knowing nothing of their situation in their native country, may apprehend, that they are naturally unsensible of the benefits of Liberty, being destitute and miserable in every respect, and that our suffering them to live amongst us (as the Gibeonites of old were permitted to live with the Israelites) tho' even on more oppressive terms, is to them a favour; but these are certainly erroneous opinions, with respect to far the greatest part of them: Altho' it is highly probable that in a country which is more than three thousand miles in extent from north to south, and as much from east to west, there will be barren parts, and many inhabitants more uncivilized and barbarous than others; as is the case in all other countries: yet, from the most authentic accounts, the inhabitants of Guinea appear, generally speaking, to be an industrious, humane, sociable people, whose capacities are naturally as enlarged, and as open to improvement, as those of the Europeans; and that their Country is fruitful, and in many places well improved, abounding in cattle, grain and fruits: And as the earth yields all the year round a fresh supply of food, and but little clothing is requisite, by reason of the continual warmth of the climate; the necessaries of life are much easier procured in most parts of Africa, than in our more northern climes. This is confirmed by many authors of note, who have resided there; among others, M. Adanson, in his account of Goree and Senegal, in the year 1754, says, ' Which way soever I turned my eyes on this pleasant spot, I beheld a perfect image of pure nature; an agreeable solitude, bounded on every side by charming landscapes, the rural situation of cottages in the midst of trees; the ease and indolence of the Negroes reclined under the shade of their spreading foliage; the simplicity of their dress and manners; the whole revived in my mind the idea of our first parents, and I seemed to contemplate the world in its primitive state: They are, generally speaking, very good-natured, sociable and obliging. I was not a little pleased with this my first reception; it convinced me, that there ought to be a considerable abatement made in the accounts I had read and heard every where of the savage character of the Africans. I observed, both in Negroes and Moors, great humanity and sociableness, which gave me strong hopes, that I should be very safe amongst them, and meet with the success I desired, in my inquiries after the curiosities of the country.'

William Bosman, a principal Factor for the Dutch, who resided fifteen years in Guinea, speaking of the natives of that part where he then was, says, 'They are generally a good sort of people, honest in their dealings'; others he describes as 'being generally friendly to strangers, of a mild conversation, affable, and easy to be overcome with reason.' He adds, 'That some Negroes, who have had an agreeable education, have manifested a brightness of understanding equal to any of us.' Speaking of the fruitfulness of the country, he says, 'It was very populous, plentifully provided with corn, potatoes and fruit, which grew close to each other; in some places a foot-path is the only ground that is not covered with them; the Negroes leaving no place, which is thought fertile, uncultivated; and immediately after they have reaped, they are sure to sow again.' Other parts he describes, as 'being full of towns and villages; the soil very rich, and so well cultivated, as to look like an entire garden, abounding in rice, corn, oxen, and poultry, and the inhabitants laborious.'

William Smith, who was sent by the African Company to visit their settlements on the coast of Guinea, in the year 1726, gives much the same account of the country of Delmina and Cape Corfe, &c. for beauty and goodness, and adds, 'The more you come downward towards that part, called Slave-Coast, the more delightful and rich the soil appears.' Speaking of their disposition, he says, 'They were a civil, good-natured people, industrious to the last degree. It is easy to perceive what happy memories they are blessed with, and how great progress they would make in the sciences, in case their genius was cultivated with study.' He adds, from the information he received of one of the Factors, who had resided ten years in that country, 'That the discerning natives account it their greatest unhappiness, that they were ever visited by the Europeans.—That the Christians introduced the traffick of Slaves; and that before our coming they lived in peace.'

Andrew Brue, a principal man in the French Factory, in the account he gives of the great river Senegal, which runs many hundred miles up the country, tells his readers, 'The farther you go from the Sea, the country on the river seems more fruitful and well improved. It abounds in Guinea and Indian corn, rice, pulse, tobacco, and indigo. Here are vast meadows, which feed large herds of great and small cattle; poultry are numerous, as well as wild fowl.' The same author, in his travels to the south of the river Gambia, expresses his surprize, 'to see the land so well cultivated; scarce a spot lay unimproved; the low grounds, divided by small canals, were all sowed with rice; the higher ground planted with Indian corn, millet, and peas of different sorts: beef and mutton very cheap, as well as all other necessaries of life.' The account this author gives of the disposition of the natives, is, 'That they are generally good-natured and civil, and may be brought to any thing by fair and soft means.' Artus, speaking of the same people, says, 'They are a sincere, inoffensive people, 'and do no injustice either to one another or strangers.'

From these accounts, both of the good disposition of the natives, and the Fruitfulness of most parts of Guinea, which are confirmed by many other authors, it may well be concluded, that their acquaintance with the Europeans would have been a happiness to them, had those last not only bore the name, but indeed been influenced by the Spirit of Christianity; but, alas! how hath the conduct of the Whites contradicted the precepts and example of Christ? Instead of promoting the end of his coming, by preaching the gospel of peace and good-will to man, they have, by their practices, contributed to enflame every noxious passion of corrupt nature in the Negroes; they have incited them to make war one upon another, and for this purpose have furnished them with prodigious quantities of ammunition and arms, whereby they have been hurried into confusion, bloodshed, and all the extremities of temporal misery, which must necessarily beget in their minds such a general detestation and scorn of the Christian name, as may deeply affect, if not wholly preclude their belief of the great truths of our holy religion. Thus an insatiable desire of gain hath become the principal and moving cause of the most abominable and dreadful scene, that was perhaps ever acted upon the face of the earth; even the power of their kings hath been made subservient to answer this wicked purpose, instead of being Protectors of their people, these rulers, allured by the tempting bait laid before them by the European Factors, &c. have invaded the Liberties of their unhappy subjects, and are become their oppressors.

*　　　*　　　*　　　*

Those who are acquainted with the Trade agree, that many Negroes on the sea-coast, who have been corrupted by their intercourse and converse with the European Factors, have learnt to stick at no act of cruelty for gain. These make it a practice to steal abundance of little Blacks of both sexes, when found on the roads or in the fields, where their parents keep them all day to watch the corn, &c. Some authors say, the Negroe Factors go six or seven hundred miles up the country with goods, bought from the Europeans, where markets of men are kept in the same manner as those of beasts with us. When the poor slaves, whether brought from far or near, come to the sea-shore, they are stripped naked, and strictly examined by the European Surgeons, both men and women, without the least distinction or modesty; those which are approved as good, are marked with a red-hot iron with the ship's mark; after which they are put on board the vessels, the men being shackled with irons two and two together. Reader, bring the matter home, and consider whether any situation in life can be more completely miserable than that of those distressed captives. When we reflect, that each individual of this number had some tender attachment which was broken by this cruel separation; some parent or wife, who had not an opportunity of mingling tears in a parting embrace; perhaps some infant or aged parent whom his labour was to feed and vigilance protect; themselves under the dreadful apprehension of an unknown perpetual slavery; pent up within the narrow confines of a vessel, sometimes six or seven hundred together, where they lie as close as possible.

Under these complicated distresses they are often reduced to a state of desperation, wherein many have leaped into the sea, and have kept themselves under water, till they were drowned; others have starved themselves to death, for the prevention whereof some masters of vessels have cut off the legs and arms of a number of those poor desperate creatures, to terrify the rest. Great numbers have also frequently been killed, and some deliberately put to death under the greatest torture, when they have attempted to rise, in order to free themselves from their present misery, and the slavery designed them.

*   *   *   *

A similar case in mentioned in Astley's Collection of Voyages, by John Atkins, Surgeon on board Admiral Ogle's squadron, 'Of one Harding, master of a vessel, in which several of the men-slaves, and a woman-slave, had attempted to rise, in order to recover their liberty; some of whom the master, of his own authority, sentenced to cruel death; making them first eat the heart and liver of one of those he killed. The woman he hoisted by the thumbs; whipped and slashed with knives before the other slaves, till she died.'

As detestable and shocking as this may appear to such, whose hearts are not yet hardened by the practice of that cruelty, which the love of wealth, by degrees, introduceth into the human mind; it will not be strange to those who have been concerned or employed in the Trade. Now here arises a necessary query to those who hold the ballance and sword of justice; and who must account to God for the use they have made of it. Since *our English law is so truly valuable for its justice*, how can they overlook these barbarous deaths of the unhappy Africans without trial, or due proof of their being guilty, of crimes adequate to their punishment? Why are those masters of vessels, (who are often not the most tender and considerate of men) thus suffered to be the sovereign arbiters of the lives of the miserable Negroes: and allowed, with impunity, thus to destroy, may I not say, murder their fellow-creatures, and that by means so cruel as cannot be even related but with shame and horror.

When the vessels arrive at their destined port in the Colonies, the poor Negroes are to be disposed of to the planters; and here they are again exposed naked, without any distinction of sexes, to the brutal examination of their purchasers; and this, it may well be judged is to many of them another occasion of deep distress, especially to the females. Add to this, that near connections must now again be separated, to go with their several purchasers: In this melancholy scene

Mothers are seen hanging over their daughters, bedewing their naked breasts with tears, and daughters clinging to their parents; not knowing what new stage of distress must follow their separation, or if ever they shall meet again; and here what sympathy, what commiseration are they to expect? why indeed, if they will not separate as readily as their owners think proper, the whipper is called for, and the lash exercised upon their naked bodies, till obliged to part.

Can any human heart, that retains a fellow-feeling for the sufferings of mankind, be unconcerned at relations of such griveous [*sic*] affliction, to which this oppressed part of our Species are subjected: God gave to man dominion over the fish of the sea, and over the fowls of the air, and over the cattle, &c. but imposed no involuntary subjection of one man to another.

*   *   *   *

How the British nation first came to be concerned in a practice, by which the rights and liberties of mankind are so violently infringed, and which is so opposite to the apprehensions Englishmen have always had of what natural justice requires, is indeed surprising. It was about the year 1563, in the reign of Queen Elizabeth, that the English first engaged in the Guinea Trade; when it appears, from an account in Hill's *Naval History*, page 293, That when Captain Hawkins returned from his first voyage to Africa, that generous spirited Princess, attentive to the interest of her subjects, sent for the Commander, to whom she expressed her concern lest any of the African Negroes should be carried off without their free consent, *declaring it would be detestable, and call down the vengeance of Heaven upon the undertakers*. Captain Hawkins promised to comply with the Queen's injunction: nevertheless, we find in the account, given in the same History, of Hawkins' second voyage, the author using these remarkable words, *Here began the horrid practice of forcing the Africans into slavery*.

Labat, a Roman Missionary, in his account of the Isles of America, at page 114, of the 4th vol. mentions, that Lewis the 13th, Father to the present French King's Grandfather, was extremely uneasy at a law by which all the Negroes of his Colonies were to be made slaves; but it being strongly urged to him, as the readiest means for their Conversion to Christianity, he acquiesced therewith.

And altho' we have not many accounts of the impressions which this piratical invasion of the rights of mankind gave to serious minded people, when first engaged in; yet it did not escape the notice of some, who might be esteemed in a peculiar manner as watchmen in their day to the different societies of Christians whereunto they belonged. Richard Baxter, an eminent preacher amongst the Nonconformists, in the last century, well known and particularly esteemed by most of the serious Presbyterians and Independents, in his Christian Directory mostly, wrote about an hundred Years ago, fully shews his detestation of this practice in the following words: 'Do you not mark how God hath followed you with plagues, and may not conscience tell you, that it is for your inhumanity to the souls and bodies of men—To go as pirates and catch up poor Negroes, or people of another land, that never forfeited life or liberty, and to make them slaves and sell them, is one of the worst kind of thievery in the world; and such persons are to be taken for the common enemies of mankind; and they that buy them, and use them as beasts, for their meer commodity, and betray, or destroy, or neglect their souls, are fitter to be called devils than Christians. It is an heinous sin to buy them, unless it be in charity to deliver them.—Undoubtedly they are presently bound to deliver them; becaues by right the man is his own; therefore no man else can have a just title to him.'

[*Extracts*]

COMMON SENSE

*W*ITH *our last two pamphlets we reach the American War of Independence, that great event in human history which sealed the inevitable destiny of the western hemisphere and anticipated to such a great extent those developments in the political thought of the Old World which we associate with the French Revolution. The revolt of Britain's American colonies, as Franklin pointed out, could be delayed but not prevented: the pace alone at which the colonial population was increasing insured that. Once the great severance took place, all other European colonies in the Americas must sooner or later follow the same path. And once this modern republic was firmly established beyond the Atlantic, republicanism ceased to be a dream of ancient Greece and Rome, of the discredited English Commonwealth or of dying Venice. Switzerland, it is true, preserved an aristocratic republican government comparable to these; but the United States of America embodied in form and theory, though not yet in reality and substance, the democratic ideals which were soon to inspire the revolutionary thought of France.*

It is significant that La Fayette, the French aristocrat who was to play so prominent a part in the early stages of the French Revolution, was among those foreigners whom chivalry induced to throw in their lot with the American colonists, in their struggle for liberation. For such knight errant types the war was a revolutionary apprenticeship. But no figure in these tumultuous times is of greater interest than Thomas Paine, who served the revolutionary cause in America and France, and became the leading figure in the radical movement of Great Britain.

Paine arrived in America in 1774. He was then 37 years of age and had tried his hand at various occupations without ostensible success at any. In some he had conspicuously failed; and even his marriage had not been a success. He had published nothing of any importance. Whatever formative influences may have been at work in those uneventful years, his public life began suddenly, soon after his arrival in Philadelphia, a year before the outbreak of war with England. The political atmosphere was already tense; and Paine, though an Englishman and a new-comer, instantly felt his sympathies to be passionately with the colonists. Almost as rapidly he found his vocation as a writer.

During the Independence War Paine's vigorous pamphlets and articles were the greatest literary stimulant, so badly needed during the darker phases, when the colonists often appeared to be facing defeat. He enlisted as a common soldier, and served in the army. He was eventually appointed Secretary for Foreign Affairs, and gave distinguished service in that department of the Revolutionary Government, fighting corruption in high places. The rest of his career is better known. He returned to England, two years before the French Revolution, intent on furthering in his own country that same cause of human liberty to which he had contributed so effectively beyond the Atlantic. When the French Revolution broke out his was the clearest voice in England that acclaimed it. When Burke wrote his Reflections on the French Revolution *it was* Tom Paine *who replied with* The Rights of Man, *a book as vigorous, lucid and logical as Burke's* Reflections *were turgid and twisted. In his time it was Paine who achieved the greater sales, in spite of prosecution and intimidation; and his is still by far the better book, though political interest and social snobbery have combined to give Burke's book the bogus title of a 'classic'. Burke had written great prose and spoken magnificently in his time—against Warren Hastings and the oppressors of India, or in defence of the American colonists, whose case he had seen almost as clearly as Paine himself. But he wrote now with prejudice rather than deep conviction; Paine had the advantage of greater integrity, clearer vision and passionate belief, which gave an incandescent quality to his literary style.*

There followed Paine's indictment for treason in 1792, and the dramatic episode when William Blake, in one of his frequent moods of prophetic insight, hustled the agitator out of the country just in time to avoid arrest. Elected to represent Calais in the French Convention, Paine distinguished himself as a deputy by his humanity where political passion regarded humanity as weakness. He saved the lives of his own political enemies, and tried to save that of the French king. Soon detested by the Jacobins, and deserted by the American Government, which owed him so much, Paine would have been executed but for another dramatic episode—the accident that saved him, a forgotten prisoner, until the fall of Robespierre. In prison he revised his great treatise, The Age of Reason, *an attack on superstition and defence of deism. When he eventually died in America, lonely and almost forgotten, Paine had given great service to three countries and left an indelible mark upon two of them. For the French Constitution was the work of Condorcet, with Paine's help; and the American* Declaration of Independence *was the direct result of an internal struggle among the colonists, in which Paine's* Common Sense *had been the most powerful statement made on behalf of those who desired a complete break with England, others being content with what we should now call 'Dominion Status'. Indeed, Paine had anticipated the* Declaration of Independence *by an earlier draft of his own.*

It is impossible to sum up briefly the importance of Paine as a thinker or as a man of action. He is the human bridge between the period with which this volume closes and the period with which our next volume will begin. Perhaps it is significant (as it is certainly symbolic) that he was, among so many other activities, the inventor of several contrivances, the discussion of which, wrote one of his biographers, 'would require a staff of specialists'. They included a crane and a smokeless candle, an internal combustion engine and an iron bridge. This last 'daring experiment', as it was long considered, was carried out at Wearmouth, to his specifications, to stand as an unintentional monument to the close connection between the Industrial Revolution and the political revolutions which accompanied it. There is little doubt that Paine could have made a fortune as an engineer, if he had abandoned politics.

But perhaps most important is the fact that Paine, like the authors of so many of the Thomason Tracts, was a 'man of the people'. His origin was humble. He was an artisan, a sailor on a privateer, an exciseman, a small shop-keeper, an 'usher' in a school, before he became famous at forty. He was self-educated. After the long interlude of monopoly culture, when most writers were born to leisure or at least achieved scholarship through the orthodox channels (as Dr. Johnson did) we have here a companion for Winstanley and the rugged giants of the seventeenth century. He is not merely slick and popular, like Defoe, but profound—well-read without a trace of academic pedantry, and better able than Pope to boast that 'The proper study of mankind is man.'

Of Paine's utter unselfishness, so rare in public men, much might be written. He made very little financially from his numerous pamphlets and articles, giving the copyrights of his American publications to the American nation, and making absolutely nothing from the vast sales of The Rights of Man. *He risked his life to save his political opponents, and lost his popularity for the integrity of his opinions—notably in the publication of* The Age of Reason. *In this connection we may notice finally a point which links him with the writer of our last pamphlet; for Paine was openly opposed to slavery, and his success in America was severely hampered by the expression of such an unpopular point of view.*

Tom Paine was born of Quaker parents; and, though at seventeen he ran away to sea, he preserved kindly recollections of 'a good father'. (It was his mother who appears to have been the difficulty, but he nevertheless supported her in her old age.) This Quaker background undoubtedly affected Paine's way of thinking, and the Encyclopaedia Britannica *rightly allows for its influence on the writing of* The Age of Reason (*though it is not literally true to say that this book was 'written from the point of view of a Quaker'). But it is in his humane view of slavery that this Quaker background is most evident. The first thing Paine ever wrote for publication—though it was not actually published until later—was on this subject. Moncure Conway considered this essay a remarkable assembly of all the arguments against slavery, 'moral, religious, military, economic', and held that it was as thorough as even William Lloyd Garrison (the great nineteenth-century abolitionist) could have made it.*

It is therefore sad to record that there was no unity between this ex-Quaker opponent of slavery and the Pennsylvania Quakers, who had so recently emancipated their slaves and become the leaders of the anti-slavery movement in America. True to their Peace Testimony, they could not take arms against Britain, any more than they had been willing to fight for Britain against the French or the Indians, or could think of fighting to free the Negroes. In one of Paine's bitterest pamphlets he attacked these potential allies—colleagues in a cause that was so near his own heart. Yet, if we are to judge by results, it is difficult to say whether Paine's sword and pen or the unarmed persuasiveness of Anthony Benezet did more to further the deepest interests of human liberty. We can only say that here were two men, living at the same place in the same period, who worked by different and apparently conflicting methods, and that each made a great contribution to a common cause.

Both were religious men, but neither indulged in what we call religio-politics. On the contrary, their conception of religious duty demanded from them a deep sense of social responsiblity, and they represent two main streams of social doctrine which were to influence the future. Paine was destined to be the chief influence in the long struggle for political democracy in Great Britain. Benezet played a similar part in the struggle against slavery, that eventually and inevitably gave rise to modern 'anti-imperialism' and the demand for colonial freedom. For empire is based upon the same arguments which Benezet had to meet in attacking slavery; and his case for slave emancipation applies equally to the emancipation of all subject races to-day. And that was precisely the reason which led Paine to identify himself with the American colonists in the 'anti-imperialist' struggle of his own time.

Common Sense *was published during the war with England, in 1776, when the American colonists were still wavering between the goal of independence (a complete break from Britain) and a policy of reconciliation, including some sort of 'dominion home rule'. Paine's views on the British Constitution make an interesting contrast to those expressed in the* Plea for Limited Monarchy *of 1660.*

COMMON SENSE

By Thomas Paine

Of the Origin and Design of GOVERNMENT *in general, with concise Remarks on the* ENGLISH CONSTITUTION

SOME writers have so confounded society with government, as to leave little or no distinction between them; whereas, they are not only different, but have different origins. Society is produced by our wants, and government by our wickedness; the former promotes our happiness possitively by uniting our affections, the latter negatively by restraining our vices. The one encourages intercourse, the other creates distinctions. The first is a patron, the last a punisher.

Society in every state is a blessing, but Government even in its best state is but a necessary evil; in its worst state an intolerable one: for when we suffer, or are exposed to the same miseries by a Government which we might expect in a country without Government, our calamity is heightened by reflecting that we furnish the means by which we suffer. Government, like dress, is the badge of lost innocence; the palaces of Kings are built on the ruins of the bowers of Paradise. For were the impulses of conscience clear, uniform, and irresistably obeyed, Man would need no other lawgiver; but that not being the case, he finds it necessary to surrender up a part of his property to furnish means for the protection of the rest; and this he is induced to do, by the same prudence which in every other case advises him, out of two evils to choose the least. Wherefore, security being the true design and end of government, it unanswerably follows, that whatever form thereof appears most likely to ensure it to us, with the least expence and greatest benefit, is preferable to all others.

In order to gain a clear and just idea of the design and end of government, let us suppose a small number of persons settled in some sequestered part of the earth, unconnected with the rest; they will then represent the first peopling of any country, or of the world. In this state of natural liberty, society will be their first thought. A thousand motives will excite them thereto, the strength of one man is so unequal to his wants, and his mind so unfitted for perpetual solitude, that he is soon obliged to seek assistance and relief of another, who in his turn requires the same. Four or five united would be able to raise a tolerable dwelling in the midst of a wilderness, but one man might labour out the common period of life without accomplishing anything; when he had felled his timber he could not remove it, nor erect it after it was removed; hunger in the mean time would urge him from his work, and every different want call him a different way. Disease, nay even misfortune, would be death; for though neither might be mortal, yet either would disable him from living, and reduce him to a state in which he might rather be said to perish, than to die.

Thus necessity, like a gravitating power, would soon form our newly arrived emigrants into society, the reciprocal blessings of which would supersede, and render the obligations of law and government unnecessary while they remained perfectly just to each other: but as nothing but Heaven is impregnable to vice, it will unavoidably happen that in proportion as they surmount the first difficulties of emigration, which bound them together in a common cause, they will begin to relax in their duty and attachment to each other: and this remissness will point out the necessity of establishing some form of government to supply the defect of moral virtue.

Some convenient Tree will afford them a State-house, under the branches of which the whole Colony may assemble to deliberate on public matters. It is more than probable that their first laws will have the title only of REGULATIONS, and be enforced by no other penalty than public dis-esteem. In this first Parliament every man by natural right will have a seat.

But as the Colony encreases, the public concerns will encrease likewise, and the distance at which the members may be separated, will render it too inconvenient for all of them to meet on every occasion as at first, when their numbers was small, their habitations near, and the public concerns few and trifling. This will point out the convenience of their consenting to leave the legislative part to be managed by a select number chosen from the whole body, who are supposed to have the same concerns at stake which those have who appointed them, and who will act in the same manner as the whole body would act were they present. If the colony continue encreasing, it will become necessary to augment the number of the representatives, and that the interest of every part of the colony may be attended to, it will be found best to divide the whole into convenient parts, each part sending its proper numbers: and that the elected might never form to themselves an interest separate from the electors, prudence will point out the propriety of having elections often: because as the elected might by that means return and mix again with the general body of the electors in a few months, their fidelity to the public will be secured by the prudent reflection of not making a rod for themselves. And as this frequent interchange will establish a common interest with every part of the community, they will mutually and naturally support each other, and on this (not on the unmeaning name of King) depends the strength of government, and the happiness of the governed.

Here then is the origin and rise of government; namely, a mode rendered necessary by the inability of moral virtue to govern the world; here too is the design and end of government, viz. Freedom and Security. And however our eyes may be dazzled with show, or our ears deceived by sound; however prejudice may warp our wills, or interest darken our understanding, the simple voice of nature and of reason will say, 'tis right.

I draw my idea of the form of government from a principle in nature which no art can overturn, viz. That the more simple any thing is, the less liable it is to be disordered, and the easier repaired when disordered; and with this maxim in view I offer a few remarks on the so much boasted constitution of England. That it was noble for the dark and slavish times in which it was erected, is granted. When the world was over-run with tyranny, the least remove therefrom was a glorious rescue. But that it is imperfect, subject to convulsions, and incapable of producing what it seems to promise is easily demonstrated.

Absolute governments, (tho' the disgrace of human nature) hath this advantage with them, that they are simple; if the people suffer, they know the head from which their suffering springs; know likewise the remedy; and are not bewildered by a variety of causes and cures. But the constitution of England is so exceedingly complex, that the nation may suffer for years together without being able to discover in which part the fault lies, some will say in one and some in another, and every political physician will advise a different medicine.

I know it is difficult to get over local or long standing prejudices, yet if we will suffer ourselves to examine the component parts of the English constitution, we shall find them to be the base remains of two ancient tyrannies, compounded with some new Republican materials.

First.—The remains of Monarchial tyranny in the person of the King.

Secondly.—The remains of Aristocratical tyranny in the persons of the Peers.

Thirdly.—The new Republican materials in the persons of the Commons, on whose virtue depends the freedom of England.

The two first by being hereditary are independent of the people; wherefore, in a constitutional sense, they contribute nothing towards the freedom of the State.

To say that the constitution of England is a union of three powers reciprocally checking each other, is farcical, either the words have no meaning, or they are flat contradictions.

To say that the Commons is a check upon the King, presupposes two things.

First.—That the King is not to be trusted without being looked after, or in other words, that a thirst for absolute power is the natural disease of Monarchy.

Secondly.—That the Commons by being appointed for that purpose, are either wiser or more worthy of confidence than the Crown.

But as the same constitution which gives the Commons a power to check the King by with-holding the supplies, gives afterwards the King a power to check the Commons by empowering him to reject their other bills; it again supposes that the King is wiser than those, whom it has already supposed to be wiser than him. A meer absurdity!

There is something exceedingly ridiculous in the composition of Monarchy; it first excludes a man from the means of information, yet empowers him to act in cases where the highest judgment is required.— The state of a King shuts him from the world, yet the business of a King requires him to know it thoroughly: wherefore, the different parts by unnaturally opposing and destroying each other, prove the whole character to be absurd and useless.

Some writers have explained the English Constitution thus: The King say they is one, the People another; the Peers are an house in be-half of the King; the Commons in behalf of the People; But this hath all the distinctions of an house divided against itself; and though the ex-pressions be pleasantly arranged, yet when examined they appear idle and ambiguous: and it will always happen, that the nicest construction that words are capable of, when applied to the description of some thing which either cannot exist, or is too incomprehensible to be within the compass of description, will be words of sound only, and though they may amuse the ear, they cannot inform the mind: for this explanation includes a previous question, viz. How came the King by a power which the People are afraid to trust, and always obliged to check? Such a power could not be the gift of a wise People, neither can any power which needs checking be from God; yet the provision which the constitution makes, supposes such a power to exist.

But the provision is unequal to the task, the means either cannot, or will not accomplish the end, and the whole affair is a *Felo de se*; for as the greater weight will always carry up the less, and as all the wheels of a machine are put in motion by one, it only remains to know which power in the constitution has the most weight, for that will govern: And though the others, or a part of them, may clog, or, as the phrase is, check the rapidity of its motion, yet so long as they cannot stop it, their endeavours will be ineffectual: The first moving power will at last have its way, and what it wants in speed is supplied by time.

That the crown is this overbearing part in the English constitution needs not be mentioned, and that it derives its whole consequence merely from being the giver of places and pensions is self-evident, wherefore, tho' we have been wise enough to shut and lock a door against absolute Monarchy, we at the same time have been foolish enough to put the Crown in possession of the key.

The prejudice of Englishmen in favor of their own government by King, Lords and Commons, arises as much or more from national pride than reason. Individuals are undoubtedly safer in England than in some other countries; but the will of the King is as much the law of the land in Britain as in France, with this difference, that instead of proceeding directly from his mouth, it is handed to the people under the more formidable shape of an act of Parliament. For the fate of Charles the first hath only made Kings more subtile—not more just.

Wherefore laying aside all national pride and prejudice in favor of modes and forms, the plain truth is, that it is wholly owing to the constitution of the People, and not to the constitution of the Government, that the Crown is not as oppressive in England as in Turkey.

An enquiry into the constitutional errors in the English form of government, is at this time highly necessary; for as we are never in a proper condition of doing justice to others, while we continue under the influence of some leading partiality, so neither are we capable of doing it to ourselves, while we remain fettered by any obstinate prejudice. And as a man who is attached to a prostitute is unfitted to choose or judge of a wife, so any prepossession in favor of a rotten constitution of government will disable us from discerning a good one.

[*Extract*]

PLAIN TRUTH

*T*HERE *would be little point in publishing extracts from this reply to Paine's* Common Sense *but for the fact that it, too, was quite widely read at the time and that it is a curiosity of absurdity—the absurdity of theories which are only plausible at the time of statement and become foolish, with the passing of the years, to those who are securely wise after the event.*

The author, a divine called William Smith, who wrote under the name of 'Candidus' (a pseudonym dear to so many anonymous nonentities), is to-day entirely unimportant; though when he wrote he was quite a formidable figure in that most ephemeral of theatres—the world of organised religion. The catalogues of the British Museum Reading Room record the labours of such pulpit heroes in countless thousands—men who meant something in their time to others, and much to themselves, but are forgotten to-day and of little interest even to the antiquarian.

We have included a few extracts from Plain Truth *merely to show how little human imbecility has changed. For here is a man arguing the impossibility of America ever surviving as an independent country, and urging the great advantage of the imperial apron strings.*

Paine's Common Sense *declared for a complete break and a declaration of independence. William Smith, D.D., though (to do him justice) he too wished the right of the colonies to be asserted and maintained against arbitrary taxation, hoped for an unworkable compromise, and advocated it with well-informed argument. As a scholar he was doubtless Paine's superior, but his scholarship was irrelevant. He was merely one of so many who have failed to follow the advice of Solomon, and to get understanding when they acquired knowledge. To read* Plain Truth *should be the duty of all political pedants who pronounce* ex cathedra *(more dogmatic than Canute, but no more fortunate on their academic thrones) the impossibility of the social tides that are about to engulf them. From every age we hear their voices, splitting moral hairs and denouncing political earthquakes on the authority of legal quibbles or historical precedents devised in the days of the dodo.*

Plain Truth *was published in 1776 and re-published while it remained of topical interest. There is no modern edition. It will be observed that it is a reply to another portion of Paine's* Common Sense, *not given in this selection. But Paine's analysis of the British Constitution, forecasting as it did the theories associated with the French Revolution, appeared to us the more interesting part of his pamphlet.*

PLAIN TRUTH

By 'Candidus', *i.e.* William Smith, D.D.

OUR author 'challenges the warmest advocate for reconciliation to shew a single advantage this continent can reap by being connected with Great Britain. I repeat the challenge. Not a single advantage is derived: our corn will fetch its price in any market in Europe.' Were the author's assertions, respecting our power, as real as delusive, a reconciliation on liberal principles with Great Britain would be most excellent policy. I wave familiarity of manners, laws, and customs, most friendly indeed to perpetual alliance. The greatest part of our plank, slaves, shingles, hoops, corn, beef, pork, herrings, and many other articles, could find no vent but in the English islands: the demand for our flour would also be considerably lessened. The Spaniards have no demand for these articles, and the French little or none. Britain would be a principal mart for our lumber, part of our grain, naval stores, tobacco, and many other articles, which perhaps are not generally wanted in any kingdom in Europe. If it is suggested, that the English islands, impelled by necessity, would trade with us, I reply, that it is not uncommon to see English flour for sale in those islands, as our merchants have more than once found to their cost. Since 1750 flour hath sold in the islands at ten and twelve per cent. the price being reduced by flour from England.

Britain is also better calculated to supply us with woollen goods, and other necessary articles, than any kingdom in Europe. Should a separation ensue, Britain will open an extensive commerce to the Baltick and Russia for all, or many of the commodities she now receives from us; the Russians, since their last glorious treaty with the Port, can now export the commodities of their most fertile Ukraine through the Mediterranean; until that period they were constrained to carry their hemp eight or nine hundred miles to the Baltick; whence, by a long and dangerous navigation, it reached the different ports in the Atlantic. I need not inform the reader that such immense land carriage precluded the subjects of Russia from raising wheat, which generally sold in the Ukraine for ten-pence per bushel, as did rye at five-pence in that extensive region, than which no country on earth is more happily adapted for that grain: the British nation, pre-eminently distinguished for industry and enterprize, will establish factories in the provinces of Russia, and animate those people to emulate our productions, which they will transport by the Mediterranean to the ports of Europe and the West Indies.—By these means, and the culture of Poland, our grain would probably be reduced to its pristine price, two shillings and six-pence. As our author is so violently bent against reconciliation, he must either suppose a constant war with the incensed power of England, or admit that he is a proper inhabitant of the domains of Ariosto (the world in the moon); now, admitting 'we have the most numerous and best disciplined army under heaven, and a navy formidable for that of England;' pray what are our resources to pay such considerable armaments? although I do not wish to mortify my countrymen, I must acknowledge, that the neat proceeds of all our produce is inadequate to that end: our author allows 'that we have a considerable check on the West India commerce of Britain, and that Great Britain has a considerable check upon our European trade.'

In case Great Britain insults therefore our European bound ships, we have only to order our admirals to seize their West Indiamen. Unfortunately, the Algerines and other piratical states of Africa have no West-India commerce; and not having the clearest distinctions of thine and mine, will be apt to seize our vessels. Our author affirms, 'that our trade will always be our protection.' I therefore crave his pardon, and shall believe, that the sight of our grain, and smell of the New England codfish, will effectually serve as a Mediterranean pass to the piratical rovers. I do humbly confess my suspicions, lest Portugal, extremely dependent on Great Britain, may not insult us. When independent, we no doubt will receive strong proofs of friendship from France and Spain; nevertheless, with the utmost humility I imagine, could we seize Gibraltar or Portmahon, and there station a formidable squadron of capital ships, we might as effectually protect our commerce, as our trade will protect us: the author of Common Sense confidently affirms, 'that our trade will always be its protection.' I cannot imagine that his purse or watch would effectually protect him on Hounslow or Blackheath from footpads or highwaymen. Hitherto we have treated of reconciliation on the principles of our being as potent as Great Britain. Let us now consider our army nearly as I have stated it, and our navy as an object by no means sublunary. It now behoves us well to consider, whether it were better to enter the harbour of peace with Great Britain, or plunge the ship into all the horrors of war—of civil war. As peace and a happy extension of commerce are objects infinitely better for Great Britain, than war and a diminution of her commerce, it therefore is her interest to grant us every species of indulgence, consistent with our constitutional dependence; should war continue, there can be no doubt of the annihilation of our ships, ports, and commerce by Great Britain. The king's ships now in New England unhappily are more than sufficient to ruin the ports and commerce of these provinces; New York is already secured; and I should be extremely grieved to hear that a small armament were destined against Philadelphia. In the opinion of the best officers of the navy, Philadelphia is accessible to a few forty and fifty gun ships, in despite of our temporary expedients to fortify the river Delaware. If such opinion is groundless, the ministry by their imbecility have befriended us, since by guarding the river Delaware with a few frigates only, they had precluded us from arming our vessels and strengthening the river Delaware. I would remind our author of the constant language and apparent purport of all ranks in opposition to Great Britain; 'we have (say they) been the happiest people on earth, and would continue to be so, should Great Britain renounce her claim of taxation; we have no sinister views, we claim not independence; no! perish the thought;' such I believe also was the tenor of the petitions from the congress to his majesty. Now I would ask every man of sentiment, what opinion our friends in Great Britain, nay the whole world will entertain of us, if ingratefully and madly adopting our author's frantic schemes, we reject reasonable terms of reconciliation? will they not most assuredly believe that our popular leaders have by infinite art deluded the unwary people into their pre-concerted schemes, on supposition that the time had found us? those acquainted with Britain must confess, that the minority in parliament hitherto have been our main prop: now independency for ever annihilates this our best resource. Let us admit a part of the minority, republicans, or what is more probable, bent on removing the present ministry from their power, our author's schemes annihilates all their consequence, all their opposition. In case of our independence, should a Barre, or Burke, patronize our government, such patrons would infallibly participate the fate of the great and good De Witts, be torn in pieces by the furious people. ——If my remarks are founded on truth, it results that the time hath

not found us; that independency is inexpedient, ruinous, and impracticable, and that reconciliation with Great Britain on good terms is our
sole resource; it is this alone will render us respectable; it is this alone
will render us numerous; it is this only will make us happy . . .

The fabricators of independency have too much influence to be entrusted in such arduous and important concerns; this reason alone were
sufficient, at present, to deter us from altering the constitution: it would
be as inconsistent in our leaders in this hour of danger to form a
government, as it were for a colonel, forming his battalion in the face
of an enemy, to stop to write an essay on war.

This author's Quixotic system is really an insult to our understanding; it is infinitely inferior to Hume's idea of a perfect commonwealth,
which, notwithstanding his acknowledged greatness of genius, is still
reprehensible: it is not our business to examine in what manner this
author's associates acquired that knowledge in national affairs; but we
may predict, that his scheme of independency would soon, very soon,
give way to a government imposed on us by some Cromwell of our
armies: nor is this sentiment unnatural, if we are attentive to constant
experience and human nature: the sublime Montesquieu, so aptly
quoted by the congress, unhappily corroborates our doctrine, 'from
(says he) a manner of thinking that prevails amongst mankind, they set
a higher value upon courage than timorousness; on activity than prudence; on strength than counsel. Hence, the army will ever despise a
senate, and respect their own officers; they will naturally slight the order
sent them by a body of men whom they look upon as cowards, and
therefore unworthy to command them; so that as soon as the army depends on the legislative body, it becomes a military one;' and if the contrary has ever happened, it has been owing to some extraordinary circumstances, such as Holland being able to drown her garrisons, and the
Venetians having it in their power to compel their troops to obedience
by the vicinity of the European armies; resources to which we for ever
must be strangers. If independence takes place, the New England men
by their consequence therein will assume a superiority impatiently to be
borne by the other colonies.

Notwithstanding our author's fine words about toleration, ye sons of
peace and true christianity, believe me, it were folly supreme, madness,
to expect angelic toleration from New England, where she has constantly been detected, persecuted, and execrated; even in vain would
our author, or our Cromwell, cherish toleration; for the people of New
England, not yet arrived in the seventeenth or eighteenth century,
would reprobate her.—It is more than probable to suppose that the

New England governments would have no objection to an Agrarian law; nor is it unreasonable to suppose that such division of property would be very agreeable to the soldiers; indeed their general could not, perhaps, with safety to his existence as a general, refuse them so reasonable a gratification, particularly, as he will have more than one occasion for their services; let us, however, admit that our general and troops, contradicting the experience of ages, do not assume the sovereignty. Released from foreign war, we would probably be plunged into all the misery of anarchy and intestine war. Can we suppose that the people of the south would submit to have the seat of empire at Philadelphia, or in New England? or that the people oppressed by a change of government, contrasting their misery with their former happy state, would not invite Britain to re-assume the sovereignty?

A failure of commerce precludes the numerous tribe of planters, farmers and others, from paying their debts contracted on the faith of peace and commerce. They cannot, nor perhaps ought not to pay their debts. A war will ensue between the creditors and their debtors, which will eventually end in a general spunge or abolition of debts, which has more than once happened in other states on occasions similar.

Ye respectable descendants of the planters from Holland and Swisserland, who acknowledge, that your fathers have instructed you to felicitate yourselves in existing under the benign British government, and have taught you to execrate the government of Holland and other popular states, where the unhappy people, unacquainted with trial by jury and other peculiar felicities of British subjects, are (to use the significant language of your fathers) under the harrow of oppressive Demagogues, do ye possess the wisdom to continue your happiness by a well regulated connection with Britain?

Volumes were insufficient to describe the horror, misery, and desolation awaiting the people at large in the Syren form of American independence. In short, I affirm that it would be most excellent policy in those who wish for true liberty, to submit by an advantageous reconciliation to the authority of Great Britain; 'to accomplish in the long run, what they cannot do by hypocrisy, fraud, and force in the short one.' Independence and slavery are synonymous terms.

[*Extracts*]

APPENDIX

Queen Elizabeth Allegorised—frontispiece

This daring caricature of the Queen as an old lady, satirising at the same time her love of fine clothes and the fashions of the period, was never published—for good reason—during Elizabeth's reign. It is a pen and ink drawing in a manuscript by a certain William Wodwall, dated about 1600—a rarity indeed in an age when caricature was almost unknown in this country.

Some information concerning this satire may be obtained from *Notes and Queries* (April 3, 1869) and from *The Connoisseur* (June, 1944). The manuscript ('The Acts of Queen Elizabeth Allegorised') was recently acquired by the Bodleian Library, and with the kind permission of the Manuscript Department we publish this reproduction. The drawing has not been previously reproduced for publication except in a catalogue of Messrs. Sotheby in 1938, and in a small plate (made from that in Sotheby's Catalogue) which accompanied the article in *The Connoisseur*.

The inscription attached to this drawing reads: 'Seaven of these foules or byrds were found and taken in Lyncolnesheere, at Croley, 1588, whereof foure died in shorte space after they were taken, the other three lyved longer, as it is to see in the ballet printed of them'.

Presentation of the Bible to Henry VIII—p. 25

This is a photographic copy of a woodcut, dated 1641, itself copied from a woodcut of 1570. The earlier version is in most respects superior, but on comparing them we found that of 1641 clearer for purposes of reproduction. This elaborate satire on the Papacy was very popular and was used by Foxe as an illustration to his *Acts and Monuments*, one of the most favoured Protestant works. A full descriptive explanation of the detail will be found in *The Catalogue of British Museum Prints, etc.*, Division I (Political and Personal Satire), Volume I, No. 6. The original woodcut of 1570, for comparison, is No. 5 in this Catalogue. The figure under the feet of Henry VIII is Pope Clement VII.

Englandes Wolfe with Eagles Clawes—p. 77

This woodcut of 1647 needs little explanation. It is a satire on the royalists in general and Prince Rupert in particular.

A Glasse for the Times—p. 124

This woodcut forms the frontispiece to a brochure of 1648. The variety, extravagance and heterodoxy of the many sects was a continued cause of alarm to many, and (though there was no agreement on the nature of orthodoxy) propagandists continued to deplore the rise of unauthorised sects and preachers. Note that in the well-conducted gathering the heads of the congregation are covered during the sermon.

The Scots holding their Young Kinges Nose to Y* Grinstone— p. 134

This refers to the 'Solemn League and Covenant' thrust upon Charles II by the Scottish Presbyterians as the price of their support. Few scenes are more amusing to contemplate than the real occasion (represented here allegorically) when the 'Merry Monarch' of later years took this dismal oath to establish Calvinism, and listened to a sermon of monumental dreariness, preached *at* him with Caledonian thoroughness. The date of the woodcut is 1651.

Collonel Sidney's Overthrow—p. 164

From a broadsheet of 1683, included among the Roxburghe Ballads. See the note on Algernon Sidney, pp. 159–160, *The Very Copy of a Paper*.

Faction Display'd—p. 185

This Tory satire of 1709 shows the celebrated divine, Richard Baxter, with Defoe and others (including the Whig 'Moderate Churchman', Bishop Hoadly). Mounted upon a peculiar beast or engine of war, they are attacking the High Church Champion, Dr. Sacheverell, who repulses them with a text from the Bible.

Baxter (extreme left) is given a label with the title of a book sometimes credited to him; but no such book is known, though one of a similar title (no doubt suggested by this legend) was written by a Welsh minister some sixty years later: 'An Effectual Shove to the

Heavy Arsed Christian', by William Bunyan. Lord Byron was among those who were 'gulled' in later days by his bogus title (as attributed to Baxter). In his *Hints from Horace* he has the lines:

> While the Lord's servant chastens whom he loves
> And Simeon kicks, where Baxter only shoves.

In a note to the above Byron wrote that the title shown in this cartoon was 'the veritable title of a book once in good repute and likely to be so again'.

The Festival of the Golden Rump—p. 233

For reasons explained in the notes to the text of this volume, there is little suitable material during the Walpole-Chatham period which we can offer for the interest of the general reader. This applies to pictorial satires (e.g. those of Gilray) as well as to pamphlets. 'The Golden Rump' (1737) is as near as anything of this period to being a self-explanatory general satire; and (though much could be written about it) the *idea* is reasonably clear without appending long personal histories.

Here the Prime Minister (Sir Robert Walpole) and his brother Horace, with Queen Caroline and Bishop Hoadly (a common subject of Tory satires—see above), are seen at the shrine of the 'Golden Rump'. In coarse symbolism the unpopular Hanoverians and their obsequious Whig ministers are lampooned in a manner hardly believable in an age when such worship is taken for granted and is above criticism. Moreover, such Rabelaisian humour is no longer permitted, even when levelled at lesser targets.